Genocide
IN THE
Desert

WRITTEN BY

EUGENE BACH AND **DR. PAUL KINGERY**

Warning: This book contains graphic material and photographs about events that might not be suitable for children.

Warning: This book contains graphic material and photographs about events that might not be suitable for children.

Genocide in the Desert
by Eugene Bach and Dr. Paul Kingery

Back to Jerusalem
277 Lower Airport Rd
Lumberton, MS 39455 USA
infor@backtojerusalem.com

Contents

Part Four: God's Solution to a World Conflict

About the Co-Author

Dr. Paul M. Kingery is an American professor, a former chairman of the board of Rwanga Organization, and briefly was a consultant to Kurdish leader Idris Barzani. He has lived in Iraq with his family since 2008, and adopted a Yazidi son three years before, Azwan Azad Elias, from Bozan.

Aid worker Dr. Paul M. Kingery and his son Charlie Phillip Kingery, in Seje Village, Iraq.

In July of 2014, just a month before ISIS's invasion on northern Iraq, Dr. Paul moved from Erbil to Dohuk to help set up the American University Kurdistan owned by Masrour Barzani, son of President Masoud Barzani. Dr.Paul was named the chair of the Academic Committee and the faculty supervisor, and was in negotiations to become the university's president when the invasion occurred. Dr. Paul delivered a keynote speech at the opening of the university, along with the newly appointed governor, Farhad Atrushi Saleem, who had been his friend and travel companion on his first trip to

Kurdistan in 2006. Dr. Paul had arranged a doctoral scholarship for Governor Saleem at the University of Hawaii before he decided to go into politics and remain in Iraq.

Following the invasion and massacre in 2014, Dr. Paul established the MedEast Organization in Iraq to aid minorities fleeing ISIS.

Introduction:
By Dr. Paul Kingery

Genocide against Christians and non-Muslims by extremist Sunni Arab Muslims is nothing new. It has been going on for years, though it hasn't always been recognized as such. Recently, the violence and persecution has grown worse and has garnered worldwide attention, resulting in an official declaration of genocide from governments around the world.

I have lived in the middle of the genocide in northern Iraq for eight years and have witnessed its escalation from palpable inter-ethnic tensions with occasional violence to a full-scale holy war. The perpetrators and their names have changed over time, from neighborhood thugs to Al Qaeda to ISIS to ISIL, but the people supporting the genocide have always been common Sunni Muslim Arabs searching for stability, power, and financial gain, using Muslim extremism as a vehicle to grab the wealth of others.

Over the years, I have watched as new jihadist groups, who were even more biased, greedy, ruthless, and organized than their predecessors, take over. Their extreme techniques and attitudes are not so different from those of Shia Muslim people seeking similar objectives, or from Hindu extremists, or from any other radical and power-hungry groups in the history of man. Ideological pretensions aside, there is a big grab for wealth and power underway by those who are willing to be extremely violent to get it.

The genocide in Iraq is different.

What makes the Iraqi genocide stand out is not that it's new or more violent than conflicts seen in the past, but that while the perpetrators are using modern warfare techniques, they have also resorted to barbaric measures of rape, torture, beheadings and crucifixions at a time when civilization was thought to have risen above this level. This genocide has grown in a vacuum of leadership regionally, nationally, and internationally with such speed that it caught many government leaders off guard. Inter-ethnic violence has been occurring in Middle Eastern countries for some time but received little attention until the scale of violence grew and claimed lands that had been liberated in previous conflicts by coalition forces. Supra-national violence has emerged on a large scale, rendering old models and tools that were used to counter more conventional forms of violence obsolete.

Through the Eyes of Iraqi Victims

In this book, we will follow the genocide in northern Iraq in 2014 through the eyes of the victims. Tragically, the stories are true and the people are real. Their terrible ordeal and their ongoing struggles are haunting. The reality of their plight is not something we can simply turn away from. The details in this book were gleaned from my daily exposure living and serving in the war zone and from hundreds of interviews with people who were terrorized and lost everything. What is happening to the minorities in Iraq today requires careful study so that the violence and hatred can be dealt with before it expands. Some fear that it has already reached into the far corners of the world.

Learning from those who have escaped the violence helps us understand the realities and lasting impact of genocide so we can better help these suffering people. The challenge is great, and their plight is not easily understood. Many credible international organizations and agencies have tried and failed.

I believe hearts can still be moved to do remarkable things in this world. We all have the capacity within us to a make a difference and help those who are suffering, regardless of how tightly the walls close in on our lives. I was moved to help Christians and Yazidis in northern Iraq beginning in 2006, leaving a career as a university professor and administrator in the United States. My previous professional publications had mostly been about violence among youth in the US. While working in Iraq for a decade, I became a witness to the genocide that would shake the entire world, and I am now immersed in the struggle to help Yazidis and Christians recover.

At the time of this writing I am still in Iraq, living in the small Christian village of Seje just fifty kilometers from the headquarters of the Islamic State. The Islamic State, also known as ISIS or IS, is responsible for the largest manmade disaster of our generation and is the culprit of mass genocide.

Yazidis are no strangers to the Islamic genocide perpetrated by ISIS. They can count seventy-four acts of genocide by Muslim invaders against them in their long history in the area of Mount Sinjar, western Iraq. Christians living in the same areas have also endured constant assaults, too numerous to count, over the last two thousand years.

As just one example in recent years, busloads of students traveling to Mosul University from Nineveh Province were stopped by terrorists, and those bearing Yazidi and Christian IDs were taken off the bus and shot dead. Truck bombs exploded in Christian villages in the area as well, killing many people.

ISIS' True Purpose in the Genocide

The land in the Middle East is being claimed by the militant members of ISIS as their own "caliphate" or fundamentalist Muslim kingdom. Their claim is that the land should be inhabited solely by radical Sunni Muslims who share their beliefs. The purpose of the ISIS invasion of northern Iraq in 2014 was to clear their growing caliphate lands of non-Sunnis, such as Yazidis and Christians, Shiite

Muslims and less radical Sunnis, like Kurds (whom they consider apostate Muslims).

The Kurds claim Yazidis are part of their ethnic group, particularly at voting time, though the Yazidis are treated as low-class Kurds and provided little aid. On the other hand, the Yazidis reject the Muslim faith and claim that the Kurds have actually descended from earlier Yazidis. This tribal disagreement has resulted in many genocidal attacks on the Yazidis for generations. But nothing has compared with the violence and brutality of ISIS.

The broader outlines of the ISIS invasion are known to the world, but many details have remained unpublished until now. On June 10, 2014, Islamic State militias overtook the northern Iraqi city of Mosul and the nearby town of Tal Afar, along with parts of Kirkuk and Diyala Provinces, Tikrit, and much of Nineveh Province, in a sweeping victory. One thousand seven hundred Iraqi soldiers who surrendered to the superior forces were massacred. The climate was ripe for ISIS. The massacre happened as a result of the hatred and conflict between the two branches of Islam.

For one thousand years, since the death of Mohammed in 632 AD, Muslims have been deeply divided over who is the rightful successor of Muhammed, whom they revere as the prophet of Allah. To explain it in simple terms, the Shiite Muslims believe that the rightful successor (or caliph) should be a direct descendant in the bloodline of Mohammed. On the other hand, the Sunni Muslims believe that the caliph or rightful successor should be elected by a Muslim Council.

Saddam Hussein was a Sunni Muslim. After the US war in Iraq, and Saddam's execution, the US made sure that the Shiite or Shia Muslims had a majority leadership in Baghdad. This meant that Shia police and officials were also sent into Mosul, where the majority of the people are Sunnis. The Shia were cruel tyrants to the Sunnis and became quickly despised. ISIS was little known then, but as a Sunni force, it was welcomed by many in Mosul and feared by the Shias, who simply ran away for fear of retribution. After overtaking Mosul,

ISIS went on to seize Fallujah, Al Qaim, Abu Ghraib, Ramadi, and other cities and villages in Iraq.

On June 29, 2014, the leader of ISIS, Abu Bakr al-Baghdadi, proclaimed that he was the new caliph of the Islamic State and that he would seek to overtake the entire world, installing Muslim Sharia law in its extremist form. On August 3, the village of Tel Azer was overtaken. That very same day, the city of Sinjar and other villages were also attacked. Over five hundred Yazidi and Christian men were executed in Sinjar alone. Seventy elderly people and children died of thirst or suffocation in the evacuation. An estimated two thousand to five thousand Yazidis, mostly men and boys, were massacred in the entire region during the first two weeks of August, 2014, and two hundred thousand Yazidis and Christians fled the area, pouring mostly into Dohuk, Erbil, and surrounding villages. In the end, a million minority residents were displaced.

The details are elusive, even now. Estimates are that three hundred men were killed in Hardan Village, two hundred in Adnaniya and Jazeera, ninety in Qiniyeh, and dozens more near al-Shimal. Hundreds were killed in other places for refusing to convert to radical Islam. On August 15, in the city of Khocho, eighty men were killed after converting to Islam because their village leader refused to convert, then four hundred more men were shot, and one thousand women and children were taken to slave markets to be sold. The same day, about two hundred Yazidi men were executed at Tal Afar prison for refusing to convert to Islam. On August 25, fourteen Yazidi leaders defending a shrine in Jidala were executed and the shrine was blown up.

I remained in Iraq the entire time and refused to leave.

An Accurate Picture of the Tragedy

No one has systematically interviewed the survivors of this genocide to gain a more accurate picture of what actually happened and how many were injured, killed, or carried away captive. The Kurdish government reports that six hundred women and girls have been repatriated from sexual slavery either by escaping or by the payment of ransoms. Over a thousand more are still held captive and repeatedly raped and resold to other ISIS fighters. There are reports that ISIS soldiers pray before raping the women, and make statements about how it is their right as soldiers of Allah to rape the "infidel" female captives. They declare that the rapes will make the women Muslim.

During the attack in 2014, as many as fifty thousand Yazidis were trapped on Sinjar Mountain without any food or water to sustain them in the brutal desert heat. They received some aid via helicopter drops from the US, Britain and Turkey before US aerial bombardment and Syrian Kurdish PKK forces on the ground cleared the escape route on the Syrian side of the mountain into Syria. On August 13, 2014, about thirty-five thousand refugees climbed down the mountain and fled to safety in Syria. That window of escape was closed on October 21 when ISIS advanced on the Syrian side of Mount Sinjar, trapping the remaining fifteen thousand.

On December 17, 2014, US bombardment, with KDP Kurdish Peshmerga fighters on the ground, retook Sinjar, allowing a southerly escape route from Sinjar Mountain, and held a line against ISIS some thirty kilometers away. All who wished to leave the mountain did so at that time. Some fifteen thousand chose to remain. On December 21, Syrian Kurdish YPG fighters fought their way to the Peshmerga lines, opening a route between Kurdish cities and Syria, which became a major conduit for food and other materials critical to the Kurdistan Region. Most of Sinjar was liberated, though many of the villages, including Tel Azer, remained under ISIS control.

By the end of the main battles, nine Yazidi mass graves had been discovered. In other places, many decomposing bodies were found on the ground where they fell in the invasion. ISIS also destroyed eighteen Yazidi shrines, the most important of which is now being rebuilt. Muslims living in nearby villages and in Sinjar had helped ISIS kill or capture Yazidis during the invasion. Masked Yazidis retaliated against the villages of Muslim collaborators of ISIS on January 25 and 26, targeting Sibaya, Chiri, Khazuga, and Sayer villages. A special unit of the Kurdish Peshmerga was formed of Yazidi soldiers after that to give them a chance to participate in the international response to ISIS. A brigade of Yazidi women, mostly former sex slaves of ISIS, also formed, and had a distinct advantage in battle. An ISIS soldier believes he will not go to heaven if he is killed by a woman.

A United Nations panel concluded tepidly and belatedly, on March 19, 2015, seven months after the genocide occurred, that ISIS "may have committed" genocide against the Yazidis. It was a weak statement, an insult to those who had suffered the genocide, reflecting the lack of vigorous and timely inquiry of the UN among the abundant witnesses sitting on the ground in Iraq waiting for someone to listen to their stories.

About six thousand of the Yazidis and Christians escaping Sinjar and its associated villages during this ongoing battle with ISIS came to the small Christian village of Seje, about ten kilometers from Dohuk, for refuge. I had just moved there with my family from Erbil days before the Christians and Yazidis began to arrive. I had come to assist in the establishment of American University four kilometers away, being briefly named its president, unofficially, before leaving to assist the six thousand displaced people pouring into my new village. I had been working in Erbil and Dohuk for seven years at that time, and operated both a Language and Computing Institute in Erbil and a non-governmental organization (NGO), MedEast, in the region.

As the news of the invasion spread, my Yazidi friend and former coworker Salim Elias, from Bozan, Iraq, arrived for a visit. Salim expressed frustration about the situation and his desire to help. I suggested he begin that moment to create the Yazidi Rescue Project under MedEast, with a Facebook page, and told him I would help him garner small donations, giving him the opportunity to begin helping immediately. He set straight to work, with assistance from his brothers Azad, Ra'ad, Farhad, Maher, and Asaad, and their sister (unnamed for privacy reasons). They all worked with my friends Jordan and Debra Greaser in the physical distributions from the very beginning, and Azad, Farhad, and Maher were later employed with MedEast for various periods of time assisting in Seje and in their home village of Bozan.

Our work in Seje Village grew rapidly as various aid organizations came to help and found us a good partner already stable on the ground there. We hired about one hundred local Sinjari and Christian workers to assist in the relief effort, eventually settling on a core group of about twenty, mostly young male workers, with some female workers sewing dresses for widows and orphans. We also opened an English school and pressed the government to open a public school to serve the village, with UN aid.

We had good access to the stories of our primary workers about their experiences escaping the Mount Sinjar area and recorded most of them, some of which are included here. These retrospective eyewitness accounts were a start for a potentially larger study of the genocide by the MedEast Organization. We also gained a cursory understanding of the Yazidi people, their religious beliefs and customs, and the history of the region, in the search to better understand how to serve them.

The following pages give a look into the history of Iraq—its place in the Old and New Testaments—and the foundational position it has held for thousands of years in the history of mankind. We will also share, for the first time, the tragic but necessary accounts of innocent men, women and children who were uprooted from their homes and their loved ones by the barbaric acts of ISIS. Finally, even in the face of recent destruction, we believe that there is still hope for the future of Iraq and biblical solutions to bring about an eternal change in the region.

PART ONE:
Iraq and Our History

ONE

The G Word
(Recognizing Genocide)

Iraqi Christians might sound like a term that is an oxymoron at first because Iraq is known as a Muslim country where it is illegal to proselytize. However, it might be surprising to know that Iraqi Christians are considered to be one of the oldest continuous Christian communities in the world.

At first glance, it would seem that Iraq's Christians are living in the wrong country. They should have never tried to settle in a Muslim country. Why would they want to be in a country that does not want them anyway? Why don't they just leave?

But the truth is, Christianity in Iraq predates Islam. Christians have been there since the days of the disciples. It is not Christianity that does not belong in Iraq. It is Islam that does not belong there. The Christian churches in Iraq were founded by the very individuals who sat at the feet of Jesus. Iraq's Christians are hardly a lonely tribe of people who ventured into the wrong country. Their churches date back to the first century, when two of Jesus' disciples—St. Thomas and St. Thaddeus—preached the Gospel in what was then Assyria.

There has been a Christian community in Iraq since the beginning of the Gospel message itself. The heartland of the Christian community in Iraq has always been in Mosul and the Nineveh Plain. And their numbers swelled as Christians from other parts of Iraq, like Basra and Baghdad, sought refuge there.

Many of the ancient Christian communities in Iraq still speak Aramaic, the same language Jesus spoke. However, these Christian communities that have lasted more than two thousand years are quickly becoming extinct. They are the last of their kind and are an endangered species. Once they are gone, their language, customs, and historical heritage will be gone forever.

Today, there are less than 300,000 Christians left in Iraq—less than a third of what there was in 2002.[1] Many of the Christians in Iraq have been murdered, enslaved, or fled. According to *Rome Reports*, 120,000 Christians were forced to convert to Islam, and in five years, there will be no more Christians left in Iraq.[2] This kind of persecution against Middle Eastern Christians is not new. Many of the Christian communities under attack in Syria today are descendants of those who were attacked and killed by the thousands in 1933.[3]

Thousands of homeless families have surged into Kurdistan, where they have found provisional shelter and security. Others have made the long and expensive trek to Europe or America looking for a safe haven. Thousands of Iraqi Christians are being killed and even more forced into slavery, but few in the West are aware of their plight.

"Can you help us get to Europe?" one Christian woman asked in November 2014. She had just escaped from ISIS after they attacked Mosul, and she was living with her family in a small classroom in a village school that had been turned into refugee housing. Her family had fled to the mountains north of Mosul and had traveled until they arrived at a village outside of the city of Dohuk. They were sharing the small space with several other families.

She had a cross around her neck and did not wish to take it off, though it was her belief in that cross that had landed her in a refugee

---

1. http://www.christianpost.com/news/christian-population-in-iraq-in-danger-of-being-eradicated-in-5-years-147947/#DhjgJMEwy17JFx3I.99.
2. http://www.romereports.com/2015/10/18/iraq-s-christian-population-will-be-gone-in-five-years-according-to-aid-to-the-church-in-need.
3. http://www.nytimes.com/2015/07/26/magazine/is-this-the-end-of-christianity-in-the-middle-east.html?_r=0.

situation. ISIS had targeted the people of Mosul like her because of their Christian belief. When ISIS attacked Mosul, the Christians living in the city were given three options: "Convert, submit to Islam by paying a tax, or die."

Once ISIS was able to secure the city, Christian and Jewish places of worship were destroyed. Church bells that had rung for hundreds of years were silenced. Wearing of crosses or other non-Islamic symbols was forbidden.

The persecution against the Christians, however, did not start with ISIS. It is only the latest trial to befall believers living in Iraq. Christians have been threatened by Baghdad's death squads and bombings. Christian leaders have been kidnapped in the middle of the night—often never being heard from again.

Christians like Walid Shamoon who had a nice job as a translator for the Australian Embassy being paid $1,500 USD per month—a good salary—had to leave Baghdad in 2011 after the Shiite militia began to persecute him because of his faith. He had a price on his head and an attempt was made on his life. He and his family could not hide at the Australian Embassy forever, and the Shiite Muslims who wanted to take his life knew that. They waited for him to come out of safety so that they could get him.[4]

Even with the international invasion of Iraq in 2003 that was supposed to bring freedom to the Iraqis, Christians continued to be persecuted. Church attacks and bombings actually became more prominent after the toppling of Saddam Hussein, like the notorious church bombing of Our Lady of Salvation Church in 2010 that killed fifty Christians and two priests.[5]

Of course, the Christians are not the only ones being targeted with a vengeance. The Yazidi minority people in Iraq have also been attacked because of their religion. In August 2014, ISIS stormed the

---

4. http://jonestream.blogspot.se/2012/03/iraq-violence-against-christians.html.
5. http://www.theguardian.com/world/2010/nov/01/baghdad-church-siege-survivors-speak.

Yazidi area of the Sinjar Mountains. An entire people group with their own religion, culture, and practices were targeted for annihilation and sex slavery.

Of those who were attacked, the Iraqi Christians and the Yazidis are the only ones without an ally in the region. The Coptic Christians have been able to flee to Egypt. The Armenian Christians have been able to flee to Armenia. The Jews were able to flee to Israel. The Sunni and Shia Muslims have had their respective communities to cling to, but where do the Iraqi Christian communities and Yazidis run? Where do they find refuge? How can they escape annihilation?

The International Community Must Recognize Genocide!

It has been a difficult road to get the international community to officially recognize that ISIS' murderous attacks on the Christians and Yazidi in Iraq is a modern act of "genocide." There were organizations beseeching Europe and the US to officially declare the acts as genocide for years before they finally did so.

Their early refusal to acknowledge the attacks against the Christians and Yazidis of Iraq as genocide seems to be the result of political correctness. In just three months in 2014, more than 800,000 people from millennia-old Christian communities were attacked, raped, forced from their homes, killed, forcefully converted, or sold into slavery.

In a deliberate campaign of hate, ISIS kidnapped thousands of women and children and killed hundreds, maybe thousands, of ethnic Christians and other religious minorities. ISIS destroyed Christian churches, temples, shrines, and other holy sites. Today, virtually no members of the targeted Christian communities can be found in Iraq's Nineveh Province.[6]

---

6. http://www.ushmm.org/information/press/press-releases/museum-releases-groundbreaking-report-on-threats-to-minorities-in-iraq.

One early voice that spoke out for the Iraqi Christians was painfully aware of the fingerprints of genocide—the United States Holocaust Memorial Museum. Their researchers published a report in the fall of 2015 that was instrumental in convincing both Europe and the United States to consider the ISIS attacks as genocide:

"ISIS perpetrated these crimes in accordance with its extreme ideology—targeting particular groups on the basis of their identity… under IS's ideology, adherents of religions considered infidel or apostate—including Yazidis—are to be converted or killed and members of other religions—such as Christians—are to be subjected to expulsion, extortion, or forced conversion."[7]

"The self-proclaimed Islamic State is carrying out a widespread, systematic, and deliberate campaign of ethnic cleansing and crimes against humanity, against religious minorities in Iraq solely because of their religious beliefs," said the museum chairman Tom Bernstein. "We have a moral responsibility not just to bear witness to these crimes but to act to prevent them."[8]

The report went on to define genocide more precisely as it pertains to the Christians and Yazidis in Iraq:

The legal definition of genocide does not require large numbers of people to have been killed or harmed for the necessary intent to exist and for genocide to have been perpetrated. While genocide sometimes involves the killing of very large numbers of people—as in the Holocaust and in Rwanda in 1994—smaller scale attacks can meet the definition of the crime of genocide. As has been shown in various cases pertaining to the genocide of Muslims in Srebrenica, Bosnia, the intent to eliminate a group within a limited area and in limited numbers can constitute genocide. The massacres of primarily men in besieged communities like the village

7. http://www.ushmm.org/confront-genocide/cases/iraq/introduction/key-findings.
8. http://www.ushmm.org/information/press/press-releases/museum-releases-groundbreaking-report-on-threats-to-minorities-in-iraq.

of Kocho and elsewhere, and the mass kidnappings, forced conversions, and enslavement of women and children are examples of the intentional destruction in part of the Yazidi people.[9]

Also in September 2015, members of the International Association of Genocide Scholars, representing the world's largest organization of experts on genocide, called upon the United States Congress to declare that the crimes against Christians and Yazidis by ISIS were "genocide" as defined by the International Convention on the Prevention and Punishment of the Crime of Genocide.[10]

Still the US and Europe held back from making an official declaration. In November 2015, renowned journalist Michael Isikoff warned that Christians were going to be excluded from an impending official United States government declaration of ISIS genocide.[11]

What has been taking place against the Christians and other minority groups in Iraq is a clear case of genocide, but was not being labeled as such. The silence of world leaders was deafening. "It is no secret that hatred of minorities has intensified in certain quarters over the past few years. It is difficult to understand this hate. We are hated because we persist in wanting to exist as Christians," His Exc. Mgr. Bashar Matti Warda, Archbishop of Erbil, Iraq, said in a statement.[12]

An entire ethnic Christian minority is being wiped off of the map, and some world leaders are still reluctant or refuse to identify it as genocide. It seems clear that there is very little intellectual,

---

9. "Our Generation Is Gone—Bearing Witness Trip Report," 21, http://www.ushmm.org/m/pdfs/Iraq-Bearing-Witness-Report-111215.pdf.
10. http://www.washingtonexaminer.com/the-islamic-state-is-committing-genocide/article/2571898.
11. https://www.yahoo.com/politics/u-s-weighs-genocide-label-1298023405674550.html.
12. http://www.christianpost.com/news/hated-because-we-want-to-exist-as-christians-tens-of-thousands-of-iraqi-christians-persecuted-by-isis-losing-hope-142536/.

emotional, or even spiritual connection to what is happening to Christians in other parts of the world.

"I am struck by the widespread apathy and indifference and ignorance concerning this issue among Christians, let alone others," said Timothy Samuel Shah, associate director of the Religious Freedom Project at the Berkley Center for Religion, Peace, and World Affairs at Georgetown University in Washington, DC.[13] Shah spoke at a Heritage Foundation panel on Christian martyrs. He did not have to go back one thousand or even one hundred years to look for examples. He had the genocide taking place in Iraq today as a reference.

"Just as a basic matter of our experiencing the suffering of our brothers and sisters in some kind of way, experiencing some kind of solidarity, we are failing the test," he said, calling his own Catholic parish "pretty indifferent" to the plight of persecuted religious minorities in Iraq. "I don't hear a lot of real outrage from Christian leaders about this issue, on a regular, consistent basis," Shah said. "Where are the widespread demonstrations? Where are letters by thousands and thousands of pastors to appropriate leaders to do more about this? Where are the spontaneous grassroots campaigns? I don't see them."[14]

Lars Adaktusson of the Christian Democrats party in Sweden recognized that ISIS clearly wants to eradicate all Christians from Iraq. He was a leading figure in bringing the EU to the place of finally recognizing that ISIS is committing genocide against Christians and other minorities in the Middle East.

"Just like their fellow Christians in Syria, the inhabitants of Mosul fled from the Islamic State's brutal and deadly rampage," Adaktusson wrote in an op-ed piece. "When faced with the demand from the terrorists' murder patrol to choose between a high penalty

---

13. http://www.catholicnewsagency.com/news/your-apathy-is-hurting-isis-victims-a-challenge-to-us-christians-91609/.
14. Ibid.

tax, converting to Islam or a beheading, an uprooting and dramatic escape was the only way out.[15]

"With this, Mosul's churches were emptied, there were no more church services and for the first time in 1,700 years the church bells were silenced. The people fleeing left their homes, their possessions and their Christian traditions, but also an invaluable cultural heritage."[16]

The patriarch of the Syriac Orthodox Church, Mor Aphrem Karim II, responded by saying, "To not call it genocide would be to double persecute the victims of the monstrous behavior of the perpetrators, the terrorist group ISIS. Atrocities that have escalated to a level not seen before in modern history. When we claim it's a genocide, we do it based on the criteria of the convention and we have no doubt that Pope Francis is right about his conclusion when he also calls it a genocide."[17]

On Thursday, February 4, 2016, the European Parliament, consisting of 781 elected representatives, finally passed a resolution declaring that the ISIS violence against Christians, Yazidis, and other religious minorities was genocide and legally punishable under the 1948 convention on genocide. One month later, on March 17, US Secretary of State John Kerry, speaking for the United States, also declared that ISIS violence in Iraq was genocide against minority people, their faith and their culture.

This book is about the genocide that has been occurring in Iraq for the last several years. We can't really understand what is happening today unless we also look at the biblical history of this Middle Eastern country and how it affects all of us.

---

15. http://www.aina.org/news/20151129140220.htm.
16. Ibid.
17. http://www.huffingtonpost.com/nuri-kino/the-g-word-matters_b_8762970.html.

TWO

We Are All Iraqi

For most people reading this book or watching Iraq in the news, Iraq can seem like a distant, remote, and completely desolate land that is so far from our daily thoughts that it might as well be on Mars. If all you know about Iraq is what is reported in the news, then it might seem like nothing more than a cesspool of violence that breeds the most extreme and brutal people on earth.

From all the pictures and movies, Iraq's terrain looks to be as inhospitable as its political environment. Endless dry deserts, unforgiving wastelands, and brown barren mountain ranges fill our mind's eye when Iraq is mentioned in any passing conversation.

It might be safe to say that we collectively imagine Iraq as a land full of confusion, contradictions, and endless wars. The land where Sunni Muslims and Baathist political parties are in constant conflict with Shia and Kurdish Muslims—all of which makes no sense to anyone not familiar with Islam and the ancient culture of Iraq. The conflicts and alliances are confusing and seem meaningless to everyone outside of Iraq.

If we are honest, Iraq is one of those countries that would be great to tuck into a corner closet somewhere and forget about. The fact that you are reading this book shows you have not yet put Iraq in the far recesses of your mind and are curious to know more.

If you are wondering about Iraq or are concerned about the present genocide, let's begin the process of removing the veil of secrecy from one of the most fascinating lands in the world today, because

Iraq is so much more than what you see in the news or read about on the internet. Before we get into the horrible genocide that is happening right now, let's get a bit of background. Truly, Iraq is a land of hidden treasures for the Christian believer and holds nuggets about the past, present, and future of God's timeless plan. Knowing more about the ancient land of Iraq will completely transform the way you read the Bible and interpret what you hear in the news.

Outside of the land of Israel, Iraq (or the many other names that it is known by in scripture) is mentioned more times in the Bible than any other nation on earth. It has been nicknamed the "cradle of civilization" because it's where most experts agree the journey for man began. Whether you believe in creationism or evolution, the current archaeological data points to Iraq as the starting point for civilization.[18]

Iraq is the home of the great Tigris and Euphrates Rivers, which are referenced frequently in the Bible, and which provided the water needed for the earliest civilizations documented throughout the Old Testament. The civilizations that emerged on the banks of these rivers are the source of the earliest stories of mankind. (It is worth noting that the course of the rivers have not always been the same as they are today.)

If most experts agree that Iraq is the cradle of civilization, then that means all the people of the world can theoretically trace their heritage back to these early societies. With that in mind, in one sense, we can say that we are all Iraqi.

Our Connection with Iraq

If you understand that, then you realize the story of Iraq is also part of your story. No longer is genocide occurring in a remote country that has no relevance to your life. When you learn more about the genocide in Iraq, in essence, you are learning more about yourself.

---

18. Charles Keith Maisels, *The Near East: Archaeology in the "Cradle of Civilization"* (London: Routledge, 1993).

This single idea that we are all Iraqi can dramatically transform the way you read about Iraq in the Bible and see Iraq in the news. Even the refugees fleeing from the conflict in Iraq will be changed in your eyes if you see them as your relatives and not as remote foreigners from a backward society.

Hopefully understanding your connection with Iraq will impact your interpretation of what you read or hear about Iraq for the rest of your life.

Of course, Iraq is not just important because it was the cradle of civilization. The events happening in Iraq are dramatically shaping the world we live in today. Though it might seem to be a small, insignificant, remote country, in reality, the storm brewing there is causing ripple effects throughout the entire world.

Iraq is the heart of the Middle East and represents the country with the most insane persecution against Christians in the world today. ISIS is arguably the most dangerous terrorist group in the world today, and not only are they operating out of Iraq, but their leader, who desires to rule the entire Middle East—Abu Bakr al-Baghdadi—was born and raised in Iraq.

For Christians who take the Great Commission seriously, Iraq represents the heart of the unreached people groups. It is in the center of the final frontier for the Gospel message located in the region of the world today commonly known as the 10/40 Window. The 10/40 Window refers to those regions of the eastern hemisphere between 10 and 40 degrees north of the equator, right where Iraq is located. This is the area of the world that has the least access to the Gospel message of Jesus Christ. It is also the area of the world that is the most violent and volatile, has the lowest quality of life, and the lowest level of socioeconomic development.

The majority of the 10/40 Window can basically be found between the borders of China and Jerusalem, and if you take a pencil and draw a line between China and Jerusalem, you will cross Iraq.

Iraq is not a country that can be easily ignored. The same group that is attacking Christians in Iraq is also launching attacks throughout the Middle East, Africa, Europe and even America. Iraq might seem far away and completely removed from our everyday lives, but their reality is quickly becoming our reality. Ignorance is no longer a luxury we can afford. Ignoring the challenges in Iraq will only fuel the problem.

In many strange ways, the country of Iraq is like a road map to understanding what is happening in the world today.

What can we learn from Iraq? What benefit would a book like this give? Why does Iraq matter?

According to biblical authors, Iraq can tell us a lot about our past, present, and future. The Bible plainly tells us many things about the beginning of time since the creation of man. The Bible also goes into great detail about Iraq as it relates to the second coming of Jesus Christ.

We will look at the history of Iraq and why it is still important to the world today.

THREE

Iraq in the Bible

There are few places on earth where Christianity is as old as it is in Iraq, and even fewer places are mentioned in the Bible as many times as Iraq. According to the Bible, the geographical location of Iraq is central to the creation of man and the end times. Iraq and the genocide against Christians are virtually impossible to understand without reflecting back on what the Bible says about the region.

Our understanding of what the Bible teaches about Iraq can be diluted with all of the news of bombings, kidnappings, and war over oil. The long, rich culture and heritage of Iraq is easily forgotten when militaries from all over the world come and go as they please and leave destruction and devastation in their wake.

War after war has been the main staple for the Iraqi diet for so long that the world cannot remember a time when there was ever anything charming about Iraq. Just the mention of someone traveling to Iraq can quickly conjure up images of kidnappings and crossfire. If a family member learns that someone they love is traveling to Iraq, they immediately try to talk them out of it.

Most countries advise their citizens not to travel to Iraq. Two ladies from the Philippines working with a ministry called Back to Jerusalem to help the women who escaped from ISIS were denied exit from Manila, because the Filipino government does not allow their citizens to travel to Iraq. There will be more important details about Back to Jerusalem in later chapters.

The EU and US issue the highest level of warnings for their citizens considering travel to Iraq. "The Department of State warns U.S. Citizens against all but essential travel to Iraq. Travel in Iraq remains very dangerous given the security situation," the US State Department warned in January 2016.[19]

The website goes on to say, "U.S. citizens in Iraq remain at high risk for kidnapping and terrorist violence. Methods of attack have included roadside improvised explosive devices (IEDs) including explosively formed penetrators (EFPs), magnetic IEDs placed on vehicles, human and vehicle-borne IEDs, mines placed on or concealed near roads, mortars and rockets, and shootings using various direct fire weapons. When such attacks occur, they frequently take place in public gathering places such as cafes, markets, and other public venues."[20]

The Australian government issued a very simple travel warning for Iraq: "Official advice: Do not travel."[21]

Reading travel warnings like this will quickly create images of Iraq that would keep anyone from ever wanting to travel to Iraq. It is especially daunting for any Christian living there, let alone wanting to travel there.

The fear of what is happening in Iraq has arguably created a vacuum of ignorance for the rest of the world, and that ignorance is a ticking time bomb for Christians worldwide. The violence that has been holding Iraqi Christians hostage for generations is beginning to spill over into the rest of the world. If we do not learn from what has happened in Iraq, we may very well be destined to experience the repetition of it on a larger scale.

Christianity, according to some experts, is about to be erased forever from the map of Iraq, and most politicians who have the power

---

19. http://travel.state.gov/content/passports/en/alertswarnings/iraq-travel-warning.html .
20. Ibid.
21. https://smartraveller.gov.au/countries/iraq.

to prevent it are either too corrupt, too ignorant, or too apathetic to stop it. The politicians are not alone in their apathy and ignorance. They are in good company with many Christian leaders as well.

If we have any chance to prevent the Iraqi genocide in Iraq from spilling over, we must first learn what is causing it. Unfortunately, trying to decipher and learn about the events in Iraq from today's news is virtually impossible. That is the bad news.

The good news is that a quick education on Iraq is just not available through recent news feeds. To learn about the events in Iraq, you don't need to enroll into a Middle Eastern evening class at a community college or read a complicated thesis paper from an expert. You merely need to wipe the dust off your Bible.

The Bible Reveals Iraq's History

The Bible goes into great detail about Iraq and explains the history, the land, the people, and the culture in ways that Wikipedia can only scratch the surface. One of the main challenges, however, is that the name *Iraq* is never actually mentioned in the sixty-six books of the Bible. Instead, you might recognize Iraq by the other names used in Scripture, such as Mesopotamia, Ur, Shinar, Chaldea, Babel, Erech (Uruk), Akkad, Calneh, Babylon, and Assyria.

Iraq has been either wholly or partially owned or controlled by the Assyrian Empire, Persian Empire, Roman Empire, Ottoman Empire, British Empire, and many others throughout history. The borders of Iraq have been established, destroyed, redrawn, reestablished, and destroyed again many times throughout history.

The land has been mostly referred to as Mesopotamia, which is a Greek word that refers to a land "between the rivers." The rivers of Mesopotamia were the Tigris and the Euphrates, and, as we said, it is considered to be the "cradle of civilization." Mesopotamia is an area about the size of California and can be found throughout the Bible. Many things took place in the Bible for the first time in Iraq. Some of these items may be debatable with some theologians, but here are a few of those that are not widely known:

+ The Garden of Eden was in Iraq (Genesis 2:10–14).

+ God created the first man and woman in Iraq (Genesis 2:7–8).

+ Satan is first mentioned in the Bible as having appeared in Iraq (Genesis 3:1–6).

+ The first sin took place in Iraq (Genesis 3:6).

+ The first birth took place in Iraq (Genesis 3:24; 4:1).

+ The first crime took place in Iraq (Genesis 4:8).

+ Cain tried to run from God for the first time and escaped to the land of Nod in Iraq (Genesis 4:16).

+ The first boat was arguably constructed in Iraq (Genesis 6:14).

+ The first boat arguably landed in Iraq after the flood (problem with translation of Mt. Ararat)

+ The world's first sacrifice before and after the flood were made in Iraq.

+ The world's first wine was arguably made in Iraq (Genesis 9:20–21).

+ After the flood, Nimrod started the world's first city in Iraq (Genesis 10:9–10).

+ Nimrod became the world's first dictator in Iraq, ruling many cities under his control (Genesis 10:10–12).

+ One of the cities that was started by Nimrod was Uruk, an ancient translation for the word *Iraq* (Genesis 10:10)

+ The confusion of the world's languages (or arguably the start of every language in the world today) took place at the Tower of Babel in Iraq (Genesis 11:5–11).

- Abraham first came from Ur—in Iraq—making him an Iraqi by birth (Genesis 11:31).

- The world's first empire was in Iraq (Daniel 1:1–2).

- The world's first great revival was recorded in Iraq when the entire kingdom of Nineveh repented (Jonah 3).

- The Israelites were first taken into slavery by a kingdom that included modern-day Iraq (2 Kings 17:6).

- The kingdom of Judah was taken into slavery to Babylon (Iraq) (Daniel 1:1–7).

Besides all of the biblical firsts that occurred in Iraq, we also see many other biblical events unfold in Iraq.

1. Isaac's bride came from Iraq (Genesis 24:10).

2. Daniel was thrown in the lions' den (most likely) in Iraq (Daniel 6).

3. Shadrach, Meshach, and Abednego were thrown in the furnace in Iraq (Daniel 3).

4. Belshazzar, king of Babylon, saw the "writing on the wall" in Iraq (Daniel 5).

5. Nebuchadnezzar was a king in Iraq (2 Kings 24).

6. Ezekiel preached in Iraq (Ezekiel 1:1–2).

7. The book of Nahum was a prophecy against Iraq (Nahum 1:8).

In addition to those past events, when it comes to prophecies, Iraq is one of the main places thought of as the subject of warnings from the book of Revelation.

A quick skim of the Iraqi events found in the Bible reveals our ignorance and knowledge at the same time. We have all heard so much about the Middle Eastern region in the Bible; we just didn't know that it was about Iraq.

According to the Bible, long before the genocide we are witnessing today, Iraq was a haven of culture and innovation, but it was not just an important incubator of the human race; it has played a central role throughout history.

When Alexander the Great conquered the known world, he, like many others before him, made Iraq the seat of his empire. One thousand years after that, the Abbasid Muslim Dynasty built Baghdad to serve as the capital of the Caliphate. Five hundred years after that, Baghdad rose to be one of the world's most populated cities. Today, al-Baghdadi, the leader of ISIS, calls Iraq the center of his caliphate.

Even though we call Iraq the "cradle of civilization," it is hard to know what that really means until we notice that it was in Iraq where the wheel was first invented. The earliest writings of man are found here indicating that the Iraqi's invented writing. Some argue that it was in Iraq, not China, that the first paper was invented.

Iraq is the country that gave us a lot of other firsts, not just biblical firsts. Iraq was the birthplace of the first laws, alchemy, trigonometry, Algebra problems, the idea of decimal points and fractions of below zero, an (accurate) calendar system, maps, sailboats, schools, the pediatric practice of medicine, and so much more.

From the ancient days of the Bible till modern history, Iraq has played a critical role. Unfortunately, that role seems to be long gone, and today it is an abyss of suffering and pain, abandoned by the rest of the world. In that way, it seems to share something in common with the most unlikely of places—Gilman, Colorado.

A Modern Comparison

In the mountains of Colorado there is a small town called Gilman. According to the town records, Gilman was founded with enthusiasm in 1886 during the Colorado Silver Boom, which started only seven years earlier in 1879.

Both the Denver and the Rio Grande Railroad helped new residents reach the vibrant little town. Soon zinc and lead were also discovered, and large companies from all over the United States began to make investments. In 1912, the New Jersey Zinc company moved into town to capitalize on the discovery. Everyone who wanted to make money from the boom flocked to the lively little town. Gilman became one of the major producers of silver in all of Colorado by 1930.

However, in 1984, the entire town was evacuated when the lead and zinc waste were discovered to be toxic to humans. Everything that was of value was taken, and everything else that was toxic was left behind. All the buildings that used to show the signs of life are still there. Schools, businesses, banks, grocery stores, homes, cul-de-sac communities, and churches can all be found in Gilman, but the people have all fled and the glory days of the boom are long gone.

In so many ways, Iraq was like that, a place where the world found the resources they needed to have a successful and thriving life, but the situation has become so toxic that it seems to be no longer suitable for human life. Families are fleeing in droves. Entire people groups are being annihilated. Wars and rumors of war are everywhere. It seems there is no safe place to live in Iraq, and like the little town of Gilman, there needs to be a forced evacuation of the entire country.

However, the Bible reveals that God has a special plan for Iraq. Iraq is serving God's purpose for the end times, and it is up to His people to search His Word to discover the meanings that lay beneath the surface. The sooner we understand, the sooner we can stop the genocide.

FOUR

Legacy Lost

An overweight man in a long black robe and thick black beard swings a sledgehammer in a video recorded and sent out by ISIS in April 2015. The man is using the sledgehammer to destroy a large grey stone tablet that was several thousand years old.

He has a black leather satchel that looks like a man's purse on his left that hangs from his right shoulder. The black leather satchel holds his handgun. It is clear that his chubby hands are not used to swinging a sledgehammer because each swing is weak and does little damage to the stone wall.

What he is unable to do, though, is being made up for by his partner, who is sitting on top of the eight-foot-high stone tablet wall cutting chunks of it with an industrial electric handsaw. He cuts the ancient tablets into blocks that are removed one by one.

Little by little the ISIS fighters tear away at the stone tablet that had lasted for several thousand years and was declared as a UNESCO world heritage site.[22]

What they are not able to do by hand is further assisted by a bull-dozer that rolls over and destroys large portions of the world heritage site. Once the bulldozer is able to make large enough openings in the building, old oil barrels that are packed full of explosives are brought in. One by one, the makeshift barrel bombs are linked together in a daisy chain along the walls of the ancient building. Moments later, a camera shot shows an aerial view of the entire ancient compound

22. http://whc.unesco.org/en/tentativelists/1463.

where the ISIS fighters are working. After a few seconds, the entire ancient heritage site explodes. The ground shakes and a plume of smoke shoots up to the sky. And just like that, an entire city that went back to the thirteenth century BC is gone forever.

Everything was destroyed. Nothing was left.

The city that the ISIS terrorists were destroying was the city of Nimrud. To those who are not familiar with the Bible, it was just another oddly named city in the Middle East, but for those who know their biblical history, it was more than that. Nimrud was known as the city of Calah or Kalhu in the book of Genesis (10:11). At first glance, the city was nothing more than old rubble in the barren northern area of Iraq, but in reality, it was the reminder for the entire world of what happens when man rebels against God. It was a remnant of the notorious leader Nimrod, who became the world's first tyrant leader.

The city of Nimrud harkened back to the days of mankind at the end of the flood. The waters of the flood had just receded back, and patches of marshes and lakes formed, exposing large swaths of land suitable for the habitation of birds and wildlife. The exposed land was productive, fertile land that was naturally irrigated with the Edenic rivers—the Tigris and Euphrates.

There was no hint of the dry, arid, desert land of today. The perfect climate of the Garden of Eden was gone forever, but the land "between the rivers" was the best that the known world at that time had to offer. God had carefully guided and protected Noah's ark until it came to rest on the perfect place for mankind to begin again.

Many believe that Noah's ark landed on Mount Ararat, on the border of Armenia and Turkey, but please consider another point of view, an ancient Iraqi point of view from Genesis 8:4, which says, "Then the ark rested in the seventh month, the seventeenth day of the month, on the mountains of Ararat."

The phrase "on the mountains of Ararat" would seem to signify a mountainous region instead of just a single mountain. Mount Ararat

on the border of Turkey and Armenia is only known as Mount Ararat
in English. The locals, both in Turkey and in Armenia, call it something completely different that sounds nothing like Ararat.

The Bible continues on and says in verse 5, "And the waters
decreased continually until the tenth month. In the tenth month,
on the first day of the month, the tops of the mountains were seen."
This indicates that other mountain tops could be seen from where
Noah's boat landed, further indicating that the ark rested in a range
of mountains, not on a single mountain.

Moses wrote in the book of Genesis in the Hebrew scriptures
of Noah that the ark landed in "rrt," which biblical translators in the
seventeenth century guessed was Armenia's Mount Ararat.

However, some locals in Iraq say the ark landed on Mount Judi,
in the kingdom of Urartia (pronounced "rrt"), a short distance north
of Iraq in Turkey. They claim that there is a specific location that is
still visible on the side of the mountain in the shape of the ship of the
proportions and dimensions mentioned in the Bible, though only the
calcified remains of animal droppings are left. The town nearest the site
was named Noa in ancient times, and is so called to this day. Kurdish
guerrilla fighters in Turkey (the PKK) occupy the site, currently block-
ing any research to verify the claims to see whether or not they are true.

Ancient Iraqi writings have their own altered form of a flood
story, which is written on clay tablets prepared by the Sumerians in
northern Iraq. According to the story, God's voice came through the
wall telling of a coming flood. He told the man to build a great ship
and carry beasts and birds on it. Winds and a great flood came. A
window was opened, sunlight came in, and the man fell down to worship. After landing he sacrificed and bowed down to worship.

The Chaldean story from southern Iraq adds that a man named
Noa lived with his three sons, Sem, Japet, and Chem, his wife, Tidea,
and their wives, Pandora, Noela, and Noegla. He foresaw destruction and began building a boat. Many years later, the oceans, inland

seas, and rivers burst forth from beneath, coinciding with many days of violent rain. The waters overflowed, and the human race drowned except for Noa and his family, who survived on his ship. The man drove his ship aground in the Corcyraean mountains. He disembarked with his wife and offered sacrifices. Afterward, men took bitumen from the remnants of the ship to make charms against evil. These stories of Noah still stir among the local population in Iraq.

After the flood, the population of the eight members from Noah's ark multiplied, and various tribes were built up. All the nations of the world can trace their roots back to the three sons of Noah. In those days, all the nations shared the same heritage, and they all shared the same language. They were slowly populating the Mesopotamian delta and were unified in their tribal spirit and unity. They were ripe for a strong leader.

Genesis 11:1 tells us that the descendants of Noah migrated to the land of Shinar, and out of the three sons, Ham was the most "fruitful." Shem had twenty-six descendants, Japheth had fourteen, but Ham had thirty. Out of the original seventy nations listed in Genesis 10 and 11, almost half or thirty of them were from Ham. Consequently, it is very easy to understand why the dominant race, language, and culture of the ancient world at that time was Hamitic.

If we pay close attention to the names of Ham's sons, we will recognize those from world history—including the history of Iraq. The descendants of Ham were Cush, Mizraim, Put, and Canaan. Basically, Cush is Ethiopia, Mizraim is Egypt, Put is Libya, and Canaan is—well—the land of Canaan. Out of the tribe of Ham, many focus on the sons of Canaan because of the continuing stories of Israel and the Holy Land, which was inhabited by the Canaanites, but none of the sons were more dominant than Nimrod.

Nimrod Led the World to Paganism

Cush was the father of Nimrod, who became the world's first great leader and was known as a mighty warrior. He was from the tribe of Cush, which many interpret that he is directly related to the Ethiopians. Nimrod came from a successful lineage. The descendants of Ham are often said to be cursed, but that can be considered a faulty interpretation based on a misreading of Genesis 9:20–25, in which Noah became drunk and Ham saw his father naked and did not cover him up. When Noah awakened from his drunk stupor, he said, "Cursed be Canaan; a servant of servants he shall be to his brethren."

From the direct reading of the verse, it would seem that Canaan, the son of Ham was cursed—not Ham. In fact, the Hamites went out and founded the first great empires of Babylon, Assyria, Egypt, Sidon, Tyre, and Carthage, and some Cushites are even thought to have gone east to establish the great empire of India.[23] During the time that these great empires were being formed, the Shemites and Japhethites maintained a very simple agrarian life. Wealth was often calculated in descendants, land, and livestock. If that is indeed the measurement, then none of the brothers had more than Ham.

And no one was greater than Nimrod. He was a mighty hunter in the eyes of the Lord and captured the attention of the known world at that time. For a thousand years many people in Egypt named their children Nimrod.[24] He is credited with founding the features of paganism and human sacrifice[25] and possibly encouraging worship of himself as a deity.

As pointed out by Olufolahan Olatoye Akintola in his book about the nations descended from Ham, "Today it is believed that all pagan gods are representations of Nimrod. For instance, the Assyrian god of war Nimurda is named directly after Nimrod. The Roman god of Bacchus is also a reference to Nimrod because it is derived from the Semitic name 'Bar-Cush,' which means 'son of Cush.' In his deified

---

23. Drusilla Dunjee Houston, *Wonderful Ethiopians of the Ancient Cushite Empire* (City: Publisher, Date, 1926), 226.
24. http://www.thechristianidentityforum.net/downloads/Chaldean-Genesis.pdf p.313.
25. http://www.biblestudentarchives.com/documents/Ham.pdf.

form, Nimrod was believed to be the incarnate of the sun god that was worshipped as Baal while his wife Semiramis was worshipped as the sun goddess Asharte."[26]

Nimrod's image was likewise incorporated very early on in the Chaldean zodiac as a child seated on his mother's lap, and both mother and child were worshipped, she as the Queen of Heaven, and he as her holy son.[27]

Nimrod was a powerful leader, and his kingdom grew to be the world's first major trading center. He led the birth of a great and powerful civilization. But he put his trust in his own powers and strength, not in God's. Remember that this was not long after the flood had taken place, and already leaders like Nimrod were taking steps that would be a repeat of history.

Nimrod was convinced he could make it on his own powers and understanding. He persuaded the people to rely on the wit and strength of man, not God.

Genesis 11:2–4 says,

> And it came to pass, as they journeyed from the east, that they found a plain in the land of Shinar, and they dwelt there. Then they said to one another, "Come, let us make bricks and bake them thoroughly." They had brick for stone, and they had asphalt for mortar. ⁴ And they said, "Come, let us build ourselves a city, and a tower whose top *is* in the heavens; *let us make a name for ourselves,* lest we be scattered abroad over the face of the whole earth." (emphasis added)

The people came to the valley of Shinar, which is in modern-day Iraq, and they said let us, "Make a name for ourselves." The phrase "make a name for ourselves" refers to reputation. They were trying to make a reputation for themselves outside of their relationship with God.

---

26. Olufolahan Olatoye Akintola, *Nations of the World…How they Evolved!: Families and Nations that came out of Ham,* 4th rev. ed. (City: Hilldew View International, 2013), 60.
27. Jessica DJ Jones, *Ask for the Ancient Paths* (City: Xulon Press, 2006), 188.

According to this passage of Scripture, their attempt to build a tower was not to merely reach the sky. The purpose was to create unity. The people wanted to show that they could accomplish unity, not under the leadership of God, but under the leadership of man. The tower was symbolic that God was obsolete and that man had amassed such superior knowledge that He was no longer needed.

The Tower of Babel was not just a construction endeavor; it was a religious duty. There is a difference. If it were merely a practical need, a construction endeavor would be determined by a benefit and loss analysis. However, a tower that is built as a religious duty abandons all ideas of self-preservation.

Nimrod needed to make building the tower and following him a religious duty. This would give him the most power. Priests and ceremonies were set up to make his control more complete.

With this kind of power, Nimrod gradually turned his government structure into a tyrannical monarchy. He influenced and forced people to rely on his power instead of the power of God. As all powerful reigns of tyranny have shown in history, when absolute power pushes ahead, deification of personality is not far behind.

From Nimrod's city of Babel, the nations of the earth adopted the foundations of idol worship, and it was from this epicenter that ceremonial idolatry was scattered all over the earth. The mysterious religions of Babylon all stem from Nimrod, and it is these religions that have influenced the world and form the standard formulation of latter pantheistic and polytheistic religions.

Again, Akintola pointed out in his book, "The high tower of Babel that was intended to reach heaven was in conformity with the procedures for Baal worship of the sun god, which requires incense and sacrifices to be offered and from a high tower to the sun god and the host of heaven, as the spirits of the zodiac."[28]

---

28. Akintola, 59.

Nimrod perverted man's relationship with God and led the people to pantheism, the belief that nature and God are in essence the same. After the flood, a new race of human beings was given a new start and reunited with the God of all creation, but Nimrod took the world away from monotheism and back into the dark world of polytheism, the belief in many gods.

"There is plentiful evidence to suggest that all forms of paganism, meaning all forms of pantheism and polytheism, trace its roots back to Ancient Babylonia. It is no secret that the assortment of gods and goddesses from Egypt, India, Greece and Rome all find their beginnings in the original pantheon of the Babylonians."[29]

This story of Iraq gives us some interesting insight. Through a personal relationship with God, man can find unity, but when man searches for unity without God, he finds chaos and confusion. When man connects to God in a personal way, he is organically connected to others who are also connected to Him. As long as mankind is inseparable with God, human beings are in essence inseparable with one another. God is the anchor point and provides connection to all that exists.

Unity, as it is artificially created by man (even through efforts of religion or humanism), is a false doctrine and creates the opposite effect of true unity under God.

The people of Babel had everything they needed for unity. They had leadership, a common goal, a vision, a purpose, a plan, and they even had the resources they needed to complete a unified task. What they did not have was connection to God—the primary ingredient needed for unity. God is the unifying agent!

The ways of man divide, separate, and destroy.

Genesis 11:6 says, "Indeed the people are one" or "echad." *Echad* is the Hebrew word meaning "which is attributed to God himself." It is the same word that is used in the Shema, "Hear, O Israel, The Lord

---

29. http://www.israel-a-history-of.com/nimrod.html.

our God, the Lord is One" (Deuteronomy 6:4). In Hebrew it would be pronounced "Sh'ma Yis'ra'eil Adonai Eloheinu Adonai echad."

The people of Babel all spoke with one language and one heart. According to paleo-linguists, all the languages of the world came from one single language.[30] However, without a relationship with God, the citizens of Babel were left with no unity because true unity, echad, only comes through a unity with God.

Today, Iraq continues to suffer because there is no unity with God. Nimrod led the people of Iraq away from God, then after the Tower of Babel, God led all of those people away from Nimrod.

---

30. http://www.sciencedaily.com/releases/2011/04/110415165500.htm.

FIVE

Iraq...Found in China

Oddly enough, a journey from Iraq's Tower of Babel to other countries in the world leads us to China. Some of the proof we have that the languages of the world diversified from the Tower of Babel can be found in the rich characters used in the Chinese language. The ancient writings of China can both confirm and enlighten us about the ancient writings of Moses. The Chinese language is fascinating and holds many secrets that the rest of the world is not aware of.

According to most population census reports, one out of every five people in the world is Chinese.[31] Apparently God loves the Chinese so much that He is making a lot of them. Chinese is the number one mother-language in the world and is one of the oldest.[32]

Today China is experiencing the world's largest revival,[33] and many Chinese are made to feel as if they are abandoning their families and heritage when they convert to Christianity. There is a common saying in China that "one more Christian in China is one less Chinese." The meaning of this saying is derived from the idea that Christianity is a "Western" religion. In the traditional mind-set of the Chinese, if someone from China converts to the Western religion of Christianity then they must abandon all of the things that make them Chinese.

31. http://afe.easia.columbia.edu/special/china_1950_population.htm.
32. http://www.ethnologue.com/statistics/size.
33. http://www.charismamag.com/spirit/revival/14745-the-biggest-revival-in-history.

"Whenever I go home to visit my parents during holidays," one BTJ (Back to Jerusalem) worker named Gina recently shared, "my parents always pressure me to take offerings to the dead elders in our family dynasty. These offerings are not just paying respects, but are a religious practice that is essentially ancestral worship, which is popular in China. When I refuse to make offerings or burn incense at the graves of my ancestors, then my family is forced to view me as a traitor who has abandoned our Chinese culture. It is a heavy burden to carry, because they do not understand that I can no longer participate in those practices as a follower of Jesus Christ."

Gina is not alone. As the number of Christians in China grows, so, too, do the number of families that feel the pain of seeing loved ones abandon the traditions of ancestral worship. But there is a secret that many Chinese do not realize.

That secret can be found hidden in the characters of their language.

Chinese is one of the oldest existing languages in the world, and if we examine it closely, it is possible to find the roots of the Chinese forefathers who first arrived in China from Iraq. If it is true that all men on earth come from Iraq, and if it is also true that the Chinese language was invented several thousand years ago, then it must be true that we can find evidence of the Chinese migrating directly from Iraq in the Chinese language.

The Chinese believe that a Chinese citizen should be a Taoist, Confucianist, or Buddhist in order to be a "real" Chinese. The problem with this idea is that the Chinese people can trace their history back to the first emperor, Huangdi, who lived 2,700 years before Christ,[34] which is more than two thousand years prior to Taoism, Confucianism, or Buddhism.

So the question becomes, what religion did the Chinese people practice during those two thousand early years?

---

34. http://www.britannica.com/topic/Huangdi.

Hold on to your seats, because to find the answer to this question, we must look to the Chinese characters, which oddly enough lead us to events that took place, not in China, but in Iraq.

No one really knows when the Chinese language actually started. We do know that it is older than most other languages. It is older than most hieroglyphics. It is, in fact, older than the pyramids in Egypt.

Prior to the flood, people lived a very long time. Adam lived 930 years (Genesis 5:5). Methuselah lived 969 years (Genesis 5:27). It was only a mere ten generations from the creation to the flood, so the events that took place from the days of Adam could have easily been passed to Noah. And if Noah knew about the events, then they could have easily been passed on to his three sons during the long, lonely journey aboard the ark with no books to read, games to play, or Facebook to update.

If it is true that all men came from Shem, Ham, and Japheth, then it is arguable that Huangdi, the first emperor of China, came from those who were scattered after the Tower of Babel and carried the stories of mankind from Iraq to China. One of those stories he carried was about the first murder ever recorded in the history of man—a story that unfolded in modern-day Iraq.

After sin had entered the Garden of Eden, Adam and Eve were expelled from paradise (Genesis 3:22–24). Adam and Eve were not just driven out of the geographical location of the garden, but they were also prevented from physically abiding in the glorious presence of the Almighty ever again as they had been accustomed to before the fall.

Adam and Eve were bound to the corruptible physical natural body that was destined for death. They tasted pain, illness, and weakness for the very first time. It must have been a frightening experience. Adam had to toil by tilling the ground to obtain enough food for himself and his wife. In the course of time, Eve tasted the pain of birth with no one to help her except for Adam. She gave birth to two sons, Cain and Abel.

Abel was the keeper of sheep, and Cain was a tiller of the ground. It soon came to pass that the two brothers brought their offering to the Lord. God accepted the offering of Abel, but rejected that of Cain. Abel offered to God his best and Cain did not. Cain was overcome with jealousy and his jealously grew to anger.

> The Lord respected Abel and his offering, but He did not respect Cain and his offering. And Cain was very angry, and his countenance fell. So the Lord said to Cain, "Why are you angry? And why has your countenance fallen? If you do well, will you not be accepted? And if you do not do well, sin lies at the door. And its desire *is* for you, but you should rule over it." (Genesis 4:4–7)

Today, just like then, sin is at the door waiting for us, to rule over us. It only needs us to give in to our desire to hate. The sin of hate leads to anger, and anger leads to the lust of destruction.

Cain tricked his brother and led him out to the field. Then he gave in to his lust to unleash his anger and killed Abel. Cain submitted himself to his own sin and desire and killed another human being who was made in the image of God Himself. God said the blood of Abel cried out to him and that the ground that received his blood would no longer be available for Cain. Cain was banished and forced to live as a foreigner, though God in His mercy placed a mark upon him that protected him from others who might try to harm him (v. 15). This is the first record of a murder ever taking place, and you might be surprised to know that every Chinese child learns about this event every day, and has for several thousand years.

Chinese history is captured in the Chinese character, and by learning the Chinese characters, you can learn Chinese history—and, in this case, Iraqi history. The Chinese language is made up of thousands of characters, and every character tells a story. In this chapter you will see that the events in history that took place in Iraq were recorded by the Chinese in the Chinese language.

Chinese: The Oldest Writing in the World

The Chinese writing system is the oldest continual writing system in the world. The Chinese language is not like English, where the sounds of the language is Romanized. Instead, it is a written language where each character represents an event and tells a story. It is a pictorial language that has been handed down for thousands of years.

The English language has twenty-six different letters (A–Z), and each letter represents a different sound. Chinese has tens of thousands of different characters, most of them small variants of major symbols. Encoded into the Chinese characters are thousands of stories that represent the origin of the word, and if you know the meaning, you can reach back in time and understand a little something more about the culture.

Even Asian cultures that do not speak the Chinese language, like Japanese and Koreans, still use the ancient Chinese characters because of the longevity of the ancient communication system and the ability to communicate history, culture, and ideas with only a single picture.

To see how the Chinese language reflects the ancient stories from the beginning of creation as told in the Bible, we can start with the story of Cain and Able. The character 兄 (*xiong*) used to represent the word for "brother" is made up of two characters: "mouth" or *kou* (口) and "son" or *er* (儿). This word is pronounced "shong." The Chinese word for "brutal murderer" is pronounced the same, "shong," but the character is different (兇). It is the character for "brother" with an X or a mark on his head.

When children in China learn the Chinese language, they are basically learning about the feud between the two brothers living east of Eden and the story of one of them brutally murdering the other and receiving a mark on his head. This is only one example, but there are many more Chinese characters that retell the same stories as those found in the book of Genesis and many connections that can be found to the God of the Bible.

Two thousand years prior to Buddhism, Taoism, and Confucianism, China was monotheistic. The Chinese worshiped one God who created all things. His name was Shangdi (上帝). The Chinese pronunciation of the word *Shangdi* is similar in pronunciation to *Shadai* or *El Shadai*.

Since the beginning of Chinese records, the emperors would offer a border sacrifice. At the border sacrifice, the emperor would make the following proclamation to the Creator of the universe. See if any of it looks familiar:

> Of old in the beginning, there was the great chaos, without form and dark. The five elements [planets] had not begun to revolve, nor the sun and moon to shine. You, O Spiritual Sovereign, first divided the grosser parts from the purer. You made heaven. You made earth. You made man. All things with their reproducing power got their being.[35]

One of the most popular tourist destinations in all of China is the Temple of Heaven, which was built for the annual sacrifice and worship of Shangdi. The Temple of Heaven is the largest existing altar in the world, and there is no image of Shangdi painted or engraved anywhere on the temple, which is in line with Exodus 20:4: "You shall not make for yourself a carved image—any likeness of anything that is in heaven above, or that is in the earth beneath, or that is in the water under the earth."

China's greatest historian was a man by the name of Si Ma Qian, and he documented the prayers said at the border sacrifice to the ancient Chinese God Shangdi, which, as evidence shows, was the same God that Noah and his three sons worshipped. Notice how the above prayer is similar to the writings found in Genesis 1. For

---

35. James Legge, *The Notions of the Chinese Concerning Gods and Spirits* (Hong Kong: publisher, date, 1852), 28.

example, look at Genesis 1:1–2: "In the beginning God created the heavens and the earth. The earth was without form, and void; and darkness was on the face of the deep. And the Spirit of God was hovering over the face of the waters."

Let's look at some other examples of how the stories of the Bible taking place in the ancient land of Iraq are reflected in the Chinese language.

Genesis 1:26 says, "Let Us make man in Our image …" The word for "make" or "create" in Chinese is *zao* (造). This character is made up of the characters for "clay" (土) and the character for "mouth" (口), from which there is breath. To these is added the character for "movement" (辶). So essentially, the character for "make"— 造— shows that God spoke (告) with His mouth (口), breathed life into the clay (土), and there was movement (辶).

Genesis 3:1 says that the serpent was more cunning than all others who came to tempt the woman. The Chinese word for "tempter" is *Mo* (魔). Interestingly, this character tells the story of a person (儿) in the garden (田) with two trees (林) telling a secret under cover (广).

The word for "boat" is chuan (船), which is eight (八) people (人) on a vessel (舟). So the character for the word boat in Chinese is telling a story about a vessel that carried eight people. The first boat ever written about was the ark, which held Noah, his wife, his three sons, and their three wives. So the basis of Noah's story is represented in the Chinese word boat.

Let's look at the character for "tower" in Chinese and see if you can identify the story that is being explained here.

The character for the word *tower* in Chinese is 塔. All the people (人) are one (一) in speech (口)＝合. This character—合—can stand alone, and it means "to unite" or "to be united." So a united people took grass (艹) and clay (土) to build the character for "tower" (塔).

Sound similar to the Tower of Babel in Iraq?

Genesis 11:9 explains that the tower received its name because the Lord "confused the language of all the earth." The Chinese character for "confusion" is 乱, which is a picture of a tongue and one leg, indicating that the tongue is only with half of the body. The languages were split up among the people of the earth, and those who spoke a different language migrated away from Babel.

The character for "migrate" is 遷, which is a big divide (㠯) from the west (西). Babel for the Chinese is known to be in the west. The Chinese migrated away from the west into the land of the Yellow River.

These are only a few examples, but the Chinese characters literally go on and on telling about the biblical stories that take place in the Mosaic writings, but these characters were being used by the Chinese people prior to the birth of Moses. It is a fascinating example of how Iraq was the cradle of civilization and that the peoples of the world moved away from that cradle carrying the early stories of creation, the flood and Nimrod's tower with them.

SIX

Cultural Genocide in the Bible?

As we mentioned earlier, in the spring of 2016, the European Union and then the United States finally recognized and declared that the mass murders and destruction taking place in Iraq were truly genocide. Months earlier, organizations with a presence in the Middle East were demanding that the world take notice of the crimes to humanity happening in Iraq.

On September 29, 2015, delegations from France and Iraq called for an emergency meeting with international leaders from around the world at UNESCO's headquarters in Paris. UNESCO is a branch of the United Nations tasked with generating peace among the cultures of the world.

The meeting was opened by Irina Bokova, director-general of UNESCO, to the ambassadors and permanent delegates of France and Iraq to UNESCO.[36]

"Islamic, Christian, Kurdish and Jewish heritage, among others, is being intentionally destroyed or attacked in what is clearly a form of cultural cleansing," warned Irina Bokova.

"Cultural cleansing, in my view, is exactly what's happening in Iraq," Bokova said in an interview with NBC News. "These extremists want to impose a different vision on the world. They want to tell

---

36. http://en.unesco.org/news/call-save-iraq%E2%80%99s-cultural-heritage.

us that there is no memory [of these sites], that there is no culture, that there is no heritage."[37]

According to the International Convention of the Prevention and Punishment of the Crime of Genocide of 1948, the United Nations defined *genocide* as an act "committed with intent to destroy, in whole or in part, a national, ethical, racial, or religious group."[38]

Part of the genocidal war on Christians being launched in Iraq by ISIS involves erasing all historical and cultural signs that Christianity ever existed in Iraq. The primary goal of ISIS is not to just rule over Iraq, Syria, and the Levant (the region from Oman to Aleppo in Syria) , but to cleanse the entire region of any group that does not ascribe to their view of Islam.

The cleansing agenda is not just a matter of mass murder—it includes an agenda of systematically eliminating anything that can be traced back to Christianity in Iraq.

French ambassador Phillip Lalliot was quoted at the meeting as saying, "We may feel uneasy about denouncing crimes against heritage when horrifying acts of violence are being committed against people. Is it right to be concerned about cultural cleansing when the dead are being counted in the tens of thousands? Yes, absolutely! Because the destruction of heritage that carries with it the identity of a people and the history of a country cannot be considered as collateral or secondary damage that we can live with."[39]

What might be shocking to many readers is that this kind of destruction of cultural icons to erase a people group from memory is not new in warfare and is certainly nothing new for Islamic fighters.

If Muhammad is to be used as the example, then the actions of ISIS as they destroy religious and cultural relics are in keeping with

---

37. http://www.nbcnews.com/storyline/isis-terror/unesco-boss-irina-bokova-laments-isis-cultural-cleansing-antiquities-n386291.
38. General Assembly Resolution 260A (III) Article 2.
39. http://en.unesco.org/news/call-save-iraq%E2%80%99s-cultural-heritage.

their religion. According to the Koran, idols and cultural relics that are part of any religion other than Islam absolutely must be destroyed.

In March 2013, ISIS destroyed an ancient Christian monastery that was described as the equivalent of Canterbury Cathedral.[40] The Mar Behnam Monastery in northern Iraq dated back to the early Christian movement in 300 AD and had one of the most valuable Syriac libraries in existence.[41] The historical significance of the monastery cannot be overstated, and the writings that were lost and destroyed can never be replaced.

To justify the destruction of Christian monasteries like Mar Behnam in northern Iraq, ISIS uses a Hadith teaching in which the Prophet Muhammad orders one of his companions to "not leave any idol without defacing it and any grave without leveling it" (Hadith 969).

In 2010, Salafi cleric Mohamed Hassan stirred a debate in Egypt after he issued a fatwa saying that individuals could sell artifacts found in their areas but should destroy them if they were statues.[42]

Mainstream Muslim clerics argue that Islam forbade actively worshipped deities, not ancient artifacts, but even with the most liberal of translations, the destruction of a Christian monastery is up for debate.

When challenged about their path of destruction, jihadi ISIS fighters easily point to the Prophet Muhammad when he marched into Mecca in the seventh century; there, he and his army destroyed all the idols and established Allah as the one and only supreme leader. Even to this day, non-Muslims are forbidden to enter into the holy city of Mecca.

However, pointing to Islam as the basis for what ISIS is doing draws a lot of criticism from all sides. Even though ISIS quotes the

---

40. http://www.huffingtonpost.com/azeem-ibrahim/by-destroying-churches-an_b_6927242.html.
41. https://www.rt.com/news/242841-isis-destroy-monastery-iraq/.
42. http://www.cultureindevelopment.nl/News/Dossier_Heritage_Egypt/591/Public_outcry_after_Salafi_preacher's_fatwa_on_antiquities.

writings of Islam in their justification and even though their leader, Abu Bakr al-Baghdadi, has a doctorate degree in the study of Islam, there is still a very large segment of political leaders and news reporters who equate Islamic teachings supporting the destruction of idols to Christians and Jews destroying idols throughout history.

David A. Graham, a staff writer at *The Atlantic*, agreed that ISIS's destruction of idols was in the footsteps of their Prophet Muhammad, but he went one step further when he joined other secular news reporters that blamed Christianity for the same atrocities. "There's a strong tradition of icon-destruction in Christianity," he wrote. "Abraham, the patriarch of Judaism, Christianity, and Islam, himself destroyed idols."[43]

Is David Graham wrong? Does ISIS receive the mandate for what they are doing from Abraham, the founding father of Islam, Christianity, and Judaism?

The answer to that question takes us back to Iraq, the birthplace of Abraham. Located in the southern part of Iraq is the famous hometown of Abraham, Ur. Ur would have been located down river from Babylon, halfway to the Persian Gulf.

The birth of Abraham would not have occurred long after the building of the tower of Babel, so the town Abraham grew up in would have been strongly influenced by the paganism established by Nimrod.

According to the Talmud, a Jewish book of holy teachings of the rabbis passed down from generation to generation, Nimrod was not only alive during the days of Abraham, but actually had Abraham thrown into a fiery furnace.[44]

Remember that Abraham, known then as Abram, is often called "Father Abraham," because he was the man God called out

---

43. http://www.theatlantic.com/international/archive/2015/02/ISIS-Video-Militants-Smashing-Ancient-Artifacts-Mosul-Museum/386198/.
44. Michael L. Rodkinson, trans., *The Babylonian Talmud*, vol. 1–10, 1918, 252.

of paganism to establish a covenant with and would one day build a nation that was dedicated to the one true God. God orchestrated the time and place of Abraham's birth. It was not as though Abraham was supposed to be born in the land of Canaan but was accidentally born in Iraq. God knew Abraham before he was formed in his mother's womb (Jeremiah 1:5), and God placed him exactly where He wanted him.

Abraham was born a Semite, in Mesopotamia, in the family of Terah, for a specific purpose. The calling that God had for Abraham would be one of the most pivotal callings in history. It would not be an easy one. At times, it would seem to be a confusing one. Abraham did not grow up in a home where he learned about the God he would one day spend his life serving. Instead, he grew up in a town that was dedicated to idols. Abraham's father, Terah, worshipped other gods (Joshua 24:2–3).

In the nineteenth century, European explorers discovered one of the large temples of Ur, which would have been a centerpiece of the town and culture Abraham grew up in.[45] The temple, or Ziggurat, was discovered in the ancient city of Abraham, which was one of the most important Sumerian Empire city states in Mesopotamia during the twenty-first century BC.

The temple was dedicated to the moon god Nanna, who was the patron deity of the city and would have most likely been one of the idols that Terah worshipped. Abraham would have been familiar with the patron deity. Nanna would have been one of the cultural idols that Abraham would have had to abandon when he entered into a covenant with the living God Jehovah.

Scripture is very clear that the Abrahamic God views idols, such as those built to worship Nanna, the god of Ur, as impotent. They are without knowledge and are powerless to save (Isaiah 45:20). They are unable to respond to prayer and are powerless against those who joke that they are sleeping (1 Kings 18:27). They are lifeless (Psalm

45. http://www.ancient-origins.net/ancient-places-asia/great-ziggurat-ur-001767.

106:28). Idols are mere fabrication, invented by the hands of man. They cannot see, hear, smell, walk, or talk (Deuteronomy 4:28; Psalm 115:5–7; Habakkuk 2:18–19).

God's first and foremost reaction to idolatry is jealousy and anger (Exodus 34:14), but the fact that God did not destroy Israel, the descendants of Abraham, because of their idolatry is evidence that while God is a jealous God, He is also merciful (Deuteronomy 4:31).

Abraham was called out of the idol worship of Ur and taken to the land that God had promised him. His journey involved teaching all those in his house to follow the God of the Covenant. Like Nimrod, Abraham had a choice to follow God. Nimrod was given all the gifts and power to lead others, but he decided to follow after idols and forced others to do the same. Abraham was given the same choice, but he chose to abandon all he knew to follow a road leading to the unknown in order to have a covenant with the one true God, and he led many others to do the same.

According to the Old Testament, God brought Abraham and his family out of the city of Ur and away from the land of his childhood idols. In the foreign land, during the twilight years of his journey, God used Abraham in amazing ways to teach the entire world about His love, grace, and care for His people. God did not send Abraham on an idol-destroying expedition, subduing those who did not agree with him as Mr. David Graham claimed in his article to equate Christianity with the actions of ISIS.

Since David Graham and the other journalists like him do not reference the source, it can only be assumed that he is referencing the Talmud or the Quran. Journalists who have an agenda of defending jihadi behavior have a tendency to throw in references to central figures like Abraham to insinuate that all religions have a problem with violence, destruction, or genocide, and therefore the solution must be a secular one. Mao Zedong, Joseph Stalin, and Kim Il Sung would have agreed with the notion that a secular, atheistic solution is needed for a religious problem.

However, the story of Abraham can teach us a lot about the genocide that is taking place in Iraq today. Aside from Moses, no other person in the Old Testament is mentioned more times in the New Testament than Abraham. James refers to Abraham as a friend of God (James 2:23). That is a title not found anywhere else in Scripture until Jesus uses it with His disciples. Believers all around the world find unity in Abraham as "children of Abraham" (Galatians 3:7).

Abraham left all that he had and followed after God (Hebrews 11:8). His family meant everything to him, and when his nephew was kidnapped by warring marauders, he put his own life and belongings at risk to go and rescue him.

When the people of Sodom and Gomorrah were about to be destroyed because of their evil and wicked ways, it wasn't a blood-thirsty Abraham who begged to go and kill the infidels with his own sword and force them into submission, but instead he tirelessly pleaded on their behalf for God's mercy.

When the sacrifice of his son was required as a test, Abraham did not take a young boy from his neighbor or force one of his workers to give up one of their children. Instead, it was his only son, the one he loved more than all others, whom Abraham was willing to give to God during this time of testing.

Abraham had many faults, and the Bible does not shirk away from sharing his many failures and times of unbelief, but in Abraham we see a faithful individual who shows us an unparalleled example of love and self-sacrifice, a foreshadowing of the love and sacrifice that Father God had in giving His Son, Jesus Christ, to be sacrificed at Calvary.

The Father of the New Testament loved us so much that He gave His Son for us (John 3:16) in the way that Abraham was willing to give his beloved son, but God the Father loved us even more than mere sacrifice. He loved us so much that He took the most precious, innocent, perfect, and pure thing in the entire cosmos and sent Him to us, laid Him at our feet, offered us His life, and allowed us the choice to reject Him.

The most powerful one in the world subjected Himself, His sacrifice, and His love to our rejection.

ISIS in Iraq is definitely not following this example. There is no interpretation from the biblical story of Abraham that would ever come close to supporting this idea that ISIS and Abraham are somehow equal in their character and approach toward faith and belief in God. ISIS offers zero self-sacrifice or choice of rejection. Hate does not offer a choice, only love does.

ISIS is following the example of Nimrod, not Abraham. God gave Nimrod a chance to choose, and when given the power, that same courtesy was not extended to others. Tyrants, in their quest to be god-like, rule in broad strokes of absolutes.

When looking at cultural genocide in Iraq, there might be individuals and events that journalists and ISIS alike could use as parallels. A thorough study of Abraham would show that he is not one of them.

SEVEN

The Second Death of Jonah

Genocide begins—A bloody plague came to Iraq from the west in 2014. ISIS fighters arrived from Syria driving vehicles and carrying weapons that were stolen from the country with the most powerful military in the world—the United States.[46] Genocide carried the black flag of ISIS jihadists in June 2014, and Iraq was the goal.

In June 2014, ISIS descended on Iraq's second-largest city of Mosul like a plague of locusts. Mosul was the Christian capital of Iraq prior to the ISIS invasion, with more Christians living there than any other Iraqi city.[47] The Iraqi military had fled from the city out of fear and abandoned the citizens to fend for themselves.[48]

The militant jihadists of the ISIS military front did not waste any time dismantling the city. They went right to work breaking into the churches, tearing down crosses, ripping religious pictures and symbols off the walls and heaping them in the middle of the city.[49]

"Overnight 100,000 people escaped from Mosul and escaped from ISIS," Father Douglas Al-Bazi, a Chaldean Catholic priest from Erbil, Iraq, recalled. "When they [ISIS] arrived and took over Mosul, they told the people we have three conditions according to

46. http://www.alternet.org/world/how-isis-ended-stocked-american-weapons.
47. http://www.bbc.com/news/world-middle-east-28686998.
48. http://edition.cnn.com/2014/06/10/world/meast/iraq-violence/.
49. http://www.independent.co.uk/news/world/middle-east/isis-attack-on-christianity-continues-in-mosul-fighters-destroy-all-religious-symbols-in-church-and-10112706.html.

Sharia. Number one was convert [to Islam]. The second was to pay Jizya (Islamic tax on non-Muslims) and they asked for each person to pay 4,000 to 8,000 US dollars. Third, they said you have to leave or you will be beheaded."[50]

Muslims and Christians who had lived beside each other in relative peace for many years were suddenly enemies. ISIS declared that all Christian property would be given to the Muslims, including the Christians themselves. Many Muslim residents, encouraged by ISIS and the implementation of Sharia Law, started to make their claims on Christian property.

One Muslim, who had been neighbors with a Christian for over thirty years, threatened to killed him if he did not leave town immediately so that he could have his house. "The Muslim guy, he went to the Christian's door and knocked and said, 'Did you hear about the decree? The announcement is to leave in 24 hours by Allah's name, and if I see you here tomorrow I'm going to kill you because I have the right to take your home.'"[51]

Crosses on top of churches were torn down, and the black flags of ISIS were raised in their place. Church buildings that used to be a sanctuary of praise, worship, and ceremony for the Christians in Mosul were now painted black and used as the headquarters to carry out terror. The best church buildings were saved from destruction and transformed into mosques.[52]

While men, women, and children were being slaughtered, churches were being stormed, and religious items were being piled up and destroyed, it was easy to miss one of the most iconic historical items in the area being blown to smithereens—Jonah's tomb.

---

50. http://www.express.co.uk/news/world/613149/ISIS-barbarity-100000-Christians-fled-Mosul-one-night.
51. http://www.express.co.uk/news/world/613149/ISIS-barbarity-100000-Christians-fled-Mosul-one-night.
52. http://www.fides.org/en/news/38178-ASIA_IRAQ_The_Chaldean_Church_of_St_Joseph_in_Mosul_transformed_into_a_mosque#.VoOw5eOriko.

Not long after storming the Christian center of Mosul, ISIS members, donning balaclavas (cloth head coverings that reveal only part of the face) and long black clothing, grabbed sledgehammers and began swinging wildly inside the tomb of Jonah.[53]

The grave they were destroying was attributed to the prophet Jonah, revered by Muslims, Christians, and Jews alike. Yes, it was that Jonah—the one swallowed by the fish described in the Old Testament. The grave site contained artifacts and remains that were several thousand years old!

Jonah is known by almost every child who has attended Sunday school as the prophet who ran away when God told him to go to Nineveh in Iraq to tell the people to repent. When Jonah tried to escape the call of God, he was swallowed up by a large fish and held in its belly for three days before finally agreeing to follow God's direction and being spit out on the beach.

The tomb also held what was considered the remains of the whale that had swallowed Jonah, including one of its teeth.[54]

The destruction of Jonah's tomb seems a little strange at first because the story of Jonah is important to Muslims as well as Christians and Jews. For starters, there is an entire section (Surah 10) of the Quran titled "Jonah," and the Prophet Muhammad is said to have declared that "one should not say that I am better than Jonah" (Hadith 4:608). Maybe it would have been safer for the Hadith to also mention that "one should not say that I will destroy the tomb of Jonah"?

It would be incredibly simple to view the attack on Jonah's tomb as just another act of cultural violence against a group that is experiencing genocide at the hands of ISIS, but there is a deeper connection here. It is a connection that can be found in the Bible.

---

53. http://www.dailymail.co.uk/news/article-2685923/Shocking-moment-ISIS-militants-sledgehammers-Mosul-tomb-Prophet-Jonah-50-blindfolded-bodies-massacred-south-Baghdad.html.
54. Ibid.

First, ISIS is part of the Salafi movement, a branch of Sunni Islam that seeks to return to the practices of the earliest Muslims—the salaf—who lived at the time of the Prophet Muhammed and shortly after.[55] This particular form of Islam has a lot of support from Saudi Arabia, where it enjoys the patronage of the Saudi royal family.[56] To really understand why a Salafi movement would want to destroy Jonah's tomb, it is important to go back to the Bible and know the significance of the story of Jonah, because some experts have associated the destruction of Jonah's tomb as part of the raging anti-Christian campaign.

On their internet blog, scholars Joel Baden and Candida Moss point out that the attack on Jonah's grave was an attempt to erase any symbolic evidence that might lead someone to believe in Jesus Christ.[57]

Sam Hardy, a professor at the American University of Rome and author of the blog Conflict Antiquities, told the *Washington Post* in an interview that ISIS is determined to destroy "basically pretty much anything in the Bible."[58]

Jonah's story is one of those biblical accounts that ignites our imagination and brings individuals face-to-face with the concept of the death and resurrection of Jesus Christ, as well as His calling for Christians worldwide.

It is doubtful that anyone went to the tomb of Jonah prior to 2014 and contemplated the international politics of Iraq. Many of the pilgrims who traveled to the tomb were more likely to meditate on the spiritual questions raised by the story of Jonah itself—questions

---

55. https://www.foreignaffairs.com/articles/syria/2015-11-24/what-salafism.
56. Jocelyn Cesari, *The Oxford Handbook of European Islam* (Oxford: Oxford University Press, 2014), 14.
57. http://www.firstthings.com/blogs/firstthoughts/2014/07/why-did-isis-destroy-the-tomb-of-jonah.
58. https://www.washingtonpost.com/news/morning-mix/wp/2014/07/25/after-leveling-iraqs-tomb-of-jonah-the-islamic-state-could-destroy-anything-in-the-bible/.

that have to do with justice, obedience, compassion, fairness, divine mercy, and the value of human beings in the eyes of God.

It is hard to imagine that anything could be worse than Iraq's plague of 2014 when genocide against minority faiths was being systematically carried out by ISIS, but there was a time when the fate of Nineveh looked much worse.

The Assyrians were like an Ancient ISIS

Built on the banks of an early Assyrian fortress was a city ruled by Nimrod. Mosul, located across the banks of the Tigris River, is the ancient city of Nineveh. Nineveh was the main city that linked the two major empires of Assyria and Persia. The city was wealthy and popular. It was the center of commerce, language, culture, and learning. It was also incredibly evil. The Assyrians fought wars without gentlemen's rules. Their traders and officials grew rich on the suffering of others.

Assyria was the most powerful nation on earth at the time, but as we see during their invasion of Israel, the Assyrians had invented another powerful tool for conquest: terror. The Assyrian army was notorious for their brutality: the mutilation of prisoners, and the genocide of entire populations. They even bragged about their atrocities in tablets of stone.[59]

In fact, the little we know about the Assyrians outside of the Bible is what has been preserved on stone tablets. Assyrian history, as it has been preserved in inscriptions and pictures, consists almost solely of military campaigns and battles, and it is one of the most bloodcurdling histories the world has known.[60]

Basically, Assyria could be compared to what it would be like if ISIS was in control of the most powerful empire in the world...but worse!

---

59. http://faculty.uml.edu/ethan_Spanier/Teaching/documents/ CP6.0AssyrianTorture.pdf.
60. Ibid.

In the book of Jonah, the prophet was sent to prophesy, not to the Israelites, as one would expect, but to the wicked people of Nineveh. Jonah was appalled. The people of Nineveh were the enemies of God and were certainly not allies of the people of Israel.

What did Jonah have to do with the people of Assyria? In short, nothing. His concern would have most likely been with his own people who were now split into two kingdoms—Israel and Judah. As noted earlier, the Assyrians were ruthless and brutal to the people they intended to conquer. Why in the world would Jonah want to make them upset by delivering bad news to them? Even more, why would Jonah want to see the hated enemies of his people repent and be forgiven for their atrocities?

At the time, Jonah was in active ministry on the heels of the prophet Elisha within the ten northern tribes of Israel. To a Jew ministering to the ten northern tribes, the destruction of Assyria would not have seemed to be a great idea. In fact, it was the Assyrian Empire that later carried the ten northern tribes away into slavery (2 Kings 18:11).

The ten tribes of Israel and the two tribes of Judah and Benjamin to the south were beginning to regain some of their former prosperity and power. Jonah became a popular preacher during a very prosperous time, and apparently he had no desire to preach to the wicked people of Assyria.

How many of us are Jonahs today? Those who would love to be obedient to God, but at the same time would prefer to be the bearer of a positive message—a message of peace and prosperity. Wouldn't most of us love to minister a message to the world that avoided all the uncomfortable negative and judgmental stuff?

Like Jonah, there are many of us who would choose to take the road that brings a message of hope and prosperity to our own countrymen, a calling of God that leads to ministering to the affluent and protected areas of the world.

It is interesting that God called Jonah instead of maybe Amos or Hosea, prophets who ministered right after Jonah and did not shy away from telling people about the judgement of God and impending doom. They were already so unpopular that it would not have made a big difference to them. What's a bit more misery to the already miserable? But God called Jonah to the hard task instead.

When we see Jonah's reaction to God's mercy upon the Iraqi people of Nineveh, we recognize that he was a true patriot of Israel (Jonah 4:1–2). He wanted to see the tribes of Israel reunited and his sanctified people succeed. Preaching a happy message of unification and cotton candy dreams was much better than going to the heart of enemy territory and preaching a message of repentance.

To put this into perspective, what would happen if God called us today out of our comfort zone and asked us to go to the Iraqi city of Mosul to proclaim the message that the established caliphate of ISIS needs to repent before God? Sounds pretty ridiculous, right? But it was not any more ridiculous than what Jonah was being asked to do.

Jonah did what any sane person would do—he ran! Jonah effectively resigned from ministry. He put in his notice with God and set sail on a one-way ticket to anywhere that would take him far from Nineveh, but God created a special fish for Jonah. Many have interpreted this "great fish" in Jonah 1:17 as a whale, but a whale is never mentioned.

In fact, that "great fish" might not exist any longer. It might have been created just for Jonah, because it was in the belly of that fish that Jonah had the time to reflect on his reliance on the Lord.

He had hit rock bottom. Death surrounded him. He was in the belly of a fish and the digestive system would kill him in a short time, but out of the pit of Hades he cried out to the Lord.

God Always Allows a Path to Mercy

"Those who regard worthless idols forsake their own mercy," prayed Jonah. "But I will sacrifice to You with the voice of thanksgiving; I will pay what I have vowed. Salvation *is* of the Lord" (Jonah 2:8–9).

Jonah realized in the belly of the fish that there is thanksgiving in the sacrifice, and after three days he was spit up by the fish on to dry shore. The fish did not deliver Jonah to Nineveh. Nineveh was still many miles away. Jonah still needed to travel for a few days to make it to the city of Nineveh from the sea. Even when he got there, the area was so big that it would take at least three days to announce God's proclamation throughout the entire city.

The Bible does not give us much information about what Jonah said, but it seems to have been the bare minimum. According to Jonah 3:4, Jonah walked around proclaiming only one sentence: "Yet forty days more, and Nineveh shall be overthrown!" The Bible does not tell us much more than that. It doesn't give us an elaborate message or a convicting sermon. In fact, more information is given about the details of Jonah's desperate prayer in the belly of the fish than what he actually preached to the people of Nineveh.

The Bible does not tell us why the people of Nineveh repented, but they did, and they did so immediately and passionately. This might have been an even bigger miracle than Jonah living for three days in the belly of the "great fish."

If Jonah being in the belly of the fish for three days represented the resurrection of Jesus after three days in the grave, then Nineveh in all of its evil was the incarnate representation of the sinful earth. Their reputation for cruelty and evil aggression was a matter of national pride. They were a ruthless people who prospered from their acts of cruelty. Their repentance was an unparalleled miracle.

Their repentance does not merely mean that the people of Nineveh (including the king) just felt sorry about the atrocities they had committed. Sorrow can come from getting caught, but it doesn't necessarily mean that one will change. The use of *repentance* in the book of Jonah begs those who heard to abandon their sins and completely change course to follow after God's way.

The Ninevites had repented and were abandoning their evil ways. The bordering nations must have breathed a sigh of relief.

Another startling fact from Jonah's history: at the very same time that Jonah was appealing to the people in the Iraqi city of Nineveh, the people of Israel themselves were knee-deep in sin and idolatry. As Israel and Judah were choosing to abandon their birthright, God was busy saving the most wicked nation on earth. Jesus said that He did not come to earth "to call the righteous, but sinners, to repentance" (Matthew 9:13).

Today, like then, the Iraqi city of Nineveh is controlled by the most evil empire on earth. Death, destruction, and pain inflicted on others are a part of the daily misery, but if the story of Jonah tells us anything, it is that God always allows a path to mercy.

Today, like then, the Iraqi city of Mosul would be a suicide mission for a Christian who attempted to share a message of repentance, but today—like then—Mosul is in desperate need of men of God who will take His message to one of the direst places on earth.

EIGHT

A Tragedy Witnessed

Have you ever seen a tragedy coming and were helpless to prevent it? It is a terrible feeling. It is that forlorn awareness of being able to see disastrous results stemming from an action currently taking place, but no matter what you do, you have no way of stopping it. You can only watch.

It is like watching a train wreck take place in slow motion.

When I was one year old, my father was killed by a train while driving across train tracks on the Fourth of July weekend in America. No one knows what really happened that day or why he didn't stop for the train. Maybe he had the music on too loud and didn't hear the train coming. Maybe he was exhausted from working day and night at two jobs to support his young family. Many assume that, because of the awkward angle of the train tracks, it was not possible for him to see clearly enough to avoid the oncoming train. In Muncie, Indiana, in 1978, there were no cross bars preventing cars from driving across the train tracks while a train was passing through.

For whatever reason, my father did not stop at the tracks as a train was coming. The train hit his vehicle with such force that there was little likelihood that anyone could have survived.

Sitting on the other side of the train tracks, facing his vehicle, was a friend and family member. He watched helplessly as my father drove in front of the train. He saw the train coming. He saw my father approaching the tracks and was aware of the approaching train, but there was nothing he could do. He could not stop my father. All he could do was witness the tragedy taking place. Even after the train hit the vehicle my father was driving, all our family friend could do was sit there. And watch. Helplessly.

Because of today's media, many of us have a front-row seat to the tragedies that are taking place in Iraq. We know the murderous intentions of ISIS. They are not trying to hide anything. They are making public declarations and fatwas against the innocent people of Iraq.We know what is coming, but we feel helpless to stop it. We are forced to watch. Children are being slaughtered, women are being raped, and entire people groups are being killed off, and most of us feel that there isn't anything we can do about it.

An Old Testament Tragedy

Reading Daniel 5 reveals that same feeling of helplessness and distress at approaching doom with Belshazzar, the king of Babylon (Iraq). From our perspective as Bible readers, we know that King Belshazzar and all those in the royal court are destined for destruction, but there is nothing we can do to prevent it. Helplessly we continue reading as the day of judgement quickly descends on the Babylonian king.

Belshazzar was having a huge, extravagant party with a thousand of his friends while an aggressive Persian army was just outside of his defensive perimeter. Instead of planning for the protection of his kingdom, he decided to use a few sacred items that were confiscated from the Jewish temple to entertain a thousand of his guests.

Suddenly, there was a mysterious hand that appeared and wrote on the wall, which of course is where we get the proverbial saying, "The writing is on the wall."

The king was struck with fear, which is odd because, as we learn from the biblical story, he did not even know the meaning of the words written on the wall. But his countenance completely changed. Daniel vividly described the level of fear that the king experienced. His knees knocked, his face turned pale, and he cried out for the astrologers, Chaldeans, and soothsayers. Before that event, the fierce Persian army was camped right outside the city gates, and King Belshazzar showed no fear. In fact, Belshazzar was showing the opposite of fear. He was having a party.

The Church Ignores the Enemy

The scene of partying while a hostile enemy force is surrounding us is not too much different from many Christians in this present age.

Militant jihadis are taking over large areas of Iraq and Syria. They are penetrating into the hearts of other countries as well like France, England and America. Christians are being threatened, persecuted, killed, and slaughtered all over the world. The members of ISIS have lined up Christians in YouTube videos and decapitated them in a formal declaration of war against "the people of the cross."

What is the general response of the church? Many today have the idea that the best response is to escape into the full pursuit of personal pleasure. Maybe throw a party like Belshazzar and retreat into the deepest recesses of desire and pleasure. Pretend it isn't happening so that they don't have to acknowledge that Christians are suffering in the name of Christ.

Why the retreat?

According to the book of Daniel, Belshazzar's party represented the careless behavior of the Babylonian leaders. It highlighted the lack of commitment to the service of the people of Babylon, as well as the selfish, egocentric cult that grew in its place. The spirit of Nimrod from generations earlier promoted the pride found in Babylon that was well nourished in the egocentric cult. The building of the Tower of Babel was a classic endeavor in revealing the sinful pride that lurks within the heart of man. Belshazzar is a picture of the heart of man recklessly indulging in his every lust.

King Belshazzar was fully enjoying himself, as were his guests, but suddenly—like a flash of lightning—his festive spirit was rudely interrupted by the ice-cold reality that his kingdom was about to fall. Belshazzar did not know the meaning of the words written on the wall, but he was certainly sober enough to know that it was not good. A sinking feeling must have dropped to the deepest pit of his stomach as was reflected in his pale, bloodless face.

In panic, he called for the dark magic introduced by Nimrod so many generations before. He summoned the astrologers, wise men, and soothsayers, but they were absolutely worthless. The astrologers, wise men, and soothsayers were great during periods of prosperity, partying, and mocking those who followed Jehovah, but when the tides turned for the worse, it was only the one true God of Daniel who was able to speak truth and give revelation.

Daniel did not require or accept personal gifts or rewards for his translation service, because he did not work for the king. He worked for the living God. By the time Daniel provided the meaning of the mystical words written on the wall, the king's life was only measurable in hours and minutes, but the one true living God was everlasting.

Without fear or trepidation, Daniel spoke the harsh truth of God's word for Belshazzar:

> And you have lifted yourself up against the Lord of heaven. They have brought the vessels of His house before you, and you and your lords, your wives and your concubines, have drunk wine from them. And you have praised the gods of silver and gold, bronze and iron, wood and stone, which do not see or hear or know; and the God who holds your breath in His hand and owns all your ways, you have not glorified. (Daniel 5:23)

The God of Daniel was the same God who created all living things, and He alone holds the power of breath and life in His hand. The spirit of pride and self-indulgent lust controlled the thoughts and extinguished the breath of Belshazzar so that he could not glorify God. He could not glorify God because he had nothing left to glorify Him with. He was depleted of all that was good. His first fruits were offered to himself instead of to the Creator. When he was fresh with spirit and energy, he did what was pleasing in his own eyes.

It would be easy for Belshazzar to believe that he was basically a good guy. It would even be feasible for him to argue that he did not do anything "that bad." However, every beast and creature on earth that has breath and life is obligated to give praise to the Creator for the breath and life that He alone provides.

Belshazzar's breath and life were offered on the altar of his own lusts, and all that was left was expended in blaspheming the one, true, living God.

Don't Ignore the Enemy at the Gate

What can be said of our own energies? Upon which altar are they spent? Have our first fruits been expended long before we find ourselves in prayer? Are the persecuted Christians of the world who also serve the one true God worth so little to us that if they get anything at all, it would merely be the scraps leftover that were not consumed even in our most gluttonous state?

When we read the story of Daniel living in Iraq under the rule of King Belshazzar, maybe it is far too easy to see Belshazzar as the black character or the bad guy in the story. Possibly we scoff at his situation in hindsight, knowing that what he was doing was reckless and ignorant. However, Belshazzar had far less information available at his fingertips about the one true God than any of us reading this book today. Every living man who is alive in the modern world has more access to the truth of the one true God and His Son Jesus Christ than Belshazzar ever did. And Christians also have constant and nearly uninterrupted access to information regarding the continual persecution of the followers of Christ.

Who will be judged with greater wrath—Belshazzar, who did not have access to Google, twenty-four-hour news channels, and the instant ability to communicate with those suffering from persecution, or the church of the twenty-first century that does?

Couldn't parts of the church today be said to be living in the spiritual state of Belshazzar's Babylon? A state of fierce independence fueled by pride? A spiritual state that mocks those who follow God with a holy passion? A spiritual Babylon that dances and celebrates worldly desires while the enemy lurks just outside the gates?

No empire of Babylon can possibly stand forever when it is built on the foundations of human strength, wisdom, and power. No wall built nor any tower erected will be strong enough to resist His judgement when the day arrives. The fall of our spiritual Babylon will be like the fall of Belshazzar's Babylon—quick, sudden, and sharply inflicting mass fear and panic.

That which brought about the destruction of Babylon can also bring about the destruction of Christian nations. The character of a nation's leaders matters. We don't know much about the character of Babylon's everyday citizens, but we do get a good view of Belshazzar's character. His character mattered. In fact, a quick study of his character will help understand the leadership traits that will destroy a nation.

According to Daniel 5, we see at least seven characteristics that will lead a nation to destruction:

- Self-indulgence (v. 1). The Persians were outside the gates of Babylon and yet the king wished to have a party with his friends.

- Addiction (v. 2). The king was under the heavy influence of alcohol. Substance abuse prohibits sound thinking.

- Blasphemy (vv. 2–3). The king sent for the gold and silver vessels used in the temple of God to be used for his own enjoyment and to show his supremacy over the Holy God of the Jews.

+ Idolatry (v. 4). Though the king refused to acknowledge or respect the God of the Jews, he was all too ready to give praise to false gods, gods that needed the hands of man to obtain existence.

+ Pride (v. 22). With the clear knowledge of what his father, Nebuchadnezzar, had experienced, and how his father had given homage to the God of heaven, Belshazzar still stubbornly served the gods of his own choosing.

+ Ignorance (v. 23). Belshazzar's life and breath were in the hands of Almighty God. Only He had the power to give life and take it back again. Only God controlled the oxygen, air, water, and trees that provided the source of life for the king and his subjects, and yet Belshazzar was incredibly ignorant of his dependence.

+ Bribery (v. 16). Belshazzar attempted to use his wealth to pay for a revelation from Daniel, the prophet of God. He promised things he could not deliver.

Shortly after Daniel revealed to the king the meaning of the writing on the wall, the entire Babylonian kingdom fell. Blasphemy is always short-lived, even if brief moments in the dark shadows feel like they will last forever.

The ancient kingdom of Iraq, which had captured the temple of God and enslaved the Jewish people, fell in the blink of an eye. Belshazzar had failed to learn the lessons of the past. He decided it was much better to eat, drink, and be merry than to learn from the lessons of his father. He was only concerned about the immediate.

Belshazzar was the last king of Babylon, and Christians have a lot to learn from him, but will we be just as unteachable? Will we walk in the footsteps of Belshazzar and ignore the enemy at the gates?

If there is anything to learn from the history of Iraq, it is that nations rise and fall, but God's Word stands forever.

PART TWO:
Iraq and the Birth of Christianity

NINE

The Gospel Arrives in Iraq

Throughout the Bible, there have been individuals who have questioned God. Those questions sometimes amaze biblical readers, because it takes an insane dose of audacity to question God Almighty. Those questions can sometimes comfort readers, because we all have our own questions.

Since the beginning of time, man has questioned God and questioned *about* God. One of the oldest books in the Bible is the book of Job, and Job had many questions for God. The further we traverse away from God, the more ignorance surrounds us and the more questions we naturally have. Even in the absence of the knowledge of God, we seek Him, because we intuitively know that we are somehow different from the animals around us. Whether you are religious or not, it does not matter. The answers still beg our questioning.

Inquisitive searches are often born out of idle curiosity, but few things ignite questions like pain, loss, suffering, and death, especially when the pain, loss, suffering, or death happens to us or the ones we love. Whether you are religious or not does not really dull the desire to seek and find answers to your questions, because the plight of every man is the plight of every man. The blood that bleeds is red from every man.

We can identify with the pain of others when we question God during our own trials and conflicts. As much as we would like to highlight our uniqueness, we are really quite similar to all the other people on earth. Our souls are all connected to the Creator, and in Him we find universal connection, and our connection brings sadness at the death and suffering of others—even those we do not know.

Our soul and the desire to be connected with our Creator make us different from the animals around us, even if we do not have the knowledge or vocabulary to explain the difference. Our souls were given to us by our Creator, and when our souls disconnect from the Creator, we become like animals without a soul. The further distance we are from our Creator, the more similarities we seem to share with the animals. This is reflected in the lack of empathy we display toward the plight of others when we are at our most fallen state.

For those who are closer to the Creator, death brings great sadness, and sadness is multiplied when death is multiplied. For those who are further away from the Creator, their ability to love, though still present, is dulled, thus the sorrow and pain of others does not bite as hard.

The coldhearted killing inflicted by ISIS can be better understood when it is acknowledged that they, by their own volition, have chosen to be far from their Creator. The ability to laugh at the pain and suffering of children, murder unarmed men begging for mercy, or rape young prepubescent girls seems like the actions of soulless animals, but it is actually the same result for all men who are separated from the Creator.

Communism in China, which enforced absolute atheism, was not any more compassionate than ISIS. The National Socialism or Nazism of Hitler's Germany certainly had similar cold and calculating characteristics. ISIS is a horrific example of godless behavior, but history is littered with them. When we are disconnected from our Creator, our ability to love is weakened and our desire to empathize is negligible.

Numerous ancient writings have attempted to describe the battle raging within the free soul of man regarding the struggle between connecting with God the Creator and retreating to the dark recesses of animalistic behavior. Ancient writings are littered with explanations attempting to answer many of man's questions. If we are truly honest about the questions we ask, then we are promised to find the answer (Matthew 7:7). Both the questions and the answers make us civilized and humane. Our own ways away from God can create a very dark chasm that turns us into barbaric, unfeeling animals where we have fewer questions and even fewer answers.

Modern societies around the world have been built or shaped by those who have chosen the laws of Jesus Christ. It is these laws or teachings of Jesus that bring us closer to our Creator. Even if we do not believe that Jesus is God, living our lives by His teachings still has social benefits that go beyond anything we can imagine. Even India's Hinduism, Saudi Arabia's Islam, Japan's Buddhism, and China's Communism have not been left to their own barbaric leaning vices. They have been shaped in part through the economic, military, political, or social influence of Christian societies, and today abide, at least in part, by the international standards set by those same Christian societies. From the Geneva Convention's rules of war to the international human rights for women and children, Christianity has paved the way for the highest ideals of justice and compassion, even if those ideals are never reached.

Creating His Own Creator

ISIS follows the example of their holy prophet, Muhammad, when they inflict genocide on the defenseless, but even Muhammad was not without influence from Jesus. When Muhammad lived among the Christians and Jews, he wrote many surahs that talked of peace, love, and justice. It was only after his heretical teachings were rejected by the Christians and the Jews that he wrote the surahs pertaining to jihad. He actively removed himself from the Creator by inventing a new deity that indulged his anger. The further he pulled away from the Creator, the more animalistic his behavior became.

Humanity, in general, has progressed technologically far beyond the primitive culture of the Mesopotamians, but the struggle is still the same basic choice given to Cain—to kill or not to kill. We might feel superior to the ancient Mesopotamians who built gods for themselves with their own hands and gave themselves over to the religions that raped them of their humanity, but we are still in the same sinful struggle as Cain. We are still in the same sinful struggle as Muhammad.

Our souls were never created by the myths that deceive us, the deities that tempt us, or the pathetic gods we attempt to create with our own hands from the images in our own feeble minds. Man can worship the cow, but it is irrefutable that the cow is controlled by man. Man can worship an idol, but the idol finds its genesis in the cradle of man's mind. Desires and needs can be manifested in the worship of sex or the sun, but they too are empty. These religions rely on man, but shouldn't man be able to rely on God and not the other way around?

Muhammad created the Allah of Islam, and his teachings of Allah required followers to force others into submission through threats of punishment and death, removing compassion, empathy, and the freedom to question. A question, for instance, that would ask, "If Muhammad's version of Allah was in fact the Creator of all mankind and all mankind has the free will of choice (which includes the option not to choose the Creator), would the Creator then choose to take away that choice by using the force of man? Is choice through force choice at all?"

The Prophet Muhammad was not the first, nor was he the last to create his own creator.

The souls that live in a land far from the Creator will inevitably find themselves in the realm of Hades where killing, rape, injustice, and pain provide constant torment. Contrary to popular belief, a sinner does not have to die to find hell. One must merely find the many places on earth that live furthest from the Creator. These are the incubators of death. These are the petri dishes of genocide. These are the places occupied by ISIS.

Hell on Earth Found Hope in Jesus

Prior to the birth of Jesus, most of the world only had residual and natural knowledge of Yahweh and were mainly guided by the law that was written on their hearts (Romans 2:14–15), but after the crucifixion and resurrection of Jesus, there was a new birth of love, compassion, forgiveness, justice, and hope. This brought Good News to the whole earth. This brought mankind closer to the Creator and His ways.

Hell on earth found hope in Jesus. The death grip of darkness and hopelessness was broken, and followers of Jesus set out to tell the entire world of this Good News. Iraq was one of the earliest destinations. Prior to the birth of Jesus, Iraq, as was mentioned earlier, played an important role in the development of Judaism, from which came the saving anchor, Jesus Christ, who keeps all mankind from losing their souls to darkness. It is this Judeo-Christian heritage that found an early home in Iraq that ISIS wants to destroy.

The people of Iraq, even though the country was not called Iraq two thousand years ago, were living in a world without justice, peace, love, and hope before the first Christian missionaries arrived. Those first missionaries were not sent by a church or a mission organization from America or Europe. They were sent by Jesus Himself.

The first missionaries to Iraq were disciples of Jesus who had walked with Him and heard the parables directly from His lips. The New Testament had not been written yet, but the stories and teachings that would one day fill books of Christian holy literature were carried in the memories of their heart.

One of those brave disciples who trekked into the land between the rivers was "doubting" Thomas. Though his disbelief, which earned him the dubious title "doubting Thomas," has been scoffed at in many sermons and Sunday school teachings, Thomas was actually not as doubting as many would have you believe. Thomas relentlessly and unselfishly took the Gospel to the darkest places on earth, pushed forward into the most unforgiving lands east of Jerusalem when others turned around, and shared the Gospel in the same land that the prophet Jonah, Noah, and Abraham had resided in.

When Jesus was crucified, all of the disciples must have felt the utter disappointment. Thomas, like Peter, surely had the same fears and angst after the death of Jesus. Naturally, his encounter with the risen Jesus was met with disbelief, which led him to ask natural questions. Instead of scolding him, Jesus gave the answers that Thomas was honestly seeking to his natural question. This encounter encourages us that an honest seeking and questioning can lead to answers that take us to deeper belief.

Thomas' faith that was gained from being with Jesus in that moment spread on the mission field from Israel to India and changed entire regions of the world forever. The disciple who would forever be known as "doubting Thomas" brought the Gospel message to the mountains of northern Iraq soon after the Great Commission was given in Acts 1:8.

In his book, *Thomas the Doubter: Uncovering the Hidden Teachings*, George Augustus Tyrrell wrote, "It may be that Thomas' critical mind compelled Jesus to explain the teachings more deeply to him than to the credulous disciples. For the prologue in the Gospel of Thomas states, 'These are the secret teachings the living Jesus spoke and Judas Thomas wrote down.'"

Thomas, walking in the power of the Holy Spirit, saw people come to Christ in considerable numbers. The Assyrian areas of modern-day Iraq quickly adopted the teachings of St. Thomas, and the modern-day Kurdish capital, Erbil, became a spiritual hub for Christianity. From Erbil, Thomas was able to build a kind of temporary headquarters and reach out to the people living in the Mesopotamian crossroads.

The Assyrian and Chaldean people who lived in the area that is now within the borders of Iraq proved to be among the most receptive early converts to Christianity, and one of the main reasons is because of language. Early Mesopotamian Christianity was Semitic linguistically, and this made evangelizing them easier. The people spoke the same language that Jesus and St. Thomas spoke, which was Aramaic.

"Thomas, being once weaker in faith than the other apostles," said St. John Chrysostom, "toiled through the grace of God more bravely, more zealously and tirelessly than them all, so that he went preaching over nearly all the earth, not fearing to proclaim the Word of God to savage nations."

There was also a sizable Jewish population among those in the area that went back to the days of the diaspora, and this proved helpful for Thomas when he arrived in the new land. Maybe it was that Thomas, who sought after the ultimate answers in life, was able to provide answers to those who lived in dire situations and sought answers to the same questions.

The church in Iraq continued to grow and became known as the Assyrian Church of the East. This church became well-known among the other disciples, and we can see that it is mentioned in 1 Peter 5:13 as Peter sends greetings from Christians in Babylon to the rest of the church. The church started by Thomas provided a powerful Christian culture in the regions of Iraq for more than two thousand years—that is, until the invasion of ISIS, when everything changed forever.

TEN

Iraq: The World's First Christian Kingdom

If you want to know how Christianity first came to Iraq, then you should talk to the priest," Jacob said. Jacob was a member of one of the few Christian families who lived in the Yazidi area of the Sinjar Mountains when ISIS invaded in 2014.

"Our Muslim neighbors came into our home and warned us that ISIS was coming," Jacob shared. "They told us to take down our crosses and pictures of Jesus and hide them in the closet. They told all of the women in our house to put on a burka and to write on the front of our house, 'We are Muslim converts.' When I heard their words, I became angry and chased them out of our house. I threatened to punch them if they didn't leave for suggesting for us to abandon our faith. We are Christian, and we will not convert to Islam," Jacob said.

Jacob took us to the home of the elderly Christian priest. They were all living in a village full of refugees from their home area of the Sinjar Mountains. "He knows everything about Christianity in Iraq," Jacob said. "I am sure he can tell you the whole story."

When we entered into the home of the priest, he was sitting on a wraparound sofa that doubled as a bed at night. More than one refugee family from Sinjar Mountain was living with the priest. The priest was frail, but excited to have visitors. He was happy, but it was apparent that running from ISIS and living as a refugee for the last several months had taken a toll on the ninety-one-year old man. He sat nervously twirling his brown wooden prayer beads and adjusting his dirty white prayer cap as he tried to remember how the Gospel message first came to his people.

"Adda the teacher was the first to bring the Gospel message to Iraq," the priest said with confidence, but then he looked down at the ground with sadness because he was not able to remember much more than that. "He would like to share more about the history of Christianity in Iraq, but he had to leave all of his books behind in Sinjar when we fled from ISIS," one of the family members sitting in the same room explained. "He has all of the history of Christianity in Iraq written in piles and piles of books that he has studied his entire life, but sadly they were all lost in the attack."

The memory of the old priest might have been vague, but he remembered one thing—the teacher Adda brought the Gospel to Iraq. Adda is another name for Addai or Thaddeus, which is one of the twelve apostles of Jesus and the author of the book of Jude. According to church records, he served as the leader of the church in Erbil from the years 66–87 AD.[61]

Both *Assyrian* and *Chaldean* are terms that are used synonymously for Christians in Iraq. Basically, they are Christians who can trace their roots back to the apostles Thomas, Bartholomew, and Jude. The Chaldean Christians have been believers since the first century AD and turned northern Iraq into a center for Christianity and Syriac literature.[62]

Theologically, the church led by Thaddeus has been labeled as Nestorian, meaning they followed the teachings of Nestorius, but the church leadership has rejected that label. They employ the Syriac dialect of the Aramaic language in their liturgy, the East Syrian Rite. Even Peter is said to have visited northern Iraq and helped with the mission work there, meaning that the origin of both the Roman church and the church of northern Iraq can claim the same mission

61. http://www.gutenberg.us/article/whebn0001675860/thaddeus%20of%20 edessa.
62. http://www.ishtartv.com/en/viewarticle,36975.html.

roots,; unfortunately, politics created a split when Persia and Rome were at war and the Christians were forced to choose sides.

Peter specifically gave his blessings to the church in Iraq when he wrote, "She who is in Babylon, elect together with you, greets you, and so does Mark my son" (1 Peter 5:13).

Because the term *Chaldean* is used in the Bible, there is often confusion about the background. But many believe the Iraqi Chaldean Christians are not ethnically related to the ancient Chaldean people. The name "Chaldeans" was used by the Catholic Church in Rome to refer to the church in Iraq, also called the Church of Chaldea and Mosul. The church from the East developed from the early Assyrian Christian communities, but when the church leadership was forced to choose sides, there was a split between the Assyrian Church of the East and those who followed the leadership in Rome who later became known as the Chaldean Christians.[63]

According to Robert Spencer, director of Jihad Watch and author of *New York Times* bestsellers *The Truth about Muhammad* and *The Politically Incorrect Guide to Islam (and the Crusades)*, the church in Iraq was much larger than it is today. "For five hundred years, from the ninth century until the bloody advent of Tamerlane, what is known today as the Assyrian Church of the East was the largest communion in the Christian world, stretching from the Levant all across Asia to India and China."[64] By some estimates, this translated to more than 20 million Christian believers.[65]

In the mind of most Westerners, Iraq is a Muslim country and has always been a Muslim country. ISIS wants very badly to reinforce this idea. However, this is a revisionist creation of history. The people of Mesopotamia were Christian long before they were Muslim.

---

63. http://christianity.stackexchange.com/questions/46068/are-iraqi-chaldean-suraye-related-to-the-chaldean-mentioned-in-old-testament.

64. http://www.crisismagazine.com/2012/the-church-that-converted-khans.

65. http://www.atour.com/forums/ed/72.html.

Iraq in the Book of Jude

Adda the Teacher, as he is known to the Christians in the Sinjar region of Iraq, is also known by many other names such as Thaddeus, Jude, Judas, and Addai. His name has been confused with others with similar names and led to confusion about Adda's identity. Adda, who was likely the disciple Thaddeus, had the unfortunate name Judas (as in Judas Iscariot, who betrayed Jesus), so other names like Thaddeus, Jude, and Addai were often used to distance him from the one who betrayed the Savior and Lord. Even Matthew and Mark dropped the name Judas and used the name Thaddeus instead when listing the twelve apostles.

The apostle Jude wrote the book of Jude, the next to last book of the Bible. Notice how the book of Jude isn't called the book of Judas so as not to confuse the reader.

The estimated dates of when the book of Jude was written are between 60 and 80 AD. This is the same time frame that Jude was ministering in Iraq, meaning that the book of Jude is most likely the only letter in the New Testament book to be written in Iraq. If this is true, then the book of Jude takes on a meaning much deeper than what many realize.

In his letter, Jude does not advertise that he is actually the son of Joseph and Mary or the younger half-brother of Jesus Christ, the Son of God. One would think this is the first way Jude would introduce himself, but he did not. Jude clung to eternal truth, not earthly relations. A person cannot choose which family they are born in or who their siblings are. Jude did not play any part in the family that he was born into, but he did choose to be born again. He spent his entire life trying to convince others to do the same.

In his letter, Jude fought for truth, and truth can be a scary thing in Mesopotamia, because the word *truth* assumes that there are non-truths. Truth can be both liberating and disruptive, peaceful and dangerous. It can bring freedom as well as uncertainty. A prisoner who has only known life behind bars might find the breath of freedom exhilarating, but become crippled at the uncertainty of the future.

This ardent desire to share the Truth eventually led Jude to the Mesopotamian kingdom of Adiabene.[66] The capital of Arbela was the modern city of Erbil on the Tigris River. Erbil was the ancient headquarters of the apostles Thomas and Jude. Today it is the capital of Kurdistan and the region where Jacob and the Christian priest now live after fleeing the Sinjar mountains.

The attacks of ISIS have split Iraq into three parts: Iraq in the South, ISIS territory in the middle, and Kurdistan to the north. As ISIS has pushed the Iraqi military further south, the Kurds have been forced to fight independent battles in the north and have gained a certain amount of autonomy for their region of Kurdistan.

About four hundred miles along the Mesopotamian mountain ridge line to the west of Erbil was the ancient capital city of Edessa. Edessa was the capital of the kingdom of Osroene. It was here that Jude would do something that would change the historical path of northern Iraq and would be forever remembered in the hearts of the Mesopotamian Christians like Jacob and his priest.

The kingdom of Osroene, in the upper course of the Euphrates with the Tigris to the east, was ruled by a famous king who became the subject of many Syriac church legends. The location has been identified as the town of Urfa, or Ur of the Chaldeans, the hometown of the patriarch Abraham.[67] Abraham was reportedly born in a cave in Edessa.[68]

The king of Edessa was an Arab called Abgar the Black, also known as Abgar of Edessa.[69]

According to tradition, King Abgar was deathly ill with a disease that had no known cure. He had heard about the healing power of a Jewish teacher named Jesus and desired for Jesus to come and

---

66. http://oca.org/saints/lives/2015/06/19/101752-apostle-jude-the-brother-of-the-lord.

67. http://www.newadvent.org/cathen/05282a.htm.

68. http://www.wfltd.com/persians/edessa.htm.

69. *The Catholic Encyclopedia*, vol. 5 (New York: Robert Appleton Company, 1909, 2012).

see him. Jesus was not able to come, but after His resurrection, Jude eventually made his way to the throne room of King Abgar. The church teaches that Jude carried with him a cloth with the image of Jesus on it. After receiving the cloth, King Abgar became a believer in Jesus Christ and declared his kingdom a Christian kingdom. If true, this would mean Jude was responsible for Edessa becoming the first Christian country in the world, long before Armenia or Ethiopia accepted Christ.

The healing cloth with the image of Jesus on it also came from Edessa. History is clear that this relic played a major part in ancient Christianity in northern Iraq, but it might go even further than that. Astoundingly, if the research of Ian Wilson is correct in his latest study, "The Shroud, Fresh Light on the 2000-year old Mystery" from 2011, then the Image of Edessa is none other than the Shroud of Turin, or the burial cloth of Jesus, which is the most studied artifact in history.

In fact, many would argue that the most famous archeological discovery that man has ever stumbled across is the Shroud of Turin, the cloth that Jesus was wrapped in when He was buried. It continues to fascinate scientists, which is why it is the most studied artifact in the world.

One can agree or disagree with the historical teachings of the Syriac church, but the fact remains that something happened to transform the ancient societies of Mesopotamia. The world's best archeologists and historians with resources at their fingertips can choose to disagree, but they can do little to academically dispute the claims of a little old ninety-one-year-old refugee priest from Sinjar.

The Christians in Sinjar count King Abgar as a saint and celebrate his life with feasts on August 1. The heritage of this story runs so deep in the area that the country of Armenia adopted a 100,000 AMD banknote in 2009 that depicts Jude handing a royal flag to King Abgar. These images and stories fly in the face of Islamic domination, and so ISIS has made it their goal to destroy these historical records forever.

ELEVEN

Iraq: A Christian Kingdom No More

What is it in the heart of man that causes him to hate so deeply or kill so passionately? Genocidal tendencies tempt us all. For the Nazis, it was the Jews. For the Turks, it was the Armenians. For the Hutu, it was the Tutsi. For ISIS, it is all "non-Muslims" the infidels, but maybe for us, it is ISIS.

How is it possible that this cancer finds dwelling in our soul? Surely God in His omniscience must have seen this coming as the result of free will. The freedom of choice is both rich with love and dark with evil. Who can know the depths of evil in a man's heart?

"The Lord saw that the wickedness of man was great in the earth, and that every intent of the thoughts of his heart was only evil continually. And the Lord was sorry that He had made man on the earth, and it grieved Him in His heart" (Genesis 6:5–6).

It is impossible to imagine the world before the flood being any worse than Iraq is today. If the Lord looked down and regretted making man then, how must He feel today? The pain and sorrow that ISIS has brought to Iraq must truly grieve the Lord.

The state of Iraq today is a far cry from the Christian worldview that existed in Iraq so many generations ago. The idea of a Christian kingdom in Iraq would be considered a joke today. Everyone knows that Iraq is a Muslim country. It has always been Muslim, or at least, that is what many Muslim leaders around the world would have us believe, but that simply is not true.

Much of the genocide that is being carried out today is because ISIS is trying to erase pre-Islamic history.

Islam was forced on the people of ancient Mesopotamia and shackled around the necks of the people. The entire region has been ripped apart and dominated by Islam since the armies of Muhammad had their first victories by raiding caravans that were traveling between Mecca and Medina. The genocide of Christians in Iraq did not start with ISIS. It actually began in the seventh century, shortly after the death of Muhammad, when Iraq was still part of the Persian Empire. Arabic Muslim armies moved into the region, establishing the dominance of their religion, and defeated the Persians. Much like ISIS' threats today, the early Muslims offered the Christian residents three choices: embrace Islam, pay a jizyah (a non-Muslim tax), or face death.

Many Christian communities were saved by the safety found in the vast deserts and endless mountain ranges of northern Iraq. They grew to know the desert areas better than anyone. The Arab conquerors that marauded through needed the resources of the nonbelieving locals to help them survive in the desert, so their unbelief was tolerated—for the time.

During the seventh and eighth centuries, the Arab Muslims did not just take Iraq from Persia; they continued on into the continent of Asia and conquered all of Persia. The Islamic expansions constituted the largest Semitic expansions in all of human history.

The Arab Muslims did not disperse and settle throughout Iraq; instead, they established their bases in the south—allowing the north to remain largely Assyrian and Christian. The Christians were important to the new Arab conquerors because the Christians were educated, literate, and gifted at governance (though they were mostly banned from government), medicine, accounting, and engineering.

The ancient land of Babylon proved to be a central location for the Caliph and became the capital city of the Abbasid Caliphate. This was the beginning of what is known as the Golden Age of Islam.

The Christian influence in the Zoroastrian Empire of Persia shifted to accommodate the new Muslim rulers very well. The newly founded Baghdadi capital had a great need for Christians and Jews. Though they were treated as conquered and inferior citizens, they were valued for their knowledge, because, as was rightly noted by Italian writer Oriana Fallaci, Islam is the "religion which produces nothing but religion."[70]

Over the next five centuries, because of the residual knowledge of the citizenry, Baghdad would become a cultural center of the Arab world where there were great contributions in science, math, art, astronomy, chemistry, literature, medicine, and more. Their museums, hospitals, and libraries were almost as famous as those in Constantinople, where Christians were also making a huge impact. Together, Constantinople and Baghdad were two of the greatest cities in the world. Students and teachers worked together to translate the Greek writings of Aristotle, Plato, and Socrates so they could be preserved for all time.

The impact of conquering societies with large numbers of Christians and Jews was readily apparent. The Christians and Jews were excellent law-abiding citizens, could be trusted in business agreements, and maintained a high level of ethics that allowed others in the community to trust them.

Muhammad's family made their living from the pilgrims who traveled to Mecca every year to pray to the gods. When Muhammad taught his new religion to the residents of Mecca, many people in his own family rejected him because his new brand of monotheism was bad for the family business. However, when Muhammad came back and conquered Mecca after being thrown out, many family members converted to save their lives.

It turns out that being dead is bad for business.

Those family members who became Muslim to save their own lives were called "Talaqaa." *Talaqaa* was a scornful term for disbelievers

---

70. Oriana Fallaci, *The Rage and the Pride* (New York: Rizzoli, 2002), 30.

who converted to save themselves. Even though they were Talaqaa, they were still family members from the same tribe as Muhammad, so they were able to rule over former Christian areas that had great wealth. That wealth was able to buy them power.

When the grandson of Muhammad, Imam Hussain, came to power, other Muslims from the same tribe as Muhammad plotted to take the power of the Caliph for themselves. They were able to travel to Iraq, trap Hussain in a town known as Karbala, and murder him, his family, and all of his close allies.

Those who followed the murderers are known today as Sunni Muslims, and those who followed the grandson of Muhammad are known as Shia. Since then, the history of Iraq has been littered with a back-and-forth leadership seesaw between the two factions of Islam. The betrayal between the two camps of Shia and Sunni has caused division that still runs deep to this day. In fact, it takes a very strong common enemy to compel the Sunni and Shia to come together in any common effort.

In 2016, ISIS attempted to take the city of Karbala,[71] but the Shia Muslims were able to repel their attack and hold on to the city.

71. http://en.abna24.com/service/middle-east-west-asia/archive/2016/01/26/732023/story.html.

TWELVE

The Woman
Who Created Iraq

Less than a hundred years ago, a group of thirty-eight men gathered together around a table to look at a map. It was March 12, 1921, and the worst world war that had ever been experienced up to that time had just ended.

The Ottoman Empire had just fallen and caused the greatest geopolitical shift since the fall of the Roman Empire. Like land developers building a new suburban housing project, the men in the smoke-filled room began to plan and carve out borders, but they were not merely setting the property lines for a few houses—they were creating entire countries.

The room was full of men, but few of them were as well known as T. E. Lawrence and Winston Churchill. Lawrence was now known around the world as "Lawrence of Arabia" because of his knowledge of the Arab language and culture which was broadcast in Lowell Thomas's multimedia show that had opened in London on August 14, 1919.[72]

However, the fame of Lawrence and the commission of Winston Churchill would mean very little to the small-framed force of nature in the room—a woman named Gertrude Bell.

Gertrude was the only woman allowed in the room, and it was not because she was serving tea or entertaining guests as a social wall

---

72. https://www.cliohistory.org/thomas-lawrence/cairo/.

flower. She knew the region well, having traveled throughout the deserts of the Ottoman Empire, Arabic Peninsula, Mesopotamia, and Persia. She had been a state official, archaeologist, officer, writer, administrator, and policy maker. Gertrude was also a British spy and possibly carried more secrets of the desert with her than any other person in the room. She was the first woman to ever be employed by British Military Intelligence.[73]

The Middle East was made up of dominant patriarchal Muslim societies which would have offered no opportunities for a female spy. However, Gertrude had an unusual advantage over her male colleagues. Because she was a woman in a patriarchal society, she was not considered to be a threat. How could a woman possibly use military information that she might be exposed to, and if she found it useful, who would be crazy enough to rely on her claims?

Many Middle Eastern men in leadership found Gertrude to be full of grace and poise and not threatening as a military strategist, so some shared information with her with relative ease, thinking she would never pose a real threat. Gertrude also used a weak point that the men were not able to exploit—their families. She was able to insert herself into the heart of the social places where women of great wealth gathered. Many of these women were either related or married to the Middle Eastern commanders and knew far more about political affairs than anyone realized. The gossip was a rich treasure trove of information that fell freely into Gertrude's hands.

In those settings with family members and wives, Gertrude was able to learn the most intimate information about the top leaders that could not be gleaned anywhere else. This information gave her indispensable insight at the table of male leaders after WWI when the borders of Middle Eastern countries were being redrawn.

Like Gertrude's secret knowledge, the Middle East was also becoming quite indispensable. Prominent figures like Winston

73. http://www.theatlantic.com/magazine/archive/2007/06/the-woman-who-made-iraq/305893/.

Churchill could already sense the importance of the oil potential and other resources available under the sand in the Middle Eastern desert. During World War I, the British had invaded the Ottoman Empire and occupied Basra and Baghdad.

In early 1921, Winston Churchill was appointed secretary of state for the colonies as well as the head of the Middle East Department, and he wanted Gertrude, with her knowledge, at his side. The British were to work together with the French, Italians, and Russians to divide up the ancient lands of the Middle East. Together they would determine the borders of all the Arab nations, including the ancient biblical land of Babylon, which would be later known as Iraq.

What these Westerns leaders were dividing up was the Islamic Promised Land—the dream of a unified Arab state from Aleppo, Syria to Oman, also known as the Levant. That dream was ripped apart with each line drawn on the map. The vision of a unified land is the backdrop of ISIS; they point back to this very meeting in 1921 when they cry out for Muhammad's land to be returned back to the "rightful" Muslim owners and all infidels to be subdued.

In all the official British diplomatic group photographs of that event in March, the men are lined up in their freshly pressed military uniforms and ceremonial bucket hats. Only the pencil silhouette of Miss Bell's dainty British dress lacks the intimidation of military metals and polished sword sheaths. She did not necessarily wish to even be there, but fate would have it that she would change the course of history forever.

From the conference, Gertrude wrote in a letter dated on March 25, 1921: "Well, now I'll tell you about our Conference. I came very reluctantly and am now so very glad I came. It has been wonderful. We covered more work in a fortnight than has ever before been got through in a year. Mr. Churchill was admirable, most ready to meet everyone half way and masterly alike in guiding a big meeting and in conducting the small political committees into which we broke up."[74]

74. http://www.gerty.ncl.ac.uk/letter_details.php?letter_id=464.

Gertrude used the leadership and assertiveness that she was well known for. It was the same boldness that the men experienced in the room that day that made her known in Baghdad for making public speeches in Arabic. She may have been bold and influential, but her instincts were not exactly right. Many people would have much preferred a different map, more like the one proposed by T. E. Lawrence.

The map of Iraq that was finally adopted had more input from Gertrude than from T. E. Lawrence. A recently uncovered 1918 map reveals that his vision for a modern Middle East was largely ignored.[75] Lawrence's map seemed to have charted a more natural ethnic division of land than that which exists today, but it was not the one everyone settled on. Instead, the final product was one that would result in continued instability throughout the region.

It would not be completely fair to blame all of the conflicts and problems of the Middle East on the arbitrary borders drawn up by the delegation. War, conflict, and genocide ravaged Iraq long before the 1921 meeting in Cairo, but it gives ISIS yet another factor to add to their grievances.

75. http://www.vanityfair.com/news/2008/01/middle-east-cultural-political-map.

THIRTEEN

The Origins of the Islamic State

What or who is ISIS and why do they have such a blood thirsty desire to kill everyone in the ancient Christian lands? Aren't they in fact a perversion of true Islam, taking the words of the Koran and twisting them as British prime minister David Cameron pointed out in September 2014 when he said, "They are killing and slaughtering thousands of people...they boast of their brutality...they claim to do this in the name of Islam; that is nonsense, Islam is a religion of peace. They are not Muslims, they are monsters."[76]

Is ISIS twisting the Koran in the way that many radical Christians have done in the past to the words of Christ? "Humanity has been grappling with these questions throughout human history," American president Barrack Obama said during a prayer breakfast in February 2015, speaking about the connection between bloody Christian history and current attacks of ISIS. "And lest we get on our high horse and think this is unique to some other place, remember that during the Crusades and the Inquisition, people committed terrible deeds in the name of Christ. In our home country, slavery and Jim Crow all too often were justified in the name of Christ."

Unfortunately for both Mr. Cameron and Mr. Obama, Islam can only be interpreted as peaceful through the eyes of cultures influenced and ruled by Christian-Judaic values that have a strong desire

---

76. http://www.breitbart.com/london/2014/09/14/no-change-as-cameron-stays-course-against-isis/.

to establish a bridge of understanding. Outside of Christian-Judiac countries, there are few other religions looking for peaceful tidbits in the Koran to justify the position claiming that Islam is peaceful.

Radical Islam is exactly in line with the history of Muhammad, the founder, who was a violent warlord who raped women, enslaved children, beheaded his enemies and encouraged all of his followers to do the same—just as ISIS is doing today. The majority of Muslims who are peaceful, are so in spite of Muhammad's teachings and actions, not because of them.

Contrarily, radical Christianity is exactly in line with the history of Jesus Christ, the founder, who never led an army, never killed another human being, never raped women or enslaved children, and instead of killing others to show His devotion to God, gave His life on a cross as a living sacrifice to show His unending love. Unfortunately, during the Crusades and the Reformation, we find people who claimed to be Christians but did not follow the example of the love of Jesus Christ. Their actions were contrary to the teachings and message of their Leader, not because of them.

The leader of ISIS, al-Baghdadi, has a PhD in Islamic studies from the University of Baghdad and knows more about Islam and the history of Muhammad than David Cameron and Barrack Obama put together.[77] Today al-Baghdadi is the leader of one of the wealthiest, most far-reaching, and powerful terrorist groups in the world— controlling more land than the country of Belgium, and his methods are exactly the same as Muhammad. Al-Baghdadi has recruited extremely intelligent and relatively well-educated foreign fighters from Canada, the USA, Australia, New Zealand, and the wealthiest countries of Western Europe.

Al-Baghdadi knows that many would-be terrorists are often stopped from inflicting harm on the West because they are somewhat handicapped by holding Middle Eastern passports that make

77. http://www.independent.co.uk/news/world/middle-east/five-things-we-do-know-about-isis-leader-abu-bakr-al-baghdadi-a6689716.html.

them vulnerable to extra scrutiny. He now has volunteers who hold Western passports and are less likely to be screened with the same level of scrutiny.

ISIS initially had a desire to establish an Islamic state to rule Iraq and Syria (ISIS = Islamic State of Iraq and Syria) and establish a caliphate as previous caliphs or Islamic rulers did during the Golden Age of Islam. That vision has grown to include the entire Levant (ISIL), or more precisely, the Middle East with parts of Europe and North Africa, and today is often just called IS—or Islamic State—which makes their vision endless to include the entire world.

Unlike other terrorist groups like Hezbollah and Al Qaeda, ISIS is willing and able to attack more than unarmed soft targets like school children, shopping centers, commercial airlines, etc. They are also willing to attack military targets and have had incredible success. What makes ISIS so dangerous is that they are able and willing to carry out both kinds of attacks.

Unlike other terrorists which operate in the shadows and do not hold any real resources of value, ISIS has a tangible, geographic headquarters with an official governing structure for overseeing the daily functions of entire cities. Many of the buildings that ISIS uses for their government functions are former churches that were captured and painted black.

In many ways, ISIS has indeed become an Islamic State as they intended to be. They have been able to carve out a small piece of land that runs as an independent region. They provide public services for water and electricity, collects taxes, implements laws, hold court trials, enforce dress codes, and set rules for schools. Enforcement officers patrol the streets and ensure Islamic order.

It seems to many learning about ISIS that they were able to establish themselves overnight, but that is not the case. ISIS had outside help and resources that enabled them to establish themselves as a regional power.

The rise of ISIS can basically be traced back to the vacuum of power left after the removal of Saddam Hussein in 2003 and the evacuation of US troops in 2011. American president Barrack Obama showed unparalleled support for the Muslim Brotherhood prior to and in the wake of the Arab Spring,[78] which eventually led to a region-wide crisis in the Middle East.

With the fall of Egypt and Libya, and the relentless attack on Syria during the Arab Spring, the United States, for reasons still not fully understood to this day, assisted the Islamic rebel forces fighting President Bashar al-Assad in Syria.[79] Among the rebel forces that were supported by the US were Al Qaeda in Iraq (AQI),[80] which eventually became too violent and too unruly for the leadership of Al Qaeda and broke off to become ISIS.

The Chinese ministry, Back to Jerusalem details the origins of ISIS in the book *ISIS—The Heart of Terror: The Unexpected Response Bringing Hope for Peac.*

The road to identify the origins of ISIS can be messy and speculative, but the religion of ISIS is a little less complicated and can lead to the *true* origin. It is not as difficult to identify the true origin of ISIS if one only listens to what the jihadists are actually saying. The problem is that many experts pussyfoot around the subject of Islam and try their best to protect it. If a kindergartner listened to the words and read the propaganda of ISIS, they would easily be able to tell you what the origins are.

It is not politically correct to repeat the mission statement of ISIS, because the conclusions are not in line with the elitist statements that Islam is a peaceful religion, but the truth is the actions of ISIS can be traced all the way back to the Prophet Muhammad.

78. http://www.nytimes.com/2012/10/23/opinion/roger-cohen-working-with-the-muslim-brotherhood.html?_r=0.
79. http://www.nytimes.com/2016/01/24/world/middleeast/us-relies-heavily-on-saudi-money-to-support-syrian-rebels.html.
80. https://medium.com/insurge-intelligence/officials-islamic-state-arose-from-us-support-for-al-qaeda-in-iraq-a37c9a60be4#.ytz3pt9ed.

It might not be the popular view among today's polished politicians, but al-Baghdadi, the leader, is attempting to walk in the historical footsteps of the founding prophet of Islam. Islam and the actions of Muhammad, whether they are being correctly interpreted or not, is the undeniable underlying dogma that is determining almost everything in the war with ISIS and fueling their continual genocide on the people that they conquer.

The more one understands Islam, the more they are able to understand the mission, the goals, and the driving force of ISIS.

This is an immutable fact.

If there is any confusion on the matter, then one only has to witness the invasion of Syria and Iraq, witness the genocide, and compare them to the examples left by the Prophet Muhammad. Examining the history and influence of Islam on ISIS helps us understand that it is the very teachings of Islam that have driven ISIS to commit horrific acts of genocide. We will see what that effect is as we read countless firsthand accounts of ISIS acts of terror.

FOURTEEN

Invasion of
a Christian City

Though the broader outline of when ISIS invaded Iraq has been published by news agencies around the world, many of the details have remain unpublished until now.

In the summer of 2011, momentum for Islamic purist ideas increased as the civil war in Syria picked up steam. The Muslims saw a greater value to the small number of Christians living in Mosul, so they did not kill them all. Instead, like a New Jersey mob forcing local businesses to pay "protection money," they made the Mosul Christians pay "protection fees," estimated to have brought in 2 million USD per month. This proved to be a war chest that helped finance some of the operations of radical Islam terrorists embedded in the city.[81]

The radical elements, connected to Al Qaeda, saw a victorious path to overtake Iraq and Syria when the rebels in Syria gained ground and the US withdrew from Iraq in December of 2011. This left a power vacuum that the Muslim radicals had been waiting for.[82]

Even though the rank and file members of ISIS come from all over the world, the leadership is almost exclusively made up of Iraqis, battle-hardened by a nearly decade-long insurgency against US forces and a grueling civil war in Syria. ISIS leaders have played a prominent role

81. http://www.telegraph.co.uk/news/worldnews/middleeast/iraq/10889832/
Analysis-why-Mosul-is-the-forgotten-insurgent-stronghold.html.
82. http://www.longwarjournal.org/archives/2014/06/isis_take_control_of.php.

in Syria's civil war, aligning with both moderate and jihadist fragmented groups and tribal alliances allied against President Bashar al-Assad.

On March 6, 2013, the Syrian city of Raqqa fell, becoming the de facto capital of ISIS during their embryonic stage. The dreams of the radical jihadists were becoming a reality, and it was the motivation they had been looking for. The battle fatigue of Western militaries meant that they were not exactly interested in investing in military operations in the Middle East to combat the gains made by the radical jihadists. So the fall of Raqqa went largely unchallenged. The innocent residents of the city were left without an advocate able to remove ISIS from their midst.

It was a perfect storm for genocide, and the leaders of ISIS could sense it. They would sweep across the ancient Levant, cleansing it of non-Muslim believers, and no one would have the backbone to stop them.

No one thought that anyone would actually be capable of the evil that ISIS represented, or at least that was the hope of the world as they observed the situation. Since the Nazis of WWII, the world has not really encountered a group that has been both willing and able to dream of global domination through mass extermination. The genocides in Rwanda, Sudan, and Croatia were all primarily local ethnic cleansing and lacked the driving passion for global control. Those conflicts also lacked the international appeal for martyrs from other nations to join the cause. ISIS had the global aspirations and the international appeal.

The rapid organization and mobility of ISIS shocked leaders around the world. The intelligence communities and global jihad monitors did not see it coming. Many leaders were secretly supporting the early stages of genocide in Syria in hopes of overthrowing the Syrian president. It was a dangerous game that backfired.

In 2012 and 2013, jihadist fighting in Syria gained massive momentum on the battlefield when they gained the unlikely support of the United States. Under the Barrack Obama administration, assistance was provided to the jihadi-led Syrian rebel groups, which included Al Qaeda in Iraq (ISIS), through a secret route known as the "Rat-line."[83]

It was not long before ISIS was in full battle mode in Syria and was able to build a bridge into Iraq.

In January 2014, ISIS moved into Iraq's Anbar Province and took control of Fallujah and Ramadi. They were not a large military force and should have been easily repelled by the Iraqi forces, but they were tenacious in their fighting and believed in their holy cause.

Their holy cause was to rid Iraq of infidels who would defy the armies of Allah. Their tactics were ruthless and instilled fear into the hearts of their enemy. The Iraqi military knew that fighting ISIS was not going to be the same as fighting the US military. The US military abided by a set of laws, rules, and guidelines that ensured that the enemy would be treated with dignity and humanity.

ISIS did not embrace such rules. They executed, used the heads of their slain enemies as trophies, raped their wives, enslaved their children, and did so without trying to hide it. They also did one other thing that other militaries did not do—they routinely and publicly executed journalists.

Not only were the Iraqi military units scared, but the journalists were also afraid to cover the atrocities too closely for fear that they might be the next victim. This was a considerable blow to International news coverage, and without the free flow of information, the world had very few ways of learning about the situation.

ISIS was bold and turned their sights on the city of Mosul. They only had a force of six thousand men, and at first that did not seem to be nearly enough to invade Mosul, which was defended by a force of thirty thousand Iraqi soldiers.[84]

83. http://www.lrb.co.uk/v36/n08/seymour-m-hersh/the-red-line-and-the-rat-line.

84. https://www.theguardian.com/world/2014/jun/10/iraq-sunni-insurgents-islamic-militants-seize-control-mosul.

However, the brutal manner with which ISIS treated those they conquered struck a psychological blow to the Iraqi Army and sucked out their will to fight. Rumors began to spread among the soldiers that ISIS was planning to attack the city. Instant fear fell upon the leadership and that flowed down into the ranks. ISIS became the mythical boogey man for the Iraqi military.

The Attack on Mosul Begins

The following story comes from an interview with a Christian living in Mosul conducted by Dr. Paul Kingery.

Muneer (55) and his wife, Mahnal Fathil Ibrahim (51), were living in Mosul in August, 2014 with their two sons and daughter. They heard the rumors that were circulating throughout the city and knew that things were dire. Muneer and his wife were Christians, so they would be one of the top targets of the Islamic jihadists.

The rumors became reality when the ISIS fighters began to attack the outer perimeter at two-thirty in the morning. Any male ISIS encountered and suspected as a soldier was killed. They were killed by execution, hanging, or beheading. Sometimes their heads were placed along the roads leading into Mosul so that others would see that resistance was futile. It had a profound psychological effect, but no one imagined that ISIS would have the power or the ambition to take control of Mosul. Many believed that ISIS only wanted to make a statement that the Baghdad government could not ignore, but by June 6, they were able to control large portions of the city.[85]

Muneer and his family did not know what to do. They wanted to flee, but they did not want to leave their only home. ISIS was not the first group of Muslims to threaten him and his family. He was all too familiar with persecution. In the summer of 2008, Muneer's cousin, Najim Abdulla Fatoohi, was killed by Muslims trying to

---

85. http://www.businessinsider.com/how-isis-managed-to-take-mosul-2014-10?IR=T.

scare Christians out of the city. Another Christian colleague, Nabil Ghanem Basheer, was killed as well. The Muslims who killed Muneer's cousin and colleague tried to accuse them of helping the US military, but there was no evidence for their claim. It was clearly the Muslims' desire to kill enough Christians in Mosul to force them to leave the city.

Although Muneer did not leave, many other Christians did. The Muslims specifically began killing Christians in every school district so they would not feel safe anywhere. An estimated one hundred Christian families left Mosul per year. They could not take the constant violence against them any longer. Muneer would not be intimidated and defiantly stayed, but something about this time with ISIS was different. Something felt more absolute about their threats.

On June 10, the unexpected happened—Mosul fell. Black flags were hoisted up all over the city. Prisoners who were sympathetic to the ISIS cause were released, and those who were not sympathetic were executed.

Not long after that, an announcement was made throughout the city demanding that everyone convert to Islam or die. The ultimatum gave no room for loose interpretation. If Muneer and his family wanted to live, they would need to convert or flee. Muneer's home was marked with a symbol that announced to everyone in the city that Christians lived there. It was an Arabic N that is used to denote Christians as "Nazarenes" or followers of Jesus of Nazareth.

Muneer and his family packed up their clothes and prepared to flee. As Muneer turned to lock the door to his home, he wondered if he would ever see it again. He and his wife left with their two sons and a daughter on June 10, 2014. Not long after their departure, ISIS took ownership of their house. A Muslim neighbor called to tell Muneer that a Turkish fighter who had volunteered with ISIS was now living in his home. He took over the downstairs. Upstairs was a Tunisian-German guy who had joined ISIS.

Most likely, Muneer has lost his home forever.

"It is no longer possible for Christians to live in Iraq," said the wife of Raad Ghanem, one of 250 Christians who fled to the picturesque Mar Mattai Monastery atop a mountain, twelve miles from Mosul. She fled from Mosul around the same time as Muneer.

Ghanem's wife, who did not want her name used because she worries about her safety, said that when she showed up one day at the hospital where she had worked for thirty years, she was told she wasn't welcome anymore. "They told me I couldn't work there because I am Christian," she said. "I told them that I am from Mosul, that this is my home."[86]

After two thousand years of Christian community in northern Iraq, the Christian church was being wiped out or driven away from their ancient homeland.

---

86. http://www.usatoday.com/story/news/world/2014/07/29/mosul-iraq-christians/13238013/.

PART THREE:

Genocide and the Sinjar Massacre

FIFTEEN

The Death Mark

ن is a symbol that most people who do not speak the Arabic language have never seen before. In June 2014, it began to appear on random houses that ISIS was invading. Nothing seemed particularly interesting about it to outsiders, but for those who were living in the areas that were occupied by ISIS, the symbol was very frightening.

ن is the fourteenth letter of the Arabic alphabet (the equivalent of the letter *N* in the Romanized alphabet) and is pronounced "noon." It is the first letter of the word *Nasara*, which means Nazarenes (نصارى). Muslims have called Christians "Nazarenes" since the beginning of their invasion of the Christian world in the seventh century. Christians under Muslim rule never called themselves Nazarenes, but Muslims used the term to portray Christians as second-class citizens who followed a contemptible text.

ن was painted on the houses of Christians in Mosul as a twenty-first century warning. It was a warning to the Christians in Mosul that the Muslims were now fully in charge, and the only mercy shown to them would be the same mercies shown by their leader—the Prophet Muhammad.

The derogatory term *Nazarene*, as it is used by the Muslims, comes from the Holy Koran in Surah 5, also known as the Al-Ma'ida—or the table spread with food. It is a Medinan surah, or a chapter of the Koran that Muhammad declared was revealed to him during the time he was in Medina.

This is extremely important to know, because there are at least twenty-four chapters or surahs in the Koran that Muhammad wrote while he was in Medina.

Those that he wrote in Mecca, when he was trying to win the hearts and minds of the Christians, Jews, and pagans, are the more peaceful surahs. Muhammad was a minority during this time in Mecca and was in no place to make demands on the Christians or Jews, so he used honey to co-exist with those of other religions. It is difficult to know if he really desired to ever have peace among the Christians and Jews, because if his desires for peace would have been true, they would have carried over when he had power, but they did not.

Peaceful intentions are not proven when one is in an inferior position, but instead, when one is in a superior one.

Once Muhammad had power in Medina, the writings in the Koran took a less peaceful tone. Surah 5 is a supreme example of that. Islam's incorporated hatred for both Jews and Christians can be found permanently embedded in Islam's most sacred text of Surah 5. Surah 5:82 is considered to be the cornerstone of hatred toward the Jews and is considered by some to be a jihad verse, or a surah that incites religious violence.[87] Surah 5 is in the beginning of the Koran, and the same surah is found again in the middle, but chronologically, Surah 5 is actually among the last of the writings of Muhammad, despite appearing so early in the Koran.

This makes it more important in the law of abrogation, which is the idea that the later laws or teachings overrule the earlier laws or teachings. Essentially, this means that the revelations Muhammad had later in his life trump those he had earlier if two revelations contradicts one another. This is why the peaceful surahs are so confusing for the innocent observers, because the later jihad surahs from

---

87. http://www.answering-islam.org/Quran/Themes/jihad_passages.html.

Medina contradict and, by abrogation, overrule the earlier ones from Mecca.

Surah 5:82 of the Koran states, "Surely thou wilt find the Jews and those who associate the bitterest of mankind in enmity toward those who believe. And surely thou wilt find the highest in affection to those who believe those who say: *we are Nazarenes*. That is, because among them are divines and monks and because they are not stiff-necked."[88] This surah, which focuses its hatred on the Jews, refers to Christians as the Nazarenes. Surah 5:82 is prefaced with commands to never ally or befriend the unbeliever (non-Muslim) and is a center-piece for what took place in Mosul in 2014.

The homes that were owned by Nazarenes (Christians) in Mosul became the exclusive property of ISIS overnight, and the terminology used for the right to claim this property was extracted directly from the Koran. The mere fact that the people were Christian made them automatically less than second-class citizens to the invading Muslims. Their houses were being marked so that the occupants could be clearly identified in the same way that the Jews were marked during the Holocaust.

Once the houses were marked, Salman al-Farisi, the ISIS-appointed governor of Mosul, sent authorized letters to the marked homes declaring that any family planning to stay in Mosul would need to pay jizyah of $470 USD (a common tax on unbelievers living in Muslim caliphates) or be killed with the sword. If they chose to leave, they would be stripped of all valuables and allowed to leave with only the clothes on their backs.

Salman al-Farisi's commands were a repeat of what the Church of the East, that was traditionally based in Syria, Iraq, and Iran, faced once the Muslim armies conquered the region 1,400 years ago when the Christians were ousted or killed. More recently, in the fourteenth century, the number of Christians in the region was reduced again when Muslim officials competed to invent new humiliations to inflict

88. Translation by Abdul Majid Daryabadi.

on the Christians who dared to remain in Muslim-owned territories. Christians were stripped of their property, horses, and land, and extreme limits were imposed on what they could wear. At times, Christians were forced to wear rags to avoid giving any impression of wealth, which could invite others to take their property.

ISIS did not just want to conquer the city of Mosul for military purposes; their leader, al-Baghdadi, wanted to go back into history when Muslims had true power over Iraq and were able to subdue the Christians or rid the land of them completely. ISIS leaders wanted to force Christians who were allowed to live to take submissive roles in society and pay jizyah. ISIS's attack on Mosul was more than a strategic venture; it was a religious conquest.

No Limits to ISIS Terror

Christians in Mosul were used to being persecuted for their faith, but, in the past, there were certain places where persecution was considered to be off limits. Among those places were hospitals and orphanages that were run by Christian believers.

ISIS did not observe any such limits to their violence and terror. Two Chaldean nuns from the Daughters of Mary Order, Sister Miskintah and Sister Utoor Joseph, were taken from the all-girls orphanage that they ran in the Khazraj neighborhood near the Miskintah Church in Mosul. The nuns were last heard from in Mosul, but have since disappeared without a trace of their whereabouts.[89]

89. http://www.aina.org/news/20140630153011.htm

Once the houses were marked as Christian homes, they were easy to identify among the soldiers when it came time to collect the jizya or the tax from Christians who did not convert. If they did not have the money to pay, then there were other ways to force payment. ISIS members entered into homes of Christian families and demanded payment. In one instance, when the family did not have the money to pay, ISIS members brutally raped the mother and daughter of the house and forced the husband and father to watch. Experiencing a trauma worse than death, the husband later committed suicide.[90]

ISIS saw Christian children as a tool that could be used to instill fear in the rest of the community. Torturing children is an effective scare tactic for ISIS. It reveals a cold heart. A cruel, monstrous heart can strike fear to the core of a community of families. They become the source of scary stories, folklore, and nightmares. Men and women tremble in fear and lose the fight before it even begins.

"There is a park in Mosul," Mark Arabo told CNN during a Skype interview from San Diego, "where they actually beheaded children and put their heads on a stick. The world hasn't seen this kind of atrocity in generations."[91]

---

90. Ibid.
91. http://www.catholic.org/news/international/middle_east/story.php?id=56481.

As these stories began to spread, many children, together with their families, went running for their lives as they tried to escape from ISIS. In the desert heat, many of them died of dehydration before they were ever able to reach safety. Some of them laid down, went to sleep, and never woke up. The stronger members of their families kept pushing on without them like the children left behind to die in the picture below posted by Catholic.org.[92]

Another Catholic.org picture shows men picking up the bodies of small children who did not make it and putting them all in one place.[93]

Additional pictures show Christians hung up and crucified in public as a warning to other believers.[94]

92. Ibid.
93. Ibid.
94. Ibid.

Sometimes the blood was collected from the Christians who were killed, like the naked woman pictured below who had her throat slowly slit and the blood drained.[95] The chilling effect that ISIS members had over the population was clear when the Iraqi military leaders laid down their weapons and fled in the middle of the night to avoid fighting, even though ISIS was outmanned and outgunned by the Iraqi Army.

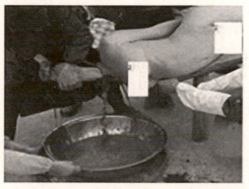

Children of Christians were not just merely killed; they were beheaded and left as a calling card to the locals like the little girl pictured here[96]:

---

95. Ibid.
96. Ibid.

They made videos that can be found on the internet of playing soccer with the heads of Christian believers. Here are two pictures that were taken from a video that can be found in full at this website.[97]:

Above, ISIS members hold up heads that they display as trophies of their victory in the Christian villages.

Below they are playing soccer with the heads. The three dark spots on the ground are heads that the members of ISIS are kicking around back and forth to one another as a kind of game.

The extent of the atrocities committed by ISIS are only partially known, but Christians have endured persecution before. Persecution

97. http://shoebat.com/2013/12/29/muslims-play-soccer-heads-victims/.

is in the fabric woven into the history of the church since its very beginning. Persecution is inseparable from following Christ. When Islamic warriors came in the seventh century or intensified their persecution in the fourteenth century, the Christians persevered. Their faith was deepened, their traditions took on new meaning, and their songs reverberated in their souls.

The irreducible core of the Christian faith is exposed during times of trial and tribulation. Christians who did not abandon their faith maintained an inner strength that blessed the communities around them. As Islam brought more darkness to Mosul, the light of the believers was even more highlighted in contrast.

This is why ISIS wants to completely destroy the Christians in Iraq. This is why their homes needed to be marked. To merely subdue the Christians and humiliate them did not change their eventual influence on the region or community for two thousand years. The believers, the true faithful believers of Jesus Christ, had a stubborn persistence under their garments of humility and grace that could persevere through the toughest of times and emerge bigger and stronger than before. ISIS knew this.

Chinese Christians have experienced this same phenomenon. The Communist government has seen the result of trying to search out, destroy, and eliminate every Christian believer. Like cockroaches, the Chinese Christians didn't die—they multiplied!

For the rulers of darkness to truly be victorious, ISIS would need to get rid of every single Christian believer in the entire region. And that is exactly what they planned to do.

Homes were marked, and Christians were killed or forced to leave. All the churches were destroyed, and the church bells were muted. And for the first time in two thousand years, the Christian voices in Mosul were silenced.

SIXTEEN

In Their Own Words

Ameer Ablahad Saman

The following story comes from an interview conducted by Dr. Paul Kingery on May 16, 2016.

Ameer Ablahad Saman (59), and his wife, Atemad Haseeb Salim (48), were Christians living in Mosul in 2014 when ISIS invaded. They had heard about the warnings that ISIS was preparing to attack areas of Iraq. Their very name (Islamic State of Iraq and Syria) indicated their desire to take over the entire country.

When Ameer's family heard the very first gunshot, they packed their bags, gathered up all of their money and valuables, and loaded their family into the car. Ameer's wife had a friend who lived in the town of Sinjar, which had no military value and would most likely be safer for them than Mosul. Once they arrived in Sinjar, they desperately missed their own home and did not have enough money to make ends meet for long. Sinjar did not offer the job opportunities they had in Mosul.

The family watched the news carefully, talked to their neighbors, and heard mixed signals about the takeover of Mosul by ISIS. After less than two weeks, Ameer felt that it was most likely safe to take his family back to their home. They had survived the days of tyrannical rule by Saddam Hussein. Surely ISIS could not be worse than Saddam Hussein.

Ameer and his family were Christians living in the Muslim country of Iraq, so they were no strangers to persecution; they had experienced it on a daily basis. Life without suffering for following Jesus was a completely foreign concept to them. Persecution of Christians did not end with the reign of Saddam Hussein. In fact, many could make the argument that it got worse. In 2004 and 2006, their church, Mar Kulos, has been attacked by radical Muslims and bombed twice.

Ameer clearly remembers the first attack against their church in 2004 when a local Muslim placed a bomb in a car parked beside the building and detonated the explosion remotely. Debris went flying everywhere, and his daughter almost died when her head was injured by the explosion. The attack occurred while they were attending a church service. According to their neighbors, ISIS had since turned the church into a car wash. That didn't seem nearly as bad as a bomb, so Ameer and his family packed up their belongings and returned to Mosul.

They didn't know what to expect, but they made sure that Ameer's wife was fully covered in the traditional Muslim burka. They went back to their home to see if they could salvage what they had left behind and create a life among the rubble. Their hardship was made even more challenging when the electricity was cut off and food was rationed for every citizen.

While life was difficult, they were able to survive for a time, but any hope of staying was quickly destroyed. At noon on July 17, the loud speakers located throughout the city hummed to life. The voice of a Muslim man came booming across and declared that all residents of Mosul would have a twenty-four-hour period to accept Islam or lose everything.

Ameer realized that life under ISIS was going to be different from Saddam Hussein. As Christians, they may have survived many hardships, but no persecution in the past could have prepared them for ISIS. He should not have returned to Mosul. He had made a tragic mistake and prayed to God that he would be able to get his family back out of Mosul alive.

Again, his family packed up all that they owned, but they knew they would not be able to take everything. ISIS now controlled checkpoints at every exit of the city. Surely they would never let them leave with the car. So they left their car parked at their house and arranged a taxi to take them out of Mosul, fearing that ISIS would steal their car at the checkpoint if they tried to drive it out of the city. Ameer gave the keys to his Muslim neighbor who promised to keep the car for him until it was safe to return it.

As they feared, when they attempted to leave, they were stopped by the ISIS guards. Ameer and his family were ordered out of the taxi and all of their belongings were taken out of the taxi and put into the custody of the Islamic jihadists. The guards ordered them to hand over every penny of currency that they had on their body or hidden in their luggage. Fearing for their safety, they did not attempt to lie or hide anything. If ISIS found money or valuables after reporting that there wasn't anything more to find, certain death would follow.

It is perfectly fine according to the Koran, under Sharia Law, for Muslims to lie to Christians, but for a Christian to lie to a Muslim was punishable by death.

"Take off your wedding ring," one female ISIS guard ordered as she searched Ameer's wife, Atemad. They literally wanted everything that had value stripped from their bodies. Wedding rings were not exempt.

"It will not come off," Atemad replied as she tried to remove it from her swollen fingers.

"If you cannot remove it from your finger, we will cut your finger from your hand. Your choice," they replied. It was clear they were completely capable of cold and brutal behavior and would not hesitate to cut off her finger.

Panicking, Atemad wrestled with the ring until it was finally removed.

Once the guards had stripped the family of all their valuables and possessions, they allowed Atemad and the family to get back into the taxi, but Ameer was not allowed to leave with them. He feared the worst, but he was glad he was facing it alone. At least his family was able to escape.

One of the guards raised his pistol and put the cold steel up against Ameer's temple. Ameer stood still. There was no way to run or resist. If they were going to shoot him, there was nothing he could do to stop them.

"Deny Christ and claim that there is no god but Allah or I will kill you," the guard ordered.

Ameer, standing alone, with no one around to provide any comfort or companionship, answered the only way that he knew how—by calmly replying, "If you kill me, it would be better than me denying the name of Jesus."

Ameer knew that was not the answer they were looking for. It was the most dangerous response he could give if he had any hope of living, but it was also the only response he could give if he had any hope of one day seeing his Savior. Surprisingly, they waved him through and allowed him to leave the Mosul checkpoint on foot. Everything he owned had been taken from him—his house, car, luggage, valuables, money, and even his wife's wedding ring—but he was alive and so was his family. That was much more than many others had.

Emad Noel Fatoohi

The following story comes from an interview conducted by Dr. Paul Kingery on May 16, 2016.

Emad Noel Fatoohi (35), his wife, Leena Elia Majid (31), and their young children, Mohed (7), Deema (5), and Zain (4), were living in Mosul when the American military brought supposed liberation from Saddam Hussein. When Saddam was defeated, there was an immediate power vacuum, and the local Muslims were given free rein to terrorize the Christians. The attacks on the Christians were never fully reported through the Western news media.

Emad lived in Mosul for as long as he could after the removal of Saddam Hussein. Even though it was the most populated Christian city in Iraq, it was becoming increasingly difficult for Christians to continue living there. Nearly all the Christians on his street in Mosul left after a bomb attack on their Dominican church in the Saa District shortly after the removal of Saddam. Emad had a good job at the local concrete factory and did not want to leave. He had high hopes that things would get better, but they never did.

Things increasingly spiraled downward after the full withdrawal of American troops. Emad and his family finally left in 2013 after a string of attacks and kidnappings. Kidnapping Christians in Mosul became a very lucrative trade for the Muslims. They would kidnap Christians and sell them back to their families for high prices and make easy money. The Christians were not armed and had no way of fighting back or retaliating. The local government and police force did not have much love for the local Christians and were useless in trying to stop the kidnappings. Some even accused the Christians of being part of the problem. If only they would convert to Islam, they would obviously no longer face persecution.

For many local law enforcement workers, the solution was easy: convert.

All the church members from Emad's church had already left. Emad and his family were the only ones remaining, but in September of 2013, he packed up his family and followed the suggestion of his friends and moved to a place in Teleskof, which is about thirty-five kilometers from Mosul. He built a house there and commuted back and forth to the concrete factory in Mosul.

Emad and his family were used to persecution from Muslims long before ISIS arrived on the scene. They had resigned themselves to being second-class citizens and did not expect anything more. Some of the Muslim neighbors could be very friendly and hospitable, but the moderation of the majority faded in the background when faced with the hostility of the minority. If the radical minority's persecution could not be stopped by the moderate majority, then the moderate majority was irrelevant.

Emad's feelings about ISIS were very much like many of his Christian neighbors: "How bad could they *really* be?" Emad and his Christian neighbors had faced extremism their entire lives, and they somehow always found a way to survive.

About a week before ISIS entered Mosul, they launched their first attack on Tel Kef around 10:00 p.m. at night, about five miles from Emad's house in Teleskof. Fortunately, the Kurdish Peshmerga military repelled them. From his house, Emad could see and hear the battle taking place. He witnessed the residents of Tel Kef fleeing on the road carrying everything they could hold. Emad yelled out to his family to pack. He didn't want to leave just yet, but he wanted everything to be ready just in case they needed to flee in a moment's notice.

Tanks, Humvees, pickup trucks, and even buses could be seen traveling on the road to provide support for the battle. It was clear that ISIS was tenaciously taking territory at a rapid rate and their sights were set on Emad's home town of Mosul. Emad's sister was still living in Mosul, and when ISIS entered the city, she immediately yelled for her children, grabbed them, and began walking. They walked all the way to Emad's house with nothing more than what they could carry in their arms.

On August 3, 2014, one of Emad's neighbors, who was a soldier with the Peshmerga, called him to tell him the Peshmerga were withdrawing from Tel Kef and that he and his family should leave immediately. Emad, his sisters, and both their families were packed up and out of their house by the same afternoon. The call saved their lives, because on August 12, ISIS entered the town and took over Emad's home.

Hakim Saadula Georgees

The following story comes from an interview conducted by Dr. Paul Kingery in 2016.

Hakim (32) and his wife, Ruaa Sabah Sadiq (26), and their sons, George Hakim Saadula (6) and Behnam Kahim Saadula (5), lived in the Noor District of Mosul, on the East bank of the Tigris River. Hakim, like many Christians in Mosul, ran his own business.

He owned an auto supply shop and business was good, but things were not always easy. Hakim lived on Death Street, a street that earned its name because so many Christians were slaughtered on that street. Hakim witnessed the murder of many of those Christians. The dead bodies of Christians littered the street in the aftermath of the US invasion of Iraq in 2003. The Muslims of Mosul blamed the Christians and took their anger out on them, killing them wherever they found them and justifying it by claiming that the Mosul Christians gave essential support to the invading US forces.

One of Hakim's friends owned a restaurant in Mosul and was well known as a Christian believer. The local Muslims were angry because he provided food to the nearby US Army base, so they used it as an excuse to try to kidnap him. They knew that if they could kidnap the restaurant owner, they would likely get a nice payday because his family had access to the finances of the restaurant. Unfortunately, the restaurant owner did not play nicely and refused to go with the kidnappers. He ran away, but he did not get very far. They shot him dead on the street known as Death Street. He was not the first Christian to be killed on the street and would not be the last.

By January 2007, Hakim could not take it any longer, so he left Mosul and moved with his family to Tel Kef. There were fewer Muslims in Tel Kef to threaten the local Christians. Hakim was happy to find that the auto parts business was even more profitable than in Mosul.

Just as things were going better in Tel Kef for Hakim and his family, ISIS prepared to attack. With much reluctance, on July 23, 2014, Hakim left the new home he had built for his family and the prosperous business he had started. It was time to flee once again.

Sabah Jameel Hanna

The following story comes from an interview conducted by Dr. Paul Kingery.

Sabah Jameel Hanna (68), his wife, Wahida Abdunoor Hanna (60), and three of their four married adult children left Mosul in three cars on July 10, 2014. When Sabah was younger, he might have put up more resistance, but he was getting tired in his older age and had already seen his share of bloodshed.

Sabah had been a prisoner of war in Iran for thirteen years after serving as a soldier in the Iraqi Army. He lived on the more dangerous west side of the Tigris River in the notorious Nebe District. Not many Christians dared to travel there, let alone live there. Sabah was the last Christian family on his street to leave Mosul. Even at sixty-eight and feeling a lot older than he used to, he was still the last man standing on his street.

He saw persecution against Christians come and go, but nothing like what was happening with ISIS. He still had vivid memories of Christians being chased down and shot dead in the streets by Muslims as far back as 1959. Whenever the Iraqi Muslims felt the number of Christians or their influence was growing in any way in Mosul, a period of killing would soon follow.

Sabah had heard the gunfire coming from the firefight with ISIS since June 6, but he didn't leave. He didn't want to fight, but he also didn't want to move. He was not ready to abandon his home, his job, and the place that held all his memories. Then, on June 8, while he was outside of his house, he was shot in the arm. Sabah did not see the attacker, but he was able to make his way to his neighbor who was a nurse and was able to treat his wound.

ISIS posted a note on his home along with a large Arabic N. The note stated that Sabah's house no longer belonged to him but was now the property of the Islamic State. It was perfectly clear what Sabah had to do. He and his family packed up all of their valuables, along with the family ID cards, and jumped in the car, but when they arrived at the checkpoint, ISIS did a complete body search and found everything. Sabah and his family could not leave Mosul until everything they had on their persons was stripped from them. Christians who chose to flee Mosul instead of convert weren't permitted to take anything of value out of the city.

ISIS was allowing people to leave, but their power was growing stronger and their patience was running out. Maybe ISIS never really thought they would be able to capture Mosul so easily. They might have thought the international community would soon react to the demise of the Christian community in Syria and Iraq. But after the first attacks, it was clear the world was not really paying close attention.

The resistance from the world community that ISIS experienced was minimal. ISIS could kill the weaker people groups like the Christians and not experience any significant pushback for their evil. This made them bolder than ever.

Talib Jameel Mammo

Talib Mammo (37), his wife, Parwin William Slewa (29), and their two young sons, Jameel Talib Jameel (5) and John Talib Jameel (3), were living on the west side of the Tigris River when ISIS entered with strength on June 10.

Talib wasn't at work as he would usually be in the middle of the afternoon. Instead, he was watching the situation closely so that he could protect his family. When ISIS began to surround Mosul, the water and electricity were cut off. Supply lines were getting backed up, and prices for daily necessities were going through the roof. Although Talib and his wife were Christians, his wife knew it was wise to wear a hijab, in case the worst happened and Mosul fell into the hands of ISIS.

Surprisingly, all of his longtime Muslim neighbors quickly aligned themselves with ISIS. They did not even try to join the resistance against them. Most of the Muslims knew they would become the direct beneficiaries of seized property once ISIS was in charge. Some of the kinder Muslim neighbors encouraged Talib to go to the mosque and pretend to be a convert.

On July 17, the city speakers sparked to life with a cackling sound as ISIS made their demands known. The announcement broadcast throughout Talib's neighborhood gave Christians the inevitable three choices: convert, leave, or die. Soon ISIS would be arriving to mark their house with the N, even though that would be unnecessary as the entire neighborhood knew where all the Christians lived. It was not a secret.

Talib and his family knew there was no use in trying to resist. They could not stay any longer. On the morning of the 18th at 10:00 a.m., Talib and his family listened to the advice of others and left Mosul. They were able to secure seats on a twenty-one-seat bus and climbed aboard with nothing more than their clothes. ISIS border guards stopped the bus on its way out of the city. Everyone was pulled off the bus and searched. Anything of value was confiscated, especially ID cards. Once ISIS was satisfied with the search, the bus was allowed to leave.

Talib has not been able to see his home since that day in 2014, and it is doubtful that he will ever see it again.

SEVENTEEN

Mount Sinjar: The Calm Before the Storm

The following story of Barakat Mahlo Khudeda, and the first-hand details of the Sinjar massacre against Iraq's Yazidi minority (August 2014) are taken directly from interviews with Dr. Paul Kingery.

Barakat Mahlo Khudeda, a young Yazidi man of eighteen, lay sleeping on a mat in the darkness on the flat roof of his father's simple mud brick house in the remote village of Tel Azer in northern Iraq, a few hours west of the Christian city of Mosul. It was Saturday, August 2, 2014. Beside him lay his young wife, Almas. Their gentle breathing was the only evidence of life in that small corner of their completely darkened and silent village. The summer heat was still in the night air, though a slight breeze of cooler air swept in from nearby Mount Sinjar.

Barakat and Almas had met at a wedding party three years before when they were both fifteen years old. Barakat told Almas he liked her and asked her to be friends. Almas agreed. It was her first time meeting a boy, and she was very shy. He told her with honest simplicity that he felt drawn to her.

For the next three years, Barakat and Almas found many opportunities to secretly see each other. Barakat bought a telephone for Almas so they could talk more often, and she hid the phone so her family would not discover it. They usually talked late at night. They always chose public venues for meetings arranged by telephone. Sometimes they exchanged little gifts. First he gave her wildflowers taken from the fields and she gave him a simple string necklace of red and white interwoven threads, as was the custom for the Yazidi New Year on the first Wednesday in April.

The village of Tel Azer, Iraq, before the ISIS invasion, 2014.

Their families didn't know about the friendship for a year, after which time their mothers discovered the secret. Both mothers were supportive and considered a prospective marriage, although Barakat never told his father. In the Yazidi culture, matchmaking is the business of mothers during the early stages, with fathers only stepping in for the final agreements.

After two years, Barakat proposed. He didn't have much money, but Almas didn't care. She loved him just as he was. They were to be married.

Sinjar Mountain in northern Iraq.

Even though the marriage was a bit hastily arranged, Barakat's family still paid the honorable price for a bride, 3,500,000 Iraqi Dinars (US $2,931) to her family, and bought seventy-five grams of gold jewelry, worth 1,500,000 Iraqi Dinars (US $1,256), as is practiced in their culture. This would be much more than the Islamic terrorists would soon be paying for unmarried girls from the same village.

Following the wedding, a party was arranged on the streets of Jedali Village on November 20, 2013. This was a few months before ISIS would invade Iraq. All their friends and family members and those in the village of Tel Azer turned out, about five hundred people in all. It was a huge celebration.

Almas was dressed in an all-white gown and modest tiara, with a train she would have to hold when she walked outside. Her hair was teased and curled, making her face seem smaller and thinner, though it was adorned with white makeup and her eyes were heavily outlined in black so she hardly resembled her modest self. She wore a long, thin red sash tied loosely around her waist and carried a medium-sized bouquet. Barakat wore a black suit and red tie and new black shoes.

Faqier Yazidis Khalaf Said Sumo and his bride, Bahar Burro Haji,
marry on the streets of Tel Azer, Iraq, in 2013.

These fond memories from their wedding were still playing out in their dreams as Barakat and Almas lay sleeping in the early-morning hours on August 2, 2014.

A single gunshot suddenly broke the silence and put an end to the fairy-tale memories of their wedding. Soon, their pictures would be all they would have left. Barakat knew the sound of a bullet discharged from a Russian Kalashnikov rifle. It was as familiar to him as the crow of his rooster at sunrise. Their eyes opened instantly, mechanically, as if connected to the lever action of the rifle's trigger. "Must have been a misfire from one of the men guarding the village," Barakat said.

Rumors had been swirling that the Islamic terrorists from ISIS were threatening to invade from their nearby stronghold of Mosul, a satellite of their headquarters in Raqqa, Syria. Upon hearing the gunshot, Almas's hand instinctively went to her abdomen, as if to calm the baby just four-months in her womb.

Barakat's mother was downstairs making flat bread in the early-morning hours. She was sixty-one, fleshy, with a tanned face and quick hands. Her eyes had been damaged seven years before in an Al Qaeda bomb blast that killed four hundred and wounded hundreds of others in the center of their village while they were shopping in the bazaar. The surgeries on her eyes had not entirely restored her vision.

His father, Mahlo Khudeda Qolo (66), and slight of build, wearing a white cotton robe and a white headdress, entered the garden with a basin of the warm water nearly touching the base with his long full white beard. It was time for his morning washing ritual. It was unusual for a man to survive to his age in Iraq. The nearby gunshots did not rattle him from his routine. Most Yazidi men die earlier in their lives in wars, have heart attacks, succumb to misdiagnosed and untreated illnesses, or die from accidents or botched surgeries, but not Mahlo. Maybe it was his routines that helped him stay sharp.

Faqier Yazidi residents of Tel Azer (left to right): Kucho Khalil Qassim, Murad Garis Ali, Barakat Zindin Hussein, Salaam Khalaf Sherif (boy), Khalaf Hussein Elias, Zindeen Hussein Elias (who died soon after in Tel Azer in the ISIS Invasion), Burro Sharaf Khuder (standing), and Ali Meesho Khalaf, in a Tel Azer, Iraq, garden prior to the ISIS invasion, in 2014.

Barakat needed to prepare for his daily duty, which was tending his uncle's sheep near Jedali on the side of Mount Sinjar; the three hundred sheep were now penned for the night in a short enclosure adjacent to his uncle's garden. There was no food stored for the sheep. They would be herded outside the rim of the village on the mountain for pasture.

The Sinjar Mountain had always been a place of refuge to the Yazidi people and other religious minorities in Iraq. The mountain's many caves had been their first homes, and they had used the caves for shelter through the genocides wrought against them in past centuries. They still drank year-round from the cool water that flowed from its many springs. The youths celebrated their holidays with picnics along its crystal streams, wearing bright colors as an antidote to the brown monotony of summer, or blending in with the bright red, purple, blue, pink, and yellow wildflowers on carpets of nibbled green grass in the spring.

The mountain was also a source of food for their bodies and souls. Old men with long white beards and flowing robes counseled them from the doors of its ornate limestone temples. They picked delicious mushrooms and bright wildflowers from among its rocks in the spring; figs, olives, and pomegranates in the late summer; and favorite herbs in all seasons, but most often in the spring.

Their sheep, like the sheep Barakat shepherded, pastured on the mountains sides and valleys, even along the rocky ridges, forming an endless grid of trails. They fertilized the soil as they were moved steadily across it by shepherds to prevent overgrazing.

The mountain was both mother and father to them. It had been the salvation of the Yazidi people through thousands of years of invasions. They counted seventy-three genocides against their people by Islamic extremists over the past millennia and a half, though before that they had also been victims of invasions from Assyrians, Babylonians, Medes, Persians, Turks, Syrians, and Greeks. Their temples were on the mountain rather than in the village, testimony to its greater safety, and they sought them out for sanctuary when they were invaded.

Smaller villages hugged tightly to the base of the mountain all around it, with larger villages between four and nine kilometers from its base in all directions. It was an ancient security system that balanced the need for farming in the flat Mesopotamian fields near the Euphrates River against the need to be able to flee to the mountain whenever the next genocide occurred. It was not as efficient as it could have been using modern technology, and it assured the survival of only a portion of the Yazidi people.

Barakat's great-grandfather had sought refuge there, traveling alone as a young man, during the Muslim Turkish genocide against the Armenian Christians and Yazidis in 1915. His entire family had been killed by the Turks, and he alone escaped with his life. He married into the local Yazidis in the Sinjar District and became part of them. He had spent his days in Sinjar in peace, living to a ripe old age. Only now was the familiar specter of genocide against Yazidis returning to haunt his grandson, Mahlo, and great-grandson, Barakat, in the place where he had once found refuge.

Barakat's family felt trapped in the village with the encroachment of ISIS, which was the term all local people used for the terrorist group now pressing against them on four sides with only narrow gaps of escape.

Two months earlier, on June 10, 2014, ISIS fighters had overtaken the northern Iraqi city of Mosul and the nearby town of Tal Afar, parts of Kirkuk and Diyala Provinces, Tikrit, and much of Nineveh Province in a sweeping victory. Rockets had fallen on Christian and Yazidi villages to frighten the people, after which ISIS operatives made telephone calls to Yazidi and Christian leaders, ordering them to convert, pay a heavy tax, or evacuate. A mass exodus of Yazidis and Christians from Nineveh Province had followed to large cities in the Iraqi Kurdistan Region: Dohuk, Erbil, and Suleimaniya. Seventeen hundred Iraqi soldiers, who had surrendered to the ISIS militants during these attacks on the moderate Muslim cities, had been massacred.

The time was ripe for a successful ISIS invasion. On June 29, 2014, Abu Bakr al-Baghdadi announced that he was the new caliph of the Islamic State, and that he would seek to overtake the entire world and install Muslim Sharia law in its extremist form. His immediate objectives were northern, western, and southern Iraq, then Jordan, and ultimately Israel. Claims to be pursuing world domination were more bluster than reality, and overthrowing Israel was their more serious ultimate objective.

With the conquered city of Tel Afar only an hour's drive from Barakat's home in Tel Azer, and with Mosul, a city of 2 million, growing into a center of operations for ISIS in Iraq just beyond Tal Afar, all the people in his village were on alert.

Muslim extremism had been taking an even harsher turn than ever before in Mosul, and Yazidis knew they would eventually become targets. Yet they clung to the hope they could escape to Mount Sinjar, as they had always done in the past if they were invaded. They knew many would die if the invasion came, but they could not afford to leave their villages, homes, and sources of income until the last moment. Their poverty gave them limited choices. Their separate peace in Tel Azer was threatened, and they knew it.

Barakat and Almas carried this knowledge heavily as they thought of bringing a new child into the world. They were determined not to convert to the Muslim religion, no matter what the cost, a determination that had grown solid as a rock within their people over time. This extreme centuries-old rejection of Islam deeply offended the Muslim extremists, and made theYazidis their most despised enemies.

The Yazidi village of Tel Azer, Iraq, prior to the invasion by ISIS, 2014.

A street wedding for Faqier Yazidis Murad Barakat Khalaf and Nofe Khalil Ibrahim in the Yazidi village of Tel Azer, Iraq, prior to the ISIS invasion, 2011.

Barakat and his father discussed the threats many Yazidis had been receiving from ISIS. Khalaf Qassim, a man who lived in Bari Village along the border with Syria, had received a warning from ISIS by text message the previous day on his cell phone:

Where are you going to go? I swear [to] God I will cut you into pieces...We are coming for you, you pig, you enemy of God. Didn't I tell you yesterday to come and repent?

The women also gathered to discuss the dangers they faced. They had seen videos on the internet of ISIS taking Yazidi girls as sex slaves in Mosul. They all agreed they would kill themselves before they would sleep with a terrorist, even with the sham of a forced marriage.

"Father, do you have enough ammunition to carry with you on duty tonight?" Barakat asked. His father would regularly take the nighttime duty, leaving Barakat free to rest at night and herd the sheep during the day. His father would return in the morning and sleep through to the afternoon before going to work laying concrete blocks when there was work to be had. "The little I have would not last long if we were assaulted, but I will use it carefully," he replied.

They had no specific plan about how long they would remain in the city after an attack, whether they would wait for him to flee to the mountain, and what they would carry. The villagers relied heavily on help from the Kurdish Peshmerga soldiers, but they also had the same old weapons and lacked adequate ammunition to defend the village from a sustained attack. The village had no plan for evacuation. It would be every man, woman, and child for him or herself on a narrow road to the mountain passing near another village that might also be under attack.

ISIS
Abu Bakir al-Baghdadi calling for a holy war, July 4, 2014.

EIGHTEEN

Life Is Devastated

Sunday, August 3, 2014

Barakat awoke to the sound of distant gunfire in the early morning hours as he had done the night before. This time it was different. His eyes flew open and he leapt to his feet, distinguishing between the single shot the night before and this lower, constant drone of distant warfare. It was 2:30 a.m. He looked out from the roof and saw the red lights of mortars being fired on the two cities on either side of Tel Azer, Jazeera to the west and Gazarik to the east.

The attack by ISIS would be three-pronged, effectively penning the people of Tel Azer against the mountain, where ISIS hoped to surround them. ISIS approached Jazeera directly from Syria, entering from the west, with support from forces in Anbar Province, a seven hours' drive to the south, and forces from Baaj, nearby to the southeast.

Jazeera was their easiest target, remote and small, and winning it fortified the terrorists to move toward Tel Azer directly to the east. A similar attack was launched at the same time against Guzarik to the east of Tel Azer. Guzarik was attacked by ISIS forces from Mosul, supported by other fighters from Baaj and Anbar. ISIS fighters were assisted by Muslim Arabs from the surrounding villages bent on killing their Yazidi neighbors. The timing of this attack was closely coordinated to affect maximum human casualties, specifically among Yazidis in this planned act of genocide.

ISIS fighters attack Guzarik in their standard beige army pickup trucks from Saudi Arabia mounted with machine guns an hour before attacking Tel Azer, August 3, 2014.

Barakat's father called him by cell phone from the front lines where he was positioned with the militia and Peshmerga soldiers.

"ISIS is coming from both sides of the village," he warned. "Gather the important things and go to the mountain quickly; I will meet you there," he instructed.

"Just a minute," Barakat said. "Mother," Barakat shouted to his mother as he turned his head away from the phone, "he says we have to go to the mountain now and he will come later."

"Nawallah!" she cried, his sister rushing to her side. "We cannot leave without him!"

Almas had joined the two women close to Barakat's side, and now all three women were crying desperate tears. Almas thought of her mother and father and longed to call them, but she would have to wait for Barakat to yield the phone.

Barakat's mother's refusal to leave, and the speed of the encroaching ISIS fighters, left no room for his father to argue with them on the telephone. He knew they would wait for him if they could. This meant he would have to evacuate his position sooner if it became clear that ISIS would breach the lines or there would be no time to get his family to the mountain before they entered the village. It was a calculated move Barakat's father had to work out in the midst of battle, and any slight error in timing would mean the end of his life and theirs.

Preparing to Flee

As Barakat hung up the phone, his mother began tasking the girls with gathering the important things for the inevitable journey to the mountain. Before they had gone for a picnic or a family reunion, but this would be something very different. The mountain was their friend so long as they rested in the arms of the gentle valleys of its lower reaches under fig, pomegranate, and olive trees by cool springs, but further up the rocks were more forbidding, the water was less abundant, and food was scarce. The upper part of the mountain had been a friend to their ancestors, in that it had saved a remnant of their bloodline from annihilation, but going there, and remaining there, would mean certain death for many, and perhaps for them, as it had for so many before them.

Almas reached her mother on the phone. They were already preparing to go to the mountain, and knowing that set her at ease. They wanted to take Almas, too, but her responsibilities were with Barakat's family now. Her fate rested with theirs, even though it put her at greater risk. She wanted to be with Barakat no matter where that was, no matter the cost.

The next five hours were tortuous for them all, knowing their father was fighting a strong force with limited ammunition. Barakat stationed himself on the roof, watching the red lights from hot bullets and mortar rounds growing closer to the side where his father was stationed, hearing the sounds of gunfire and mortars growing louder. He could also see the people scurrying around the neighborhood, preparing to leave, and men grabbing their rifles and running to join the fight. He could see families being separated in the chaos as people ran for their lives, screaming, shouting orders to children, and crying. The mass exodus gradually changed shape from the chaotic swarm within the village into a single line of evacuation on the road toward Jedali and the mountain beyond, composed of people, sheep, and every kind of vehicle.

Growing more anxious, and unable to reach his father again by phone, Barakat called several of the other men fighting on the front line to assess the situation. They all felt they could hold ISIS back. When Barakat called again, they had become less sure of themselves. The Yazidis on the front lines did not seem to know, or effectively communicate to the village, when the Kurds pulled out. No one seemed to know if the Kurdish fighters were wounded or killed in the battle that day.

The Peshmerga kept their big guns at the police station, so some of Barakat's neighbors went to make sure the guns were being used in the battle. They found that the Peshmerga had pulled out of the village, taking the guns with them. Barakat's friend Ismail Shammo called the Peshmerga to find out what was going on, and the Peshmerga said not to worry, they were fighting ISIS. Later he found out that the Peshmerga had already fled but were apparently too ashamed to tell him. They could have reported their retreat orders to the leaders of the village, also known as muqtars (and may have), but the people didn't get the word.

Barakat called some of his cousins who were Yazidi Peshmerga soldiers stationed in Solaq Village and found that the Kurdish Peshmerga had abandoned the fight there at about 5:00 a.m., and the Yazidi soldiers were now evacuating with their families, leaving no force to protect the village. He presumed the same was happening in Tel Azer.

The people were left alone to be taken by ISIS.

The Peshmerga soldiers fought bravely and left when ordered to do so, and if they hadn't they would have needlessly died, but the system for getting that word out to the people of Tel Azer broke down somewhere along the line, leaving thousands at higher risk. The people were lulled into the false hope that the Kurds were guarding them even long after the Kurds had abandoned the field to the safety of the Kurdistan Region.

Many Yazidi fighters were heroic in their situation. Men like Khalaf Suleiman Hokay were killed August 3, 2014, by ISIS while fighting on the front lines. Others, like Farhan Haji Khalaf (24) and Hammo Hamid Khalaf (35), made their way safely to the mountain with their families, then returned to fight the enemy. Farhan was killed in Tel Azer fighting ISIS, and Hammo was captured in Tel Azer and never heard from again.

Another man, Ezdeen Ibrahim, stayed behind in Solaq to fight, an hour away from Tel Azer, while his family escaped with relatives. His wife called him at one point, and one of his friends answered the phone. He told her that he was busy and would call her later. The next day her husband's brother came to tell her in person that her husband had been killed in the fighting. He had killed five ISIS soldiers before his death. A sniper had shot him in the ear, which angered him, and he had stood up and started shooting wildly without seeking cover, taking down several of the enemy. The sniper then shot him between the eyes, and he died instantly.

Twenty-four-year-old Faqier Yazidi Farhan Haji Khalaf, who was shot and killed by ISIS while fighting them at Zorava, Iraq, on the north side of Mount Sinjar, 2014.

From the roof Barakat saw families running toward them from Jazeera and Guzarik villages on either side of Tel Azer with blood on their faces, warning them to leave. Their weak mud-brick, mud-mortared, pole and thatched-roofed houses had collapsed on top of them when shelled by ISIS, wounding many and killing others.

Barakat's mother, grandmother, and sisters gathered the most important things, taking photos out of albums so they would be lighter to carry, checking to see that all their IDs were together, taking money from its hiding place, and choosing carefully what little food and water they would carry and what vessels or bags they would use to carry it. They chose only the most essential clothes to carry with them. They had no car or other vehicle to transport them, so they would have to walk all the way to the mountain.

Yazidis Evacuating Tel Azer through the outskirts of Jedali, Iraq, in their private cars toward Mount Sinjar, August 3, 2014.

Barakat's grandmother, Shereen, was seventy, and somewhat frail, so Barakat knew they were going to have to help her. He could see people in the village carrying their elderly and infirmed in wheelbarrows or on their backs, but he felt this would be too jarring for his elderly grandmother. Some were leaving their elderly and sick behind as they were unable to walk, and others who were weak chose to take their chances with the Peshmerga and militia instead of slowing down their fleeing family members. Barakat and his family were not willing to leave his grandmother behind. Shereen would have to endure the five-hour, nine-kilometer walk to the mountain and the long climb up the side of the rocky terrain, between their arms, even if it meant the group would move more slowly and take on the additional risk that ISIS would catch up with them in the chase. Of course this meant an impossible journey for her, and they all knew it, but they were not willing to leave her behind.

A Faqier Yazidi man from Tel Azer, Iraq, carries his elderly grandmother on his back fleeing ISIS at Mount Sinjar, August 2014.

Thousands Flee to the Mountains

His father's friend called three hours later on the telephone to say that ISIS was entering Tel Azer. Barakat rushed to the other side of the house and saw ISIS invading in fifty trucks from two directions, trying to circle the people to prevent them from fleeing to Mount Sinjar. The ISIS fighters were distinguishable by their all-black clothing, captured US army vehicles, and black flags with white Arabic words proclaiming they were the army of God.

As they approached, they were shooting every man they encountered and every child who ran away, and capturing the women and children who didn't run away to put on a bus for sale as sex slaves or to hold for ransom. They had buses waiting behind their forces for the swift processing and relocation of female slaves and their children, and excavation machines for the mass burials of men, older boys, and many of the elderly and disabled.

Barakat's family hid inside their house and bolted the door—as if that would help anything. It was 7:30 a.m. when his father arrived from the front lines, covered in dirt and splattered with the blood of his fellow fighters. He called through the locked door. They opened the door to him and threw their arms around him. They were thankful he had been spared.

"The front lines have been breached, and I think most of the Kurds left before I did," he said. "I ran out of bullets, and the others had little to spare," he reported, more to calm his own feelings of having abandoned the field than to calm theirs. "Some of the local men are still fighting there, but they won't be able to hold out much longer."

A man of his age did not need to excuse himself for having fought terrorists on the front line for a shorter time than younger men. He was an exceptional man and brought pride to his family.

They quickly distributed the items prepared for carrying, assigning Faisal and Basse to steady his mother as she walked while carrying what they could. Barakat and his parents carried clothes, food, and water, and his father carried his Kalashnikov in case he could get bullets somewhere. Within a few minutes, they were on their way, walking as quickly as they could toward the mountain in a scene of ultimate terror, a mix of people and sheep running in every direction on foot or trying to load up and flee in vehicles.

As they left their home, they were taking a big step deeper into poverty. The house they left behind was their own, though it was not much. They would have no means to get another. The loss of the sheep would leave them with no source of milk or meat or cash from the hides. There would be no bread oven, no household items for cooking, no beds and blankets for sleeping, and no extra clothes. Years would pass before they would see their house and village again, if ever. They would be psychologically traumatized. Many, including some they loved, would be killed, wounded, or captured and raped repeatedly by their captors in the name of Islam. It was a dark hour, the darkest most of them would ever know, though many dark days were yet ahead of them.

It was clear. The manifestation of hell had arrived.

Azad Murad/Paul M. Kingery

The last people leaving Tel Azer, Iraq, on foot toward Mount Sinjar, who were soon to be slaughtered, on the morning of August 3, 2014.

As Barakat walked away from his home, he thought they would return later, maybe even the same day, if the Kurds rallied to their defense. Many never left their homes for the same reason. It would prove to be a fatal mistake for most of those who stayed.

Barakat saw a little neighbor girl named Shareen, just five years old, from a Sheik caste family, (the Yazidi's have several levels of casts in their society). She was alone and crying in the street, lost in the chaos of thousands of people fleeing for their lives. She was one of eight children in her family who had started for the mountain with their mother without the help of their father. He was fighting on the front lines and had remained too long or had been wounded or killed. Shareen had been separated from the rest of her family, frightened beyond imagination, too afraid to move in any direction, and was calling out for her mother in tears.

Barakat picked her up in his arms, passing his load to others, and tried to comfort her. She asked him where her mother was, and he assured her that she was up ahead, walking toward the mountain, where they could meet her. When she calmed down, he let her walk beside him, holding his hand, and as she grew tired, he carried her again. They slowly made their way toward the mountain with Barakat's family and thousands of others. He would call her "little Shareen" because his grandmother had the same name.

The family who lived next door to Barakat had decided to stay and not take the dangerous trek to the mountains. They opted to yield to the terrorists, thinking their rule would be no different from Saddam's. Little did they know how wrong their choice would be.

The march of seven thousand Yazidis was reminiscent of a story from the book of Exodus. As they walked in a single straight line, their formation extended four kilometers long. A cacophony of sounds arose from the village: the shooting of guns, yelling of ISIS fighters, screaming of women and children, crying of babies, honking of cars trying to merge with haste into a single line, noise of truck engines, explosions on and around houses, and the intense shouting of seven thousand people trying to escape. There was no rapid evacuation system in place. The road leading to the mountain was a single lane, and quickly jammed with traffic, leaving those at the end of the line more exposed to the oncoming ISIS fighters.

Some tried to avoid the endurance test of climbing the mountain, which had been the salvation of the Yazidi people for thousands of years. That proved to be a mistake.

Murad Aedo and his family tried to make an end run in their car around the base of Mount Sinjar and into the Kurdistan Region, rather than leaving all behind and seeking refuge on Mount Sinjar without adequate food and water. All of them were captured. The parents were let go at some point, but their two daughters, Noohad Murad Aedo (thirteen) and Leila Murad Aedo (eleven), were captured and have not been seen since they were taken to Raqqa, Syria.

The only order to the evacuation was the direction in which the people ran, as all hopes were on reaching the mountain. People were struggling under their burdens, carrying the elderly and sick on their backs and their small children in their arms, pushing the elderly and their possessions in wheelbarrows, walking, running, dragging, and crying, all at once. Few stopped to rest or take pictures or video clips on their cell phones. It was time to simply run.

Traffic jam at the base of Sinjar Mountain near abandoned Qandil Village during evacuation from Tel Azer, Iraq, on the morning of August 3, 2014.

Barakat's family knew the terrain and the distances well enough to know it would be an odyssey for all of them, particularly for Shareen, at the age of seventy, and for Mahlo, at the age of sixty-six. Their journey would involve walking 27 miles, climbing 3,155 feet to reach the top of Mount Sinjar, then descending to the Syrian border. They would walk 11 miles to the base of the mountain. Their route would take them along the only road toward the mountain, 7.5 miles to Jedali, then 2.2 miles to Shekhmand Temple, and another 1.2 miles to the base of the mountain before beginning their ascent. They would face a steep climb of 2,315 feet in just 2.3 miles up the southern ridge.

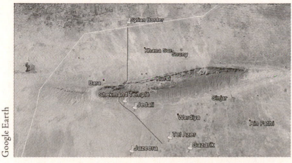

A map of the Sinjar District showing the escape route from Tel Azer, Iraq, over Mount Sinjar to the Iraqi-Syrian border.

Barakat Mahlo Khudeda

Barakat Mahlo Khudeda, his wife, Almas Khalaf Qassim, and their daughter, Vean from Tel Azer in Lalish, Iraq, one year after the ISIS invasion of the Sinjar District, August 2015.

NINETEEN

Iraqi Nightmare

Barakat's father looked through his binoculars to see that fifty trucks filled with ISIS soldiers were leaving Jazeera, ten of them heading straight toward the fleeing refugees, the remainder traveling toward Sinjar. Quickly, his father pulled the family off the road, and they ran behind some farms some distance away. They and others near the end of the line were hiding in sheep pens and crawling face down on the ground to avoid detection. In the bare desert mountains, the hiding places were few.

As a line of refugees streamed out of the village, a truck approached from a distance filled with ISIS fighters dressed in black with long beards and no mustaches, with black bandanas on their heads. There was a large gun mounted on top of the truck. The lone ISIS driver, having moved too far from the cover of his comrades in the village, was frightened by the large number of vehicles heading to the mountain, so he changed course and headed toward the village to join the other fighters. Upon seeing him, the people quickened their pace.

The same scene was playing out in all the villages around Sinjar Mountain as ISIS swept from Tel Azer around both sides toward Sununi. In Zorava, Salim Ziad Hussein (51) and his wife, Nasreen Kuto Ali (48), and their two daughters, Shama (16) and Noora (32), and four boys, Barakat (20), Ahmed (14), Azwan (12), and Reward (10), left for Mount Sinjar at 8:00 a.m. (not their actual names). ISIS overtook them, cut off their escape, shot their oldest son, Khudeda, because he shot at them with a Kalashnikov, and then captured the

153

rest. They were put into vehicles and taken to Sinjar, to a building that had been formerly used by the Kurdish government.

Once herded inside, ISIS separated the younger girls from the larger group and took Shama and the other young women with them to another location. A US airplane suddenly appeared overhead and dropped a bomb on the ISIS soldiers gathered there, injuring and killing some while many of the others escaped to the mountain to Garbara, then to Jedali, and from there to Sinjar Mountain. Shama was then taken to Sununi, Iraq, on the north side of Mount Sinjar, then to Raqqa, Syria. Another captive who had seen her was ransomed and returned months later to report that Shama was still alive in Raqqa. Her family has not heard from her.

This Was Their Own Genocide

Back on the road between Jedali and Tel Azer, Barakat's father took his family farther off the road, hoping that would save them from an ISIS attack at the end of the line. Several ISIS fighters had already careened through some of the farms near the village, killing and wounding many. Barakat found seven or eight men lying dead on the farmland just ten meters off the road.

He met a frantic older woman who begged him to help her adult son who was lying injured under a nearby tree. Barakat left little Shereen with his mother and went to the man. He had been shot in the thigh. His brothers and father had been killed, and his sisters had been taken away by ISIS, leaving him alone with his mother. She was beside herself in her grief as her last remaining family member lay wounded before her eyes, his blood draining slowly out on the ground.

Barakat tied a cloth around his leg and urged the woman to hold her hand on it to stem the bleeding. He flagged a passing pickup that was already overloaded, and managed to get the mother and her son safely on the back to flee to the mountain, not expecting the man to survive his extreme blood loss.

Barakat gathered little Shareen into his arms again and reassured her once more. His grandmother rose up to walk again, and they continued forward, seeing fewer shooting victims as they moved nearer the mountain. As they grew tired, they dropped clothes and less critical items along the way. They had been walking for about two hours when the little girl recognized her mother up ahead. Her eyes had been completely devoted to that one purpose—looking for her momma. She cried out in a desperate, shrill voice, "Mama, Mama, Mama!" Her mother stopped and turned, her tortured face transforming with tearful joy.

Little Shareen wiggled until Barakat set her down, then she ran to meet her mother, who moved slowly in her utter disbelief. The reality of her daughter's salvation slowly replaced the grief that had overtaken her when she realized an hour earlier that her daughter was not with her fleeing brood. They ran to one another and embraced as if both had returned from the dead, the other children gathering around them and hugging the little girl, too.

Her mother thanked Barakat profusely, and the two families quickly resumed their journey together, side by side. They were now more a part of one another than they had ever been before as neighbors.

Before them and behind them for a kilometer were the opposite ends of the long line of frightened, fleeing people facing imminent death. The tales of ISIS stealing Yazidi girls and raping them, hanging babies by the neck, and beheading men without mercy had filled their lives for weeks, playing out on their smart phones and on a few computers many shared. Now what had happened to others was coming to touch them as well. They knew what they were up against. This was a genocide in the making, one more in a string of seventy-three that had come before. But *this was their own genocide, and not merely a story* told by old men about others who had suffered and died before them.

Their small children and elderly were exhausted. More were stopping to rest with spent legs, pains in their chests, sores on their feet, and dryness in their mouths. Most families stopped with those weaker members who rested, resisting the urging of their elderly for the younger family members to go on without them.

The more fearful among them did not always wait for their loved ones, and, in very few cases, even small children, elderly, and disabled people who were too weak to walk were left behind.

Sometimes others would gather them up and help them, but other times they would die where their families left them. As they lay on the dusty ground, they watched the images of their families fade off into the distance until there were no other people around.

Later, safely reaching the mountain, the families would contemplate their choice of saving the healthier young ones at the expense of the old or the weaker children, and grief would overtake them. They would pray that some stronger person would help those they had left, as Barakat had done with little Shareen and with the wounded man and his distraught mother. In many cases, the weak were helped up the mountain, and the reunions were even more joyful because their choice had been so devastating.

Barakat's family finally reached the base of Mount Sinjar and started the grueling ascent. Gaining elevation, they could see more clearly what was going on behind them, seeing those who were the last to leave, waiting for their husbands and fathers to return from the fighting, or those with small children or the sick, elderly, and disabled struggling to catch up.

ISIS was advancing in increasing numbers, having wreaked their havoc and murder upon the villages of Jazeera, Guzarik, Tel Azer, and Jedali in short order, with a preference for death over capture, except in the case of pretty young girls and women. Most had been killed quickly with machine guns, dispatched with cruel economy due to the blood lust of the young ISIS fighters, instead of slow and theatrical beheadings and hangings. Others were killed with hand-guns by single fighters moving among the houses or along the roads.

The ISIS fighters were time sensitive, feeling the need to kill those in the villages quickly so they would have enough time left to kill those fleeing to the mountain before they reached it and formed any line of defense against them. The militants then proceeded to circle the mountain, cutting off any means of escape, in order to complete the genocide.

A few ISIS fighters had been left in the villages to herd the surviving girls, women, and young boys who had not run from them. They were gathered onto large buses. It was a carefully calculated plan to rape, sell for rape, or train as fighters those they had captured.

The ISIS attack on those last poor souls approaching the mountain came suddenly and with strong force. Six large, armor-plated, open-top vehicles with mounted machine guns, taken from Iraqi soldiers fleeing Mosul, approached from Jedali. As they drew closer to the end of the line of evacuees, they shot people indiscriminately: men, women, children, the elderly, and the disabled. They fell where they were hit, dead or wounded, with no one to help them. Their families scattered, running ahead, dropping everything but their small babies and grandparents.

Another twenty-five or more vehicles with ISIS soldiers approached from the two sides, flanking the line of those trying to escape toward the mountain. Together, ISIS fighters fired upon the people from three sides. Barakat watched with horror as about sixty Yazidis of all ages, including many of the weakest, were slaughtered in a hail of bullets. It was exactly what ISIS planned for all the Yazidi people once they were herded up the mountain, circled on all sides, and hemmed together for a single great act of ultimate genocide. Some of the bodies would be buried in mass graves; others would lie unburied at the base of the mountain for a year and a half, until the area was reclaimed by the Kurdish Peshmerga. Those who survived this massacre raced up the mountain as fast as they could.

TWENTY

The Fate of the Late

The Yazidi refugees at the back of the lines, and those left behind in their homes or on the road, were there for many reasons. Some had conflicting emotions, unwilling to let go of their sheep or markets, farms, or homes. Sardar Khalil Rasho (33) sent his family ahead to the mountain, staying behind to tend to some business. He didn't leave Tel Azer until 10:00 a.m., and then had to walk as all the cars had left. He made it safely to the mountain and stopped to rest before going farther up, but ISIS caught up with him and shot him dead.

Murad Jurdo Hassan (45) had a big market full of goods in Tel Azer. He had two cars, so he sent one with his family to the mountain, and he stayed behind with the other. He was hoping the Peshmerga would return. After waiting too long after ISIS entered the village, at about 10:00 a.m., he fled to the mountain in his car. He didn't make it far before ISIS fighters overtook him and shot him in the head. Two days later, the family, learning of his death, retrieved and buried his body near Jedali.

Many who had disabilities lost their lives in the invasion. The ISIS religious leaders had declared that all people with Down Syndrome should be killed. This attitude toward those with disabilities was pervasive. They were deficient, to be slaughtered, as if their lameness were infectious or would be passed on to the next generation of children.

Hanif Khalil Khuder, an unmarried nineteen-year-old girl, had been lame from birth and her mother had died accidentally by electrocution years earlier. Her family was poor and didn't have a car, so they had to walk to the mountain. Her family believed they had no choice but to run ahead and leave her to proceed slowly on her own. She was dragging her legs on the ground, pulling herself forward with her hands, attempting the seven-kilometer journey from Tel Azer to the mountain alone. ISIS caught up with her and, showing no pity, shot her dead, leaving her body on the road.

Barakat Hussein Khalaf (14) had a mental disability from the age of two. He was often seen in the village attacking children and animals with sticks of wood, and was known to be violent and uncontrollable, so he could not travel in a car without endangering himself and others. When the family fled to the mountain, they had to leave him behind. An elderly neighbor woman who had not been able to travel to the mountain gave him bits of bread for several days, and ISIS fighters made sport of him, sometimes feeding him and mock-fighting with him. After five days, one of the ISIS fighters tired of him and shot him. The woman called to report his death to the family. She was not able to retrieve his body, so it lay in the streets where he fell.

Khalaf Hassan Shammo (20) had been lame in one leg from birth. He and his family made the journey safely to the mountain in their car. His family continued going up the mountain on foot, but he chose to stay behind with their car to protect it from ISIS, along with several of his friends, who were also protecting their cars. After two days, knowing ISIS was in the area, his friends abandoned their cars and climbed up the mountain on foot. They offered to help him go up as well, but he refused and stayed with his car. After two more days, ISIS caught up with Khalaf and shot him dead. His friends had hidden a short distance away and heard the shots. They waited until ISIS left, then went sadly back down to retrieve and bury their friend's body.

Sharrow Hussein Hassan (47) and his wife, Wadhan Derwesh Hassan (69), were in Tel Azer when ISIS invaded. Wadhan was ill with palsy, unable to walk to the mountain, and they had no car.

Their daughter, Kochar Sharrow Hussein, had just enough room for her own children in the car, and felt there was no mortal danger for their parents, as the Peshmerga were expected to protect them. The family never saw or heard from Sharrow and Wadhan again.

Murad Hameed Haider (67) had lost one leg to diabetes and could not imagine climbing the mountain with crutches, so he stayed behind in Tel Azer when his family left for the mountain. ISIS found him and murdered him in his home.

Many of the elderly also lost their lives or were captured because they were unable to endure the journey to the mountain or were too slow in walking there. Khuder Svouk Mahmoud (71) died on the road because he was walking so slowly and fell behind. Many more of the elderly did not attempt the journey to the mountain at all.

Khonaf Murad Elias, age one hundred, was left behind by her family in her home because she couldn't walk. She was taken from her home by ISIS after one month and held for seven months in Mosul before being released by ransom in a group of twenty other refugees.

Azan Usman Bukker (70) and Haishan Hassan Kanqi (80) were both left behind by their families, and were seen being taken from their homes by ISIS. Their fate is not known. Many other elderly were killed by ISIS in Tel Azer after their families fled to the mountain, but no one knows which of them may have survived, since, as of this writing, the village is still in the hands of ISIS.

Barakat Qassim Barakat (70) was unable to walk, so his two sons waited for the last minute when it was clear ISIS was in the village, then attempted to walk to the mountain. His son Ziad left carrying his mother, Kamel Kalaf Murad (60), walking with his brother, Khudeda (25). ISIS caught up with the three, killed the two boys, and captured Kamel, taking her to Mosul. Meanwhile, some other Yazidis found Barakat in his house alone and successfully transported him to the mountain in their car. Kamel was ransomed back with a group of three hundred other Yazidis about eight months later. The two parents, though deeply grieved by the loss of their children, were reunited and are now living in Khanqi Camp about thirty minutes from Seje Village near Lake Mosul.

Kune Haji Barakat (70) was also unable to walk to the mountain, and her family had no car so they had to leave her behind. ISIS captured her and put her with Kamel and the other older women in Mosul. Thankfully, she was also ransomed back to the Kurdistan Region and was reunited with her family. She is now living in Kabartu Camp outside Semel, about twenty minutes from Seje Village.

Defending women cost the lives of some men as well as the women they protected. Khuro Khuder Suleiman (60) and his sister, Kavani (40), were late to leave and were overtaken by ISIS on the road to the mountain near Jedali. Khuro was infuriated when he saw ISIS fighters fondling the breasts of Yazidi girls and so shot one of the ISIS fighters. Both he and his sister were then slaughtered by the militants, and their bodies were left on the roadside.

Khalil Chato Khuro (55) and his brother, Atto Chato Khuro (45), were also in this group of men infuriated by the ISIS fighters touching their female family members sexually, and also responded violently. Atto's throat was slit by an ISIS soldier, and his brother was shot.

Sammy Jindo Khuro, age 20, was shot while defending his teenage wife on the road near Jedali.

Others who were late to leave for unknown reasons were killed or captured on the end of the line of fleeing people on the road near Jedali. These included Khalaf Suleiman Khoke (40) and his sons, Farhan (17), Khatan (15), and Sufian (13), all of whom were killed by ISIS in a hail of machine-gun fire. Ibrahim Agab Khoke (24) also died there. Khalaf Rasho Qassim (50) and his son were captured and taken out of Tel Azer and killed, and his wife, Honaf Rasho Qasso, and other children were taken captive. Khalaf Gharib (34) was captured, along with Khery Khalil Suleiman (11).

Farman Khalaf Khuto (25) and his young wife, Nofa, already had ten children, and his wife was pregnant with the eleventh. It is common for Yazidis in that distant area to marry at thirteen years old, or as soon as they are sexually mature, and not using birth control, they have a child every nine months to a year. Farman was on the front lines of Tel Azer fighting the ISIS invasion while his wife waited in their home with their ten children. She didn't feel she could walk to the mountain without her husband in her state of advanced pregnancy with so many small children and no car or relative to take them to safety. Farman stayed too long on the front lines and could not get past the ISIS fighters to his wife, so he evacuated to the mountain with other soldiers, hoping someone else had been able to help his family. There he was caught by ISIS and held for an hour before making a phenomenal escape.

ISIS came to their home in Tel Azer, and finding Nofa pregnant, left her there (ISIS fighters are not permitted to have sex with pregnant women). Sadly, all of her children were taken away from her, and she was left alone. She managed to make her way to the mountain with help from others so late in the day that it was very dangerous.

There she found her husband, Farman, and the two, their lives shattered, made it across the mountain in a terrible state, and eventually over to the other side and into a camp near Zakho.

From there, they managed, without help from anyone, to ransom back their eleven-year-old daughter, Sherivan, and their nine-year-old daughter, Basse, for $5,000 each. The other seven daughters and one son remain in captivity, if they are still alive:

First Name	Father	Grandfather	Age	Sex
Ghalia	Farman	Khalaf	7	F
Diljean	Farman	Khalaf	8	F
Dalal	Farman	Khalaf	4	F
Mareen	Farman	Khalaf	13	F
Haio	Farman	Khalaf	12	F

First Name	Father	Grandfather	Age	Sex
Berivan	Farman	Khalaf	8	F
Hariman	Farman	Khalaf	2	F
Dilshad	Farman	Khalaf	5	M

ISIS fighters continued killing all of the men they found who had hair on their faces (mostly aged 14 and up), killing the younger boys who ran away or refused to convert to Islam and join them as Muslim child soldiers, and carrying away the women and girls to sell as sex slaves or to ransom back to their relatives.

One group with two middle-aged men, Khalaf Rasho Elias (50) and Khery Sheik Khuder (50) and six young men were caught, lined up on the ground, and executed. ISIS fighters posted a photo of the killing on the Internet. The young men included the following:

Naiv	Khalaf	Rasho	22
Khalil	Khalaf	Rasho	21
Majed	Maho	Khalaf	20
Zedo	Barakat	Qasim	22
Khalaf	Barakat	Qassim	32
Saeed	Kamal	Ibrahim	27

Nazzar Jameel Khudeda (55) and his wife, Gule (50), their two sons, Maho (20) and Mendo (25), their daughter, Hatam (18), Khalil's pregnant wife, Nasreen, and Nasreen's little boy, Salaam, were caught by ISIS while fleeing Tel Azer (not their actual names). Gule, Hatam, and Nasreen were captured and taken to Mosul as slaves.

Nazzar and his sons, Maho and Mendo, were all killed by ISIS. A live video of Maho and Mendo was filmed as they lay face down in the dirt with six other Yazidi boys from Tel Azer . They were executed by ISIS and the live video was posted on the Internet with the militants bragging of their achievement. The jihadists are cruel and bloodthirsty enemies.

Eighteen year old Hatam was taken to Talafar for fifteen months. In a photo that ISIS posted on the internet, Hatam was pictured with the Arab man who raped her. Hatam, her mother, and her sister-in-law were ransomed in January 2016 and returned to their relatives in Kabarto Camp near Semel before moving to Germany. No one knows what happened to Nasreen's little boy, Salaam.

Those with larger families that could not fit into one car often had to make two trips to take all members of their family to the mountain, which put them at great risk. One woman, Shereen Suleiman Khudeda (not her actual name), unmarried, took her parents to the mountain on the first trip and was returning to Tel Azer to pick up her six younger sisters for a second trip. As she drew close to Tel Azer, she could see her sisters were already being taken captive by ISIS, so she had no choice but to return to her parents on the mountain with the devastating news of their loss.

Her six sisters were all captured by ISIS, ages eight to twenty-three. Shereen made it over the mountain with her parents and settled in Seje Village, where her father had a heart attack in his grief and died. A year and a half after she came to Seje, two of her sisters were ransomed back to their family and went to Germany with their mother, while Shereen waited alone in Seje, Iraq, trying to ransom back her other four sisters.

Many men went missing during the invasion and no one knows whether they were killed or captured. A few of the names from Tel Azer were:

Sabri	Khudedo	Khalil	43
Faisal	Sabri	Khudedo	25
Naiv	Khalaf	Rasho	20
Khalaf	Rasho	Qassim	55
Naiv	Khalaf	Rasho	24
Khalil	Khalaf	Rasho	20

TWENTY-ONE

Fleeing to the Mountain

Back on the south side of Mount Sinjar, Barakat and his family climbed up the base of the mountain and into a valley that would provide some protection. The Yazidi men who stayed at the mountain's base formed a line to protect their beloved holy site, the Shekhmand Temple, and to protect the thousands who were gatherer there. Avoiding this resistance, ISIS fighters scattered to attack those who had fled from the main road and were hiding in outbuildings on farms or crawling through the mud to avoid detection. They moved in step with their diabolical plan to murder all of the men that they found in the outlying areas and to gather up all of the fleeing women and children to take away to nearby Muslim towns for processing as slaves.

Khalid Naiv Maher (35) tried to escape the village of Tel Azer with his family of four daughters and two sons. He had also been caring for his two nephews, Ahmed (15) and Mahlo (13) (not their real names), when ISIS invaded. The militants caught up with them as they fled, shot Khalid in the leg, and then captured him, along with his nephews Ahmed and Mahlo, but the rest of the family escaped to the mountain.

Sometime later, several ransomed sex slaves recounted how Ahmed, Mahlo, and Khalid had been taken to Raqqa, Syria, the headquarters for ISIS, where they refused to let Khalid bathe or have food and water, trying to force him to agree to train to fight with them. Khalid became so desperate and suicidal at one point, the witnesses said, that he had grabbed a gun from an ISIS soldier and started shooting them, so they shot and killed him.

A fifteen-year-old Yazidi boy who was captured by ISIS while fleeing Tel Azer, Iraq, and forced into training as an ISIS terrorist in Mosul but tried to run away and was shot dead, August 2014.

Khalid's two nephews, Ahmed and Mahlo, were eventually taken to Mosul and pressed into training as ISIS soldiers. Ahmed tried to run away and was killed. Fourteen-year-old Mahlo was able to get to a cell phone after a year of ISIS training and, remembering his uncle's phone number, called him in a desperate plea for help. After learning that his uncle was dead, Mahlo was able to call his father and has been able to call him once every week or two. He is deeply and emotionally traumatized.

Sabri Khudeda Khalil heard that his brother-in-law was behind them making the same dangerous journey and had been shot in the leg. Sabri borrowed a car and returned to the village through the marauding ISIS fighters in a heroic attempt to rescue his brother-in-law. When Sabri didn't return in an hour and a half as he had promised, his family called his phone. Sabri didn't answer.

Sabri's son, Haji Sabri Khudeda, and his nineteen-year-old cousin took two Kalashnikov rifles from relatives and moved secretly between the farms to go back to the village to find him. About two kilometers before they reached the village, they saw an ISIS vehicle with markings in the village and another nine vehicles chasing people who were fleeing to the mountain. Haji and his cousin hid to avoid being seen by the ISIS soldiers who were approaching. Two other boys nearby were also hiding, and one of them called out to the other that the ISIS fighters were gone. They thought the coast was all clear. As they emerged from their hiding place, they were immediately spotted by an ISIS fighter only fifteen meters away.

The ISIS fighter moved toward them menacingly, shouting at them in Arabic, then pressed them to the ground with his rifle. They surrendered. The ISIS soldier called for his comrade to come over and cuff their hands. They were loaded on the back of a truck with other captives. As they drove out of the village, they saw hundreds of people, men, women, and children, lying dead along the roads leading from the village to the mountain.

They were taken to the Arabic Muslim village of Baaj, four or five kilometers away, and left under guard outside a house until the ISIS team leader arrived. The man pondered the situation, then told the boys to go back to the mountain to convince their families to return to the village. They promised ISIS would help them if they returned to the village.

The boys were going to be driven to Jadali where they would be directed up the mountain to retrieve their families. As they were leaving in a truck, not far from the village of Baaj, they witnessed some ISIS fighters pointing rifles at a group of about a hundred young men with their arms tied behind their back. Many of them were shirtless and lying face down in the dirt. They were forced to stand and line up in a single file.

They were all executed by a firing squad. After each of the bodies fell to the dusty ground, several of the fighters gleefully pulled out their mobile phones and took pictures of their exploits. The jihadists seemed to have no method to their cruel madness. While some young Yazidi men were captured, kept alive and taken to other villages, others were cruelly executed without any particular reason.

As the captured boys were driven to Jadali, they continued to see the ghastly scenes of dead bodies lying everywhere by the roadside.

*Yazidis fleeing the ISIS invasion seek shelter near a cave on Sinjar Mountain,
August 5, 2014.*

Once they arrived at the base of the mountain, the truck stopped
and the two boys were hurriedly dropped off. They did not waste any
time putting distance between themselves and the ISIS invaders.

Haji and his cousin found Haji's father, Sabri, on the road in his
car and joined him. Sabri told them of the hundreds of dead he saw
lying in the streets. He had walked among the many bodies, looking
for his brother-in-law, until he couldn't take it any longer. So many
of the faces of the dead were those of family, neighbors, and friends.
Many of them were elderly who could not get away fast enough. They
were easy targets.

At the base of the mountain was the Yazidi Shekhmand Temple.
About one thousand people sought shade under the trees surrounding the holy site.

Eighteen-year-old Ismail Rasho Khudeda was among the thousands trying to find a moment of refuge at the holy temple before
making their way farther up. He saw four women crying loudly over
the deaths of their husbands. Between them, they had seven daughters who had been kidnapped and taken away to be sold as sex slaves.

He listened and watched as he held his little brother in his arms.
He was surrounded by fifteen other younger brothers, sisters, and
cousins. Ismail had to be strong for them, even though he too was
fatherless from an Al Qaeda attack years earlier.

He was not sure what to do next. If he continued up the mountain, he and the young children he was given charge over might die of starvation, dehydration, or hypothermia. If they choose to stay at the temple, they could easily turn into low-hanging fruit for ISIS.

The world was only beginning to hear about the plight of the Yazidi people. On August 3, 2014, the hereditary secular Yazidi leader, Prince Tahseen Said, issued an appeal to the world for aid from his quarters in Germany and for help to save the Yazidi people who were being systematically targeted in the largest genocide of the twenty-first century. The aid came, but not as quickly as it was needed.

TWENTY-TWO

Massacre: Day Two

August 4, 2014 marked the second day of the ISIS attacks on the Yazidi people in Sinjar. Those who had made it to the top of the mountain had quickly run out of supplies. The need for food and water was critical. What use was it to survive ISIS only to die a slow death of starvation or dehydration in the intense desert heat?

Some of the men were already secretly making their way back down the mountain to find desperately needed food and water to bring back to their families. Everyone who had stayed behind and resisted ISIS had already been killed, and the captives were in the process of being carried away.

The jihad fighters were busy raiding the homes of any valuables they could find, including ID cards and travel documents that they could use later to assume a different identity. The IDs also helped ISIS to make fake ID cards later to smuggle fighters into Europe and America. In some of the homes, they found people who had chosen not to flee. They were all executed.

The Sinjari villages were buzzing with the arrival of more than a hundred trucks, heavily armor-plated Humvees, bulldozers, and excavators being used to dig mass graves. ISIS had several military tanks as well to reinforce their presence in Sinjar. Almost all of the vehicles had been captured from the Iraqi Army.

Senior ISIS leaders talked to two muqtars (village mayors), asking them to return back home and submit to their rule and to convert to Islam, falsely promising they would be spared. Most of the Yazidis did not believe the false promises of ISIS, but a few did.

Khudeda Jurdo, age 35, his wife, Khalida, and his four siblings were caught on the mountain by ISIS. They were told they would be safe if they returned to their home in Tel Azer. They believed the fighters and returned to their home, only to be captured and taken away.

Jurdo Khalaf, age 55, his wife, Bara (40), their sons, Shahab (25), Ali (16), Saied (17), Azad (14), and Nozad (8), and a daughter (23) also returned back to their home believing in the false promises of ISIS. They were all taken away from their village to a fate unknown.

Some of the prisoner processing of ISIS was done in such haste that several people were able to secretly hide their mobile phones and alert others of what was happening to them. Vian (not her real name) was a fifteen-year-old girl from the mountain village of Zorava. She was taken to the Raqqa headquarters in Syria. She was able to stay in contact with her relatives and was later ransomed back for $200 USD.

The family of Tamo Ravo Murad was attacked in their home at the base of Mount Sinjar. They fled up the mountain with the others for safety. On the mountain, not far from their home, they were having lunch. When they felt things were safer, they returned to their home. ISIS came, trapped them, and blocked their escaped. One family member was away fighting ISIS and another successfully hid behind a door, but twenty-eight out of thirty of their family members were captured. Their location or status are unknown.

First Name	Father	Grandfather	Age	Sex	Relationship
Tamo	Ravo	Murad	55	M	Husband of Sabri
Sabri	Ezdo	Qassim	62	F	Wife of Tamo

First Name	Father	Grandfather	Age	Sex	Relationship
Gule	Ravo	Murad	60	F	Sister of Tamo
Jamal	Mahlo	Ravo	27	M	Nephew of Tamo
?	?	?	23	F	Wife of Jamal
?	Jamal	Mahlo	2		Child of Jamal
?	Jamal	Mahlo	3		Child of Jamal
Mishko	Tamo	Ravo	35	M	Son of Tamo
Nofa	Mahlo	Ravo	36	F	Wife of Mishko
Nashwan	Mishko	Tamo	13	M	Unmarried son of Mishko Tamo
Emad	Mishko	Tamo	12	M	Unmarried son of Mishko Tamo
Maher	Mishko	Tamo	5	M	Unmarried son of Mishko Tamo
Eman	Mishko	Tamo	11	F	Unmarried daughter of Mishko Tamo
Vian	Mishko	Tamo	7	F	Unmarried daughter of Mishko Tamo
Rebar	Mishko	Tamo	3	M	Unmarried son of Mishko Tamo
Nader/ Zozan	Tamo	Ravo	21	F	Unmarried daughter of Tamo
Shame	Tamo	Ravo	15	F	Unmarried daughter of Tamo

First Name	Father	Grandfather	Age	Sex	Relationship
Zatoon	Sasho	Qassim	27	F	Wife of Haji Tamo Ravo
Saadia	Haji	Tamo	13	F	Daughter of Haji and Zatoon
Rojean	Haji	Tamo	8	F	Daughter of Haji and Zatoon
Aiman	Haji	Tamo	7	M	Son of Haji and Zatoon
Saadi	Haji	Tamo	5	M	Son of Haji and Zatoon
Renas	Haji	Tamo	4	M	Son of Haji and Zatoon
Shaabas	Haji	Tamo	3	F	Son of Haji and Zatoon
Kheria	Selo	Khalaf	27	F	Wife of Hadi Tamo Ravo
Mateen	Hadi	Tamo	5	M	Unmarried son of Hadi Tamo Ravo
Warveen	Hadi	Tamo	6	F	Unmarried daughter of Hadi Tamo Ravo
Jager	Hadi	Tamo	2	M	Unmarried son of Hadi Tamo Ravo

Their relatives are still hoping that one day they will get a phone call and find out that they are all alive. At the writing of this book, ISIS has raised the going price of ransom in order to sponsor their trips to sneak into Europe and America. The average price to return a family member is $4,000 USD, which is also about the same price as passage to Europe via Turkey.

The family of Khalil (36) and his wife, Kochar Rasho Hussein (28), and their six children had one home in Tel Azer and a retreat in Wardia Village at the base of Mount Sinjar. They sought shelter from ISIS at their home in Wardia Village, thinking ISIS would not come there. They were overtaken in their retreat home by ISIS, and all were taken into captivity. Their four-year-old son, Hawas, and two-year-old daughter, Nadia, and four other children were separated from the rest and have not been heard from since.

A group of five families made it safely from Kaberto Village to the mountain, but they did not have food or water to survive. The oldest, and their leader, was Khalaf Elias Bakker, age 45. He came together with five other men who were the elders of their tribe to decide what to do. Their families were desperate, so desperate that the men decided to risk their lives and go back to the village for food.

The risk proved to be too much and they were all caught by ISIS.

Khalaf	Elias	Bakker	45		
Khalid	Qassim	Elias	20		
Hazer	Murad	Elias	24		
Bapir	Sabri	Elias	18		
Nawaf	Hamat	Saido	30		

Khalaf Elias Bakker and his men share the same story as hundreds of others who were desperate for food and decided to go back to their villages to get supplies. Once their families were safe on the mountain, the men had little choice but to go back if they wanted to get the necessary items for their families to survive.

Ibrahim Agab Khoke, age 24, was one of these men. Another was Dilsher Khudeda Hadi, age 24.

Defending the Temples

Day two of the fighting also proved to be the last stand for the holy Shekmand Temple. Barakat had been hiding out at the temple. He knew that the Yazidi men would fight hard to protect the holy shrine. He was not expecting the level of determination that ISIS was showing. Barakat saw three ISIS trucks about two kilometers away from the temple. They were filled with jihadi soldiers and mounted with large guns on top.

At the sight of the trucks, the Yazidis began to scatter. Many ran in different directions away from the fighters. Others ran into the shrine and bolted the doors, locking themselves inside. An Iraqi Army helicopter appeared overhead. Signs of the Iraqi military were rare. The helicopter only observed and did not engage the jihadi fighters, so an hour and half later ISIS approached the holy temple again.

The sight of any foreign temple in Iraq angered ISIS to the core. They saw the temple as a clear sign of blasphemy, an affront to Allah. The zealous cry of the warriors rang out as they slowly overpowered the temple guards.

Barakat's family was farther up the mountain, but they could see the fighting taking place and the plume of smoke raising up from the gunfire all around the temple. Shamoo Rasho Ali, age 40, was one of the men valiantly guarding the temple against the overwhelming forces of ISIS. He stayed behind as his family continued up the mountain. He died "with his boots on," as they say in the military. ISIS would not take the temple without a fight from the true believers of the Yazidi faith.

Once ISIS was able to break through the main barrier of poorly armed militia fighters, there was nothing else to stop them. They charged the temple and broke through the doors. Inside they found elderly men and women who were screaming, crying, and praying. Many of them were disabled and did not have a chance to escape or make it up the mountain. All of the people were forced outside.

Those who could not walk were carried. Their clothes were stripped off of them.

Shamo Rasho Ali/Paul M. Kingery

A Faqier Yazidi man, Shamo Rasho Ali, who delivered his family safely from Tel Azer, Iraq, to Mount Sinjar and fought to defend Sheikmand Temple, where he was killed on August 4, 2014.

It was like a scene from the nature channel, where seals grab vulnerable baby penguins from their families on the beach. Instead of eating the penguins right away and putting them out of their misery, they drag the defenseless babies into the surf and fling them around, playing with their prized catch. The baby penguins have zero chance to escape, so the seals are free to do with them as they wish.

The elderly in the temple were completely defenseless and unable to escape. When they were dragged from the temple to the courtyard, there was nowhere for them to run. When their clothes were stripped from them, there was nothing they could do to stop it. Their only escape was to pray for a quick death. They were soon granted their wish. They were lined up, and one by one they were shot. Those who were killed last suffered the most because they had to watch the others gunned down.

Sometimes the mention of genocide conjures up the ideas of death, but it is more than just death. It is also the destruction of religion and cultural icons. Total genocide would not be complete with only the death of the people. The temple represented hundreds of years of religion and culture. The temple was the center of the Yazidi people and ISIS was determined: it had to be destroyed.

The militants had planned for this moment. They brought TNT with them and were able to put charges throughout the temple. All of the jihadi soldiers were ordered to get out of the blast zone as the charges were set.

In one enormous blast, the temple went up in smoke. The Yazidis farther up the mountain felt the mountain shake and heard the blast. Those who were close enough could see the plume of smoke rise into the air. It was the sign telling them that their beloved temple was gone.

On the north side of the mountain, the same scene was playing out. The Shefadeen Temple was under attack, and the men guarding the temple were hungry, thirsty, tired, and scared, but they were able to hold out against ISIS for a little longer. Then, ISIS cut off the electricity and water, so those in the Shefadeen Temple would need to leave to get water and food. Hundreds of Yazidi fighters died near the temple that day, but mostly from lack of food and water, others from wounds sustained during their exodus to the mountain.

The bodies of the dead were wrapped up in carpets. When there were no more carpets, then sheets were used until they were gone. When there were no more sheets, then the dead were just left in their clothes. They were buried in the ground or under rocks near the temple.

About seven hundred meters away at another site on the mountain, known as Taboot Temple, a completely different story was unfolding. A young mother was going into labor. Kochar was married to Barakat's cousin and was nine months pregnant. She was exhausted from struggling to escape up the mountain with her five children. In her condition, it was amazing that she was able to make it as far up as she did.

As the evening closed, Kochar went into labor. She was bigger than she had been during her previous pregnancies because she was having twins. Two babies were inside her womb relying on her to keep them safe. They had no idea what was going on in the evil world they were about to enter.

Kochar's five children were worried. They were scared for their mother, and her labor pains were intensifying. Most women give birth to their babies in the safe and sanitized rooms of a hospital, staffed with medical professionals who are prepared for almost any situation. Even with all the support one usually finds at a hospital, the event of delivering a baby can still be extremely scary.

Kochar was surrounded by flying dust and germs with no running water. If she delivered her babies right there on the mountain, they were sure to be exposed to a smorgasbord of bacteria. Kochar knew that she should be trying to find a way to get her and her five children to safety, but she was no longer able to move.

An hour later, Kochar gave birth to two little baby boys. They were a delightful sign of new life in a place that only seemed to promise death. Kochar was tired and dehydrated. She was unable to nurse the babies because her breasts had no milk. She held both of the infants close to her as she drifted off to sleep. With no pain killers and no guarantee of safety, she was not able to sleep any longer than a few moments at a time.

Four hours after she gave birth, she checked on the babies, only to find that they were no longer sleeping. They had both stopped breathing and were dead. Their bodies were cold and lifeless. Kochar's heart shattered. The babies she had carried for nine long months in her womb never had a chance. She emptied herself into her own grief. Her dehydrated body had no more tears to cry.

When the morning came, she began the unimaginable task of burying the newly born infants in the shallow rocky ground in the shadow of Taboot Temple. Soon after she would continue her journey so that she and her other children could survive.

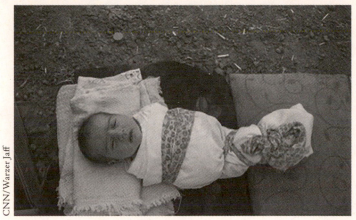

CNN/Warzer Jaff

A Yazidi baby born on Mount Sinjar in August 2014.

TWENTY-THREE

Beautiful Zere and Sexual Victims

Kochar had just lost her beautiful newborn sons, but thankfully she and her five surviving children made it up the mountain. There were many women who might have chosen to be in the mountains with her. Many women did not make it up the mountain to escape ISIS.

One young lady, Zere, had not been married long and was in the Sinjar town of Tel Azer when ISIS invaded. Her husband's family decided that it was best to try and wait it out. They were among the ones who did not want to leave all that they owned behind.

Many had put their trust in the promises ISIS was making to those who were fleeing in an effort to get them to stay or to return back to their home. Zere's family remembered all too well the broken promises of the Saddam Hussain regime, but they were able to survive his tyrant rule. Many Yazidi families assumed the same about ISIS. If they could survive Saddam Hussein, then surely they would be able to withstand the short rule of a ragtag group like ISIS.

Or at least, that is what they thought.

Even though no one believed the promises of the ISIS leaders, there were still many who hoped against all hope and stayed in their homes. Zere and her family soon realized the horrible mistake they had made once ISIS entered their village. They had underestimated the evil intentions of the jihadi fighters. Any hope of letting Zere or her husband's family remain in possession of their property was gone. Staying alive was the only thing left to hope for.

Zere's father-in-law was the first to be killed. There was no warning. It was done and over before anyone had time to think. Zere's brothers-in-law were not that old, but they already had hair on their faces, so they too were murdered on the spot. Once the men were gone, there was no more hope for the women and children. No one could even think of providing any meaningful resistance.

The small boys were snatched up and taken away to be trained as soldiers, and all the women in the house with Zere were taken to Talafar and then to the police station in Sinjar. The police station had already been overrun by ISIS and was their local headquarters for operations. All of the women were going through a kind of processing at the police station. From there Zere was loaded on to a bus with other women and sent to the city of Mosul. When Zere was put on the bus, the jihadis hastily looked her over, but did not do so thoroughly. They missed the cell phone that she had hidden in her clothes.

Zere was singled out from all the other girls for her beauty. Like many Yazidi women, she was fair- skinned and had wide eyes that men found attractive. Her hair had a light blonde tint to it that easily made her stand out in a sea of brunettes. Zere had a sweet, friendly face that relaxed others around her and is evident even in her photos.

Zere was put with a group of young women and taken to a house owned by one of the ISIS leaders. The top leaders usually got the prettiest, most sought-after girls for themselves. All of the women were frightened. The men were all speaking in Arabic, which is different from the Yazidi mother language. The house had obviously belonged to another family prior to the fall of Mosul and the soldiers took what they wanted. They also wanted Zere.

Once Zere and the other girls were at the house, the jihadi soldiers began to debate who would get her. Rank was obviously a subject that was an important part of the debate, because there was more than one soldier who claimed the "right" to have Zere as his "wife."

Finally, one of the soldiers yelled at Zere and commanded her to go to the bathroom and wash herself to prepare for "marriage."

Marriage is always the term used by Muslim militants to condone rape. For them, the women did not have the choice whether to marry or not to marry. The marriage did not even have to last for very long. In fact, according to Sharia Law in Islam, a marriage can be established for just hours at a time. This is often done as a legal form of prostitution. Islam also permits multiple wives and condones divorce at the sole discretion of the man. Therefore, short-term marriages have become a way for Muslim men to be sexually promiscuous without being "sinful" in the eyes of Allah.

Many Muslim men, as they travel for work, will enter into contractual marriages with women for the duration of their travel and then divorce them as they move on to another location. This can be seen in longer, less obvious ways like in the case of the Muslim father of American president Barrack Obama. He had a family in his home country of Kenya, but when he left them, he felt free to marry again when he traveled to Hawaii to attend the university. When he left Hawaii, he left that family behind and moved on to another marriage to father another family.

According to the ideas of Sharia Law, Muslim imams will create contracts (which are essentially a payment for services) and perform the ceremonies for short-term marriages. Once the marriage is annulled, then the woman will be available to be married to another who can pay for her services.

The commanders for ISIS had a desperate demand to provide women for their men. Many of the men did not want to wait for the virgins they would receive in paradise. They wanted payment of immediate gratification like the soldiers of Muhammad were given 1,400 years ago.

Zere was not aware of all the details of Sharia Law, but she knew enough to know that she was not going to the bathroom to get cleaned up for an actual marriage. She was going to be raped. She pretended to calmly obey, but she had no intention of letting the soldiers rape her. The women of Mosul had already become sex slaves and were often bound hand and foot and beaten during their "wedding" ceremonies. She knew that she would not be able to fight them off. Trying to make an escape by running away also seemed futile. In that final moment, she decided to escape through the only means she had at her disposal—death.

Quickly Zere searched around in the hallway and found a rope, climbed the stairs, tied one end of the rope around her throat and the other to the railing, and jumped off the stairs, breaking her neck.

Zere was one of several hundred Yazidi girls who chose suicide when they saw no other way to escape. In their culture, if women are raped, they can expect to be rejected by their families and communities, who blame the female victim and not the male for the rape. Young women are routinely stoned to death for having sex or even being intimate with someone who is not a Yazidi and who is not her husband, while the man is merely banished.

There is no concept of rape in Middle Eastern cultures that would count the man as the perpetrator and the woman as innocent. The woman is considered evil for "allowing" the man to rape her. The women had reason to expect harsh treatment. The honor of the family rested on the purity of their young women, rather than on the character and achievements of the men, as it does in nearly all Middle Eastern ethnic groups. It is a cultural travesty that is centuries old and seems even more bizarre and horrific when it is communicated through modern technology and social media.

Suspicious that Zere was taking so long, the soldiers ran into the hallway and discovered their prized "catch" hanging by her neck in the stairwell. The life had already left her body. They were furious that she left on her own terms, which was shown when one of the soldiers took out a knife, sliced her neck, took a picture, and posted it on her family's Facebook page.

Zere's family wailed with grief when they received the news through the Facebook message. Thousands of Yazidis would come to know this same kind of profound grief and utter devastation of losing family members to rape and suicide. This aspect of their experience would be hidden from cameras and from televisions around the world. No one could ever capture their deepest moments of suffering.

Zere Khuder Ismail, and her husband, Adnan Jameel Chato, in Tel Azer, Iraq, July 2014 just one month before the massacre.

TWENTY-FOUR

Tragedies on Mount Sinjar

One of the elderly women fortunate enough to have family members willing to push her up the mountain in a wheelbarrow was almost near the top. But the man pushing her had lost his strength and was struggling to do it alone. He needed the help of others. The rocks along the path were so large that it was almost impossible for him to maneuver around them by himself. Exhausted and dehydrated, he stopped and rested for a moment. He realized that it might not be possible to continue alone, so he left her to go find another person to help push the wheelbarrow.

The wheelbarrow was not made to carry people, and after many hours riding in it and bouncing up and down rocky mounds, the woman tried to readjust her position. Her weight shifted and tipped the wheelbarrow over. The wheelbarrow and the elderly woman rolled down the mountain and over a cliff. She and the wheelbarrow flipped over eight or nine times until finally she stopped.

Those who saw it would have normally run to her rescue, but this was not a normal day. Dead bodies littered the entire route up and down the mountain. No one wanted to expend the energy they needed to survive to see if she was still alive. Everyone just presumed she was dead. In their minds, maybe she was better off that way. She would no longer have to suffer the future of dying from starvation, dehydration, or worse.

A Yazidi man fleeing ISIS stops to rest from pushing his elderly relative in a wheelbarrow up Sinjar Mountain, August 2014.

Those who walked by the scene knew that they could be next. Just down the mountain, the fighting was escalating. ISIS moved in greater concentrated strength to Sinjar and its eighty-eight thousand residents. The approach was again from three sides, forcing people to evacuate toward the mountain where they could be circled and later systematically killed.

The villagers fleeing up the mountain were joining the rest of the people who had already started the long treacherous trek. The ISIS fighters who had taken Jazeera, Guzarik, and Tel Azer and associated small villages moved toward Sinjar from the west. Additional fighters from Mosul, the ISIS stronghold in Iraq, moved in from the east. Fighters from Baaj and other Sunni Arab villages south of Sinjar added recruits from those villages and attacked from the south. The city was quickly overrun, in a fashion similar to what the residents of Tel Azer had experienced. The same systematic killing of men and boys with hair on their faces, the elderly and disabled, and the capture and removal of younger women and children was seen. Captives from other villages were brought in for processing, and the Shiite shrine there was blown up and its priests were executed.

Many people had lingered behind on the south slopes of the mountain. Some wanted to be close enough to shorten the needed journey back to their homes to quickly gather food and race back to the mountain.

Abu Jan Khairi Aldomli

Ali Jameel Khalaf, age 23, and Suleiman Ali Khalaf, age 22, waited on the mountain for three days before attempting to return to Tel Azer to get some food for their families, only to be shot and killed there, leaving their families to proceed over the mountain without them.

According to firsthand accounts, as many as 100,000 Yazidis had taken refuge on the mountain, and they were weakening, and many were dying, from the ongoing attacks and from lack of food and water. Those who survived did so against remarkable odds. If death did not find you by gunshot, beheading by sword, hunger, or dehydration, then the nearly 50-degree-Celsius heat (122 degree F) would do its best to finish the job.

For the aid workers who wanted to provide more help, there was no way to bring aid over land. Iraqi helicopters were able to drop small amounts of food and water on the mountain, but many families were not able to reach the supplies. Water was difficult to find on the mountain, and springs were more abundant on the south and north slopes than in the valley between the two ridges where people felt the most protected from shelling and were farther away from ISIS.

Dead bodies lay out on the open ground in plain view. There was no material left to cover them other than the clothes they wore, and no one had the energy any longer to bury them. As a result, dogs, set loose from shepherding all over the mountain and in the villages below, were eating the corpses. One cave held fifty corpses and the stench of death was in everyone's nostrils.

A Yazidi family takes refuge in a cave on the slopes of Mount Sinjar after fleeing ISIS, August 2014.

On Friday, August 15, nearly two weeks after the attack began, ISIS lined up four hundred Yazidi men four kilometers from the village of Kocho. They staged a mass execution and systematically killed each one of them. About one thousand women and children were rounded up and taken away as prisoners. Once again, the young boys would be trained as Islamic soldiers and the women would be given to the soldiers as sex slaves.

A Yazidi family rests under a shade tree on Mount Sinjar after fleeing ISIS, August 2014.

Just down the road from where the elderly woman rolled down the mountain to her death was a mother sitting with her children. She sat down under the shade of a large boulder. Her baby children were dying of thirst and were in agony, unable to escape from the heat. The mother had no water for them and did not have anywhere to get it.

Other mothers had already begun to throw their children off the cliffs of the mountains. They could not bear the thought of their children dying a slow and gruesome death. Many of them were in temporary states of insanity. Nothing seemed real. It all seemed like a nightmare that would never end.

The mother sat in the small shade provided by the boulder. Soon the sun would be directly above them and there would be no more shade. She did not know what she would do then. She contemplated doing what the other mothers were doing and ending the misery for her children by throwing them off the top of a cliff.

There is a long tradition in the history of the Kurdish people of women throwing themselves from the tops of mountains when things are desperate, but throwing children from the cliff was something that not even the most gruesome stories foreshadowed.

The woman was not able to bring herself to kill her children. She did what she thought would be better than throwing them off of the cliff. She pulled out a knife she had been carrying. She knew she might need it for cooking, but did not know that it would serve another purpose as well.

She gripped the blade with her hand, closed her eyes, and pulled the blade through her hand until it sliced through her skin. As the blood poured out, she put her hands over the mouth of her children and let them drink her blood.

Barakat heard about what this woman had done from women who were close by, and he shuddered in disbelief, but he realized that to her it must have seemed the only option left. He didn't see her family again and doesn't know whether the children survived.

TWENTY-FIVE

The World Responds

At the same time that the Yazidis were fleeing from their homes, there was one voice in the Iraqi government trying to get them aid that was louder than all of the others—Iraqi member of Parliament, Vian Dakhil. Vian is the only female Yazidi member in the Iraqi Parliament.

She was tracking the unfolding crisis closely in Sinjar. Vian became the lone voice and champion of her people. Within the first two days of the attacks, she reported, "Seventy children have already died of thirst and 30 elderly people have also died. Over the past 48 hours, 30,000 families have been besieged in the Sinjar Mountains, with no water and no food."[98]

Vian Dakhil, official MP Facebook Photo

Four days after the ISIS invasion, on August 6, the US and Iraqi Army helicopters started dropping desperately needed water and food, with some of the early aid supplied by Turkey, to those stranded on the mountain. The helicopters were fired upon by ISIS, just two

98. https://www.rt.com/news/178548-thousands-iraqis-trapped-mountains/.

kilometers from the drop zone, and they returned fire, but were not hit. Turkey's early role would be largely supplanted by the Iraqi, Kurdish, American, and British entrance on the scene. The Turks and the nearby Kurds have been in a lengthy feud so the Turkish government's aid was limited.

The next day the US started bombing ISIS convoys in the Sinjar area as well as ISIS positions that threatened US personnel at the consulate in Erbil. They used both drones and manned flights. This provided air cover for future aid drops by the US and other nations, and supported the YPG (Syrian Kurdish militia) on the ground in their attempts to clear a pathway to allow Yazidis to descend from the mountain to safety. Barakat and his family could hear the bombs in the distance. They noticed that none of the bombs were close enough to shake the ground.

The same day, aid was supplied by the private Kurdish Rwanga Organization, based in Erbil, and delivered by Kurdish Peshmerga soldiers in Iraqi Army helicopters. The speed of this action was possible because the organization was under the direction of the Prime Minister Nechirvan Barzani's eighteen-year-old son, Idris, and was supported by other key staffers from the PM's office. It was licensed as a non-governmental organization (NGO), but it had all the right government connections and funding. Rwanga was also preparing Qadia Camp between Dohuk and Zakho to receive Yazidis fleeing the invasion. A small group of twenty people were evacuated off the mountain on the return trip. This flight was also fired upon by ISIS, making it a very risky and dangerous journey for all.

British intelligence officers were in contact with Barakat's cousin on the mountain by cell phone that same day. They spoke urgently through Kurdish-speaking interpreters imbedded with them. "Where are you? How long can you survive? How much water do you have? Where are the ISIS fighters?" They were desperate for information to facilitate the air drops. They didn't have any other intelligence on the ground.

A plan was made by phone for a nighttime aid drop by airplane. Those who spoke with the officers on the ground agreed to position flashlights to mark the zone to facilitate the drop. Some daring Yazidis traveled down the pathway cleared on the north side of the mountain facing Syria. Once they were positioned, they called back to say they had arrived in safe places.

Few other Yazidis were ready to follow the first team, knowing ISIS would fortify their response. Many just felt too weak, too traumatized, and too distrustful of Muslims who might be in the area on the north side of the mountain, so they didn't go.

The ISIS response to the aerial traffic on the north side of Mount Sinjar was becoming more focused and powerful, making it more dangerous for anyone to fly the aid missions for a time. The US military was responding to the attacks and trying to destroy ISIS's ability to fire on aircraft, but it was only partially successful. Flying in aid, while the US was bombing ISIS, was very risky.

As a result, the aid drops decreased and the food and water was inadequate to sustain those who remained on the mountain. The aid was not reaching all the people in hiding there, particularly on the south slopes facing Tel Azer where there were many elderly and people with disabilities. People were spread out for at least thirty-five kilometers across the length of Mount Sinjar, and for several kilometers across its width.

Finally, the United Nations declared the humanitarian crisis faced by the Yazidis and other minorities in the area to be on the highest level. This would pave the way for their broader role in the coming relief effort to those who escaped the Sinjar area, primarily through UNICEF and the UNHCR, assisting with the establishment of camps in the Dohuk area. They would provide only limited aid to Yazidis seeking refuge outside their camps, where they preferred to live, as this was not the UN's chief mandate.

Aid: Sometimes Helpful, Sometimes Tragic

On Saturday, August 9, US airplanes made their first high-altitude aid drop over Sinjar Mountain. A single C17 Globemaster III cargo plane with a crew from the 816th Expeditionary Airlift Squadron dropped forty containment delivery systems full of ready-to-eat meals weighing eight hundred pounds each on wooden pallets. Central Command posted a video of the drop from inside the aircraft on YouTube. The parachutes used to deliver the pallets would be used for tents.

Unfortunately, some of the aid was severely damaged in the drop.

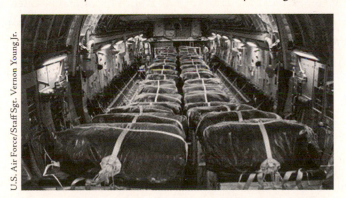

U.S. Air Force/Staff Sgt. Vernon Young Jr.

Straps secure water bundles aboard a C-17 Globemaster III before a humanitarian airdrop over Iraq on August 8, 2014.

The first British aid mission flew the same day. A British Royal Air Force Hercules cargo plane dropped 1,200 reusable water containers, providing 6,000 liters of water in total, and 240 solar lanterns that could also be used to recharge mobile phones. The British RAF were very clever and strategic with their aid drop. They dropped mobile phones that, when switched on, connected the people on the mountain directly with the British officers.

That same day, an Iraqi Army helicopter pilot dropped aid in three daring day-time rescue missions on the mountain, using the code-name Fox 1. The pilot had called ahead to identify the best drop zone.

Thousands of people were gathered where the helicopter arrived. The aid was dropped, despite the interference of countless desperate people rushing the helicopter, seeking to board it. The pilot had declared that their stop was limited to a brief window of five minutes, no more.

John Irvine, senior international correspondent for ITV News, was aboard the flight and reported the events. Many Yazidis attempted to climb aboard, beating out others who struggled against them. A mother and father literally threw their two little girls across a crowd clamoring to board the helicopter and into the arms of people already on board.

There was panic in the air. People were desperate to get out. They wanted to get to safety, and they knew they could reach a safe place if they were able to secure a seat on the helicopter.

The pilot announced that the helicopter's capacity was only fifteen people. Soon, fifty people fought their way on board, but the pilot could not lift off. The pilot yelled out for the crew chief to get people off of the aircraft. A number of men were forced off the helicopter before the pilot felt it was safe to attempt a lift-off.

A middle-aged man stood and said farewell to his wife and children, then walked back down the ramp. All lives were at risk. As the helicopter lifted off, a young woman ran up and grabbed on to the bottom of the helicopter in a desperate attempt to get off the mountain. She dangled from the bottom before aid workers pulled her up and inside. A man attempted the same thing. He grabbed on to the platform of the helicopter as it was lifting off. Those inside were not able to lift him up. He lost his grip and fell from the helicopter, plunging to his death in the mountains below.

On Sunday, August 10, the US made their second high-altitude aid drop over Sinjar Mountain. The first two American aid flights dropped off more than thirty-six thousand meals and seven thousand gallons of drinking water. This time, the aid was dropped from high enough in the air to avoid risk of gunfire and RPGs, but some of the water exploded upon impact, despite the use of parachutes. While much of the food was salvaged for consumption, a significant portion was scattered about on the ground and damaged. Unfortunately, the aid that day would hardly put a dent in the tremendous need.

The British Royal Air Force also made a second drop that day from two C130 cargo airplanes that provided 3,180 reusable water purification containers filled with clean water (15,900 litres of water in total), tents, tarps, and 816 solar lamps that could also be used to charge mobile phones. In the early hours of the following Monday morning, under cover of darkness, the US made their third high-altitude aid drop over Sinjar Mountain.

Also that day, a joint Iraqi Air Force and Kurdish Peshmerga mission commanded by Iraqi general Ahmed Ithwany sent four army helicopters from Zakho, on the Turkish-Iraqi border, to drop aid and evacuate refugees from Mount Sinjar. A Kurdish commander led the mission and steered them toward people who had not accessed the aid from the British and American aid drops in the previous days. They started dropping bags and boxes of water, flour, biscuits, dehydration salts, and shoes from as high as a hundred feet in the air without parachutes as they approached, and many of the plastic water bottles broke as they fell and spilled their precious contents in front of the thirsty people. People near the helicopter were more interested in being air-lifted off the mountain than taking the aid.

In the beginning, each helicopter touched down for five brief minutes on the mountain to deliver food, water, milk, and diapers, nearly causing a riot. Old men pushed themselves aboard as the aid was still being pushed out. Families pushed their small children into the arms of those on board the helicopter, and their dehydrated and weak bodies were briefly trapped in the press before being pulled aboard to safety in the back of the cargo section. One of the aid workers began kicking and punching Yazidi men who were pressing aggressively to get aboard, pushing themselves over the little children, trapping some of them under their struggling bodies.

It was an ugly scene, showing the nearly complete depletion of humanity in some of these desperate men. They were willing to do anything to escape the genocide. About twenty-five refugees were taken on one helicopter, another forty on three others. As they lifted off, people of every age cried on their way to safety. Sometimes to avoid riot, or because there were no flat landing areas near the people, aid was dropped from the air and did not evacuate people from the mountain.

One night another aid drop by the British Royal Air Force was conducted. Tragically, it was surrounded by confusion and the fog of war. A Hercules cargo plane flew at night to avoid the bullets and rockets of ISIS fighters in the area. The Yazidis placed the lights as instructed to show the pilot where it was safe to make the drop without hurting people camped in the area. However, so much time had passed that the people on guard fell asleep with their lights on. Other unsuspecting families moved into the drop zone with their children to find rest.

The unthinkable happened. The British RAF dropped hundreds of one-ton aid boxes directly on the people below while they were sleeping. When the darkness lifted, there were more than fifty people, mostly women and children, who had been crushed to death by the cargo.

NY Times/Adam Ferguson

Yazidis stranded on Mount Sinjar await evacuation by Iraqi Army helicopters.

As aid was beginning to pour in, the world was just beginning to understand the slaughter that was taking place in Iraq.

TWENTY-SIX

Escaping the Mountain Alive

After fifteen days on Mount Sinjar, on August 18, about six hundred people walked down the mountain together, thinking there would be strength in numbers if they faced the enemy. They could no longer survive where they were. They had to do something. It was either face death on the mountain or face death with ISIS. At least with ISIS they could fight back.

Everyone decided to begin in the early-morning hours before the sun rose so that it would not be so hot. At four o'clock in the morning they started off and walked for five hours. It was not much easier going down the mountain than it had been to go up, because their ability to move was diminished, they were severely sleep deprived and psychologically traumatized, their shoes were worn out, and their feet were damaged from walking barefoot or with shirts wrapped around them.

The journey down was more difficult than the journey up had been, given their weakened state, their profound grief, and their concern about the possibility of walking into another massacre by ISIS terrorists. They realized that even if they survived the journey, they would face the danger and undesirability of seeking refuge in a Sunni Muslim–controlled area, even among the moderate Kurds, whose failed efforts to protect them were still fresh in their memory.

Some of the men were carrying Kalashnikov rifles and a few bullets in case they encountered ISIS.

Yazidi people escaping the siege on Mount Sinjar, walking toward Syria, August 2014.

The group was a sad sight, utterly shaken in every way, mentally, physically, and emotionally. Their hair was matted with dust and dirt from the mountain and sticking out in all directions.

Their hands were rough from picking up rocks, climbing over rocks, taking water from rocky springs, moving rocks to lie down, and throwing rocks at dogs to keep them away. Their eyes were drooped from exhaustion, and they no longer tried to cover them to protect them from the intense sunlight, as that would require lifting their tired arms. Their faces, necks, and hands were brown and dehydrated, fingernails long and filled with brown dirt. Every crack, crevice, and fold in their skin was filled with dirt and dust.

The children and elderly were being carried down, just as they had been carried up. The widows and their children were barely able to make their own way down the rocky slopes. They struggled alone over the rocks, the distances between them growing over time as the weaker ones lagged, and those with a little strength moved forward with such economy of movement that they did not turn their heads back to see who was behind or how far back the others were.

At long last they reached the place where they could see tire tracks that indicated where the trucks had passed. They decided to sit by the road tracks and wait. If that was the place of resupply, then hopefully another supply would come or another rescue mission. No one in the group wanted to move more than necessary. As they waited for the trucks, they found some stored water in a concrete tank at a nearby farm to wash their faces, but it was too dirty to drink. They had a small amount of drinking water left from the air drops.

The farm house was the only place for miles around that provided any sort of shade. The elderly, the sick, and the children were all brought there to find rest. The men stood watch in the noon-day sun and risked overexposure, dehydration, and heat exhaustion. Unfortunately, the trucks never arrived, the drinking water ran out, and they were all becoming seriously dehydrated in the intense heat. Eventually the people gave up waiting, feeling their lives were threatened by dehydration. The men came together and decided that they had to keep moving. It was not an easy decision, but if they wanted to survive they had to go.

Everyone got up, faced the Syrian border, and continued moving. After several more hours dragging through the desert, the motley crew finally arrived at the border. Not long after their arrival, they could see dust clouds rising from the road in the distance toward them. The women and children became frightened, worried that it might mean ISIS was approaching.

Many of them had frightening, reoccurring dreams of that moment when the ISIS vehicles would finally catch up with them. It was the nightmare that returned night after night while on the mountain. There was nowhere to run. They were completely exposed in the open desert. They were too far from the mountain for it to provide any protection. Even if there was a place to run, they had no more run left in them. If the vehicles were driven by ISIS, this would be the end.

As the vehicles came closer, everyone looked for signs. They looked for ISIS's black flag of death that was often mounted on the vehicles and flown with pride. When the trucks got close enough, a few of them were able to see the flags. "It is not ISIS," one of the young men yelled out. Others joined them in the cry, "It is not ISIS! It is not ISIS!"

Soon, most of the refugees were able to make out the bright yellow and green colors of the YPG flag of the Syrian Kurdish forces showing through the dusk. A feeling of joy swept over everyone. This would not be a final massacre of ISIS, but salvation from the Syrian Kurds.

As the dust cloud drew closer, they could make out some big trucks, several busses, and small cars driven by Syrian volunteers who had received free fuel from the YPG to use in their cars. The trucks were empty to take the tired and devastated group to a safe place. Only the drivers knew where they would be going, but the people figured that anywhere was better than here.

Men helped women and children climb into the trucks. It was tight and there wasn't much space, but no one wanted to be left behind. A few men climbed into the trucks before all the women and children had been loaded. The others rebuked them, but everyone was too tired to fight. A few hours later, more trucks arrived for those who could not fit in the first caravan. This time there was more space than people, and even though there was a wait, it was worth it to have the extra space while driving over the harsh terrain. The majority of those who were on the last trucks were men—real men who allowed the women and children to go first.

The exhausted but relieved Yazidis traveled the dusty road away from Mount Sinjar, watching it grow smaller and less imposing as they progressed. Their memory of suffering there was the only portion of the experience that did not diminish with the passing of distance and time. Those who rode in the trucks were safely evacuated across the border into Syria to the YPG military station, and were taken into an official office that provided water and food for all, and medical exams for the injured.

Volunteers were there to assist, compassionately caring for each of the refugees. A few cameramen and news crews were able to capture the moment. These scenes would become the stuff of music videos lamenting the suffering of the Kurdish people, sung in Badini, in their common bid for aid and independence from Iraq, Syria, and Turkey. The plight of the suffering Yazidis, their Kurmanji language, and their dim future would not be featured in the Kurdish films. The desperate plight of the Yazidi was still being hidden from the world.

TWENTY-SEVEN

The Horrific Truth of ISIS and Sex Trade

We find a lot of…maybe not a lot, because it has been awhile since it all went down, but you can still see the blood stains," says Ramon (not his real name) as he and his team of Christians go into Sinjar Village to help the people rebuild after ISIS is partially pushed out by the Peshmerga military forces in northern Iraq.

In May, 2016, Ramon gave an interview about the things his missionary team had found in the houses abandoned by ISIS. "It can be different torture devices, just different things. We see tunnels that ISIS dug. I took some video footage of a tunnel where ISIS had hidden the girls."

Ramon was talking about the girls who had been taken by ISIS to be sex slaves for the jihadi fighters. Inside the tunnels Ramon found many needles, because, as he pointed out, "They would put these girls on steroids, because it was humanly impossible for them to endure the assaults at night and then work during the day. So they put them on steroids so they could continue serving digging tunnels—digging tunnels during the day and at night they are [sex slaves]."

ISIS needed tunnels in Sinjar to maneuver underground from house to house without being seen by the observation drones of the United States and other allies. The young women were used for this purpose because they were expendable. They were slaves. They were an asset to use until they could not be used any longer. From the very beginning of the attacks by ISIS, the women and young girls were subjected to the horrible atrocities of rape and slavery. Most people who are not familiar with the history of Islam might tend to think that this barbarity is unique to ISIS—it is not.

ISIS is walking in the footsteps of the Prophet Muhammad and the history of ancient Islam.

In the Koran, Allah tells Muhammad that he has given him girls to receive as sex slaves: "O Prophet! We have made lawful to thee thy wives to whom thou hast paid their dowers; and those whom thy right hand possesses out of the prisoners of war whom Allah has assigned to thee" (Surah 33:50a).

Slavery is not an anomaly in Islam, and it continues to be supported by Muslims in the modern world. ISIS's view on slavery is in line with the mainstream scholarly view of the Koran on the subject. Both the Koran and the Hadith repeatedly, both in action and in written words, support taking sex slaves from among the conquered people.

In Islamic Sharia law, *Ma malakat aymanukum* is a term specifically used for slaves or captives of war. The purchase of female slaves for sex is lawful under Islamic law and has been one of the most common motives for the slave trade in Islamic history.

This is a topic of supreme importance, because many people attempting to find common ground with Muslims will throw their hands into the air and moan, "But this kind of thing doesn't happen anymore, so stop being so Islamaphobic and ignorant!" Unfortunately, they are deceived. Even though their motivation to reach out to understand Muslims is good, they are misinformed.

Sex slavery happens all over the Islamic world today, and it is not limited to ISIS. This is a vital issue that most of the world is extremely ignorant about. The Muslim world is enslaving tens of thousands of women worldwide.

Muslim countries, such as Mauritania, have as many as one out of every five people living in slavery.[99] More than thirty-five thousand

99. http://edition.cnn.com/interactive/2012/03/world/mauritania.slaverys.last.stronghold/.

slaves, many of them sex slaves, live on the border of north and south Sudan, where Christians are captured by Muslims and taken to the north to be enslaved. This is on top of an ethnic cleansing campaign, much like what we have seen in Iraq, that has left four million men, women, and children dead.[100]

Slavery is still openly practiced by Muslims in Mali, Chad, Niger, Nigeria, and according to a very disturbing 2009 US State Department report, Iran, Kuwait, and the United Arab Emirates also help facilitate slavery.[101] Slavery has been so openly practiced in the Muslim world that in Saudi Arabia a man tried to sell his African slave on Facebook![102]

When ISIS first began to take ground in Iraq and conquer communities, the slave trade of women became a number one priority. Both women and young girls were forced into marriages with ISIS members who were being "rewarded" for their bravery and loyalty. The women and young girls who were made available were sold at open markets and inspected in the crudest manner. Christian and Yazidi women were made available for purchase by the jihadi fighters. They were presented with a price list that looked like a menu from a restaurant.

One market pamphlet price list stated:

In the name of Allah, most gracious and merciful. We have received news that the demand in women and cattle markets has sharply decreased and that will affect Islamic State revenues as well as the funding of the Mujaheddin in the battlefield. We have made some changes. Below are the prices of Yazidi and Christian women.[103]

In case there was any doubt about where ISIS members received the idea about selling women, ISIS further wrote, "One should

100. http://www.huffingtonpost.ca/diane-bederman/slavery-africa_b_3975881. html.
101. http://www.state.gov/documents/organization/123357.pdf.
102. http://www.frontpagemag.com/point/167540/saudi-offers-castrated-african-slave-sale-facebook-daniel-greenfield.
103. http://www.ibtimes.co.in/shocking-isis-official-slave-price-list-shows-yazidi-christian-girls-aged-1-9-being-sold-613160.

remember that enslaving the families of the kuffar—the infidels—and taking their women as concubines is a firmly established aspect of the Shariah, or Islamic law."[104]

Here is a copy of the price list provided by Iraqi News:[105]

The information provided by *Iraqi News* was translated into the following list for women to be sold as sex slaves.

+ A (Yazidi or Christian) woman, aged 40 to 50 years, is for 50,000 dinars [$43 USD].

+ A (Yazidi or Christian) woman, aged 30 to 40 years, is 75,000 dinars [$64 USD].

+ A (Yazidi or Christian) woman, aged 20 to 30 years, is 100,000 dinars [$86 USD].

+ A (Yazidi or Christian) girl, aged 10 to 20 years, is for 150,000 dinars [$129 USD].

+ A (Yazidi or Christian) child's price, aged 1 to 9 years, is 200,000 dinars [$172 USD].

104. http://edition.cnn.com/2014/10/12/world/meast/isis-justification-slavery/.
105. http://www.iraqinews.com/features/exclusive-isis-document-sets-prices-christian-yazidi-slaves/.

That last price point should be the most shocking to everyone. Innocent little girls between the ages of one and nine are being sold on the open market to blood-hungry jihadists who want to use them. This one price list alone shows the horrific extent of the slave situation.

First Prize: A Slave Girl

Every year, as the time for the holy month of Ramadan comes around, things intensify, because this is the time when the fighters rejoice over their spoils of war and make plans for new conquests. It is the time of the year that Muslims rejuvenate their faith and practice pious exercises that are often rewarded. And with ISIS the rewards would horrify people in western nations.

Fasting and praying during the month of Ramadan is one of the five main pillars of Islam. Koran reading and memorization competitions are held around the world, and in ISIS-controlled areas of Iraq and Syria, the prizes can be horribly different from other places.

"In honor of the holy month of Ramadan, the Islamic State launched a Quran memorization competition, with slave girls as prizes."[106]

Translated by the Clarion Project's Arab Affairs Analyst Anwer Al-Iraqi

---

106. http://www.clarionproject.org/news/memorize-quran-get-free-slave-girl-isis-competition.

This was the notice advertising the competition in the al-Barakah Province of Syria. The links to the chapters of the Koran chosen for the competition were provided (the translation was the Sahih International version).

Partial translation is below:

Province al-Barakah
ISIS
Announcement

To the soldiers of the Islamic State in all of the departments in the province of el-Baraqa

We congratulate you for the blessed Ramadan month and may the Lord accept from us and from you the fast …

May god deliver us and you from the fire.

The department of Dawa in the mosques announces the beginning of a tournament to memorize suras from the book of Allah.

From the 1st of Ramadan 1436 until the 20th of Ramadan.

Whoever wants to participate must register with the Imams of the following mosques.

The Mosque of Abu Bakr el-Sadiq

The Mosque of Osama Bin Laden

The Mosque of Abu Musab el-Zarqawi

The Mosque of el-Taqwa

In the name of Allah, the competitors will be divided and marked between the dates Ramadan 21st until Ramadan 27th. The prizes will be distributed on the first day of Eid el-Fitr in the name of Allah.

The Prizes for this competition are:

1st prize: A slave girl

2nd prize: A slave girl

3rd prize: A slave girl

4th prize: 100,000 Syrian lira ($462)

We ask Allah to make your life easier and to grant you with what he loves and what pleases him.

The Dept. of Dawa and Mosques.

For the memorization competition, ISIS chose the surahs in the Koran which emphasized jihad; it was a key part of the Ramadan festivities. The reward for accomplishing the memorization goals was a slave girl from among the "infidels" that will serve as the winner's sex slave. This is his reward for honoring Allah.

Ramadan is extremely important to ISIS because on June 28, 2014, the first day of Ramadan that year, ISIS announced the return of the Muslim Caliphate "to rule all of the Muslim people of the world." The militants declared that Abu Bakr al-Baghdadi would be "the first 'caliph of Islam' in this new era." [107]

The emphasis that ISIS places on sex slaves and the role this plays in their jihadist terrorism is incomprehensible to most of us. As painful as it is to learn about the details, it is important to listen to and read about the stories of those who are have escaped this horrific slavery so that we can truly understand the horror and prayerfully do something to see it come to an end.

The following are testimonies from several women who were able to escape. As painful as they are to read, they are stories with better endings than those who still remain in slavery today.

Zena

The details in this story have been gathered from an interview with the mother of Zena.

---

107. http://www.al-monitor.com/pulse/security/2014/06/iraq-syria-isis-announcement-islamic-caliphate-name-change.html.

Zena was only sixteen years old when ISIS invaded Tel Azer in 2014, but, as was the custom of her tribe, she was already married.

Zena's husband, who was just twenty, joined his father to fight ISIS and protect their village. Zena and the rest of the family did not leave their house; instead, they waited for Zena's husband and father-in-law to return. They did not want to flee up the mountain without them.

Unfortunately, as ISIS entered the village, it was apparent that they would have to leave before the men returned. They did not have a car and had to escape on foot. Without mobile phones, they were not able to tell anyone where they were going.

Zena's mother-in-law and two sisters-in-law ran ahead and found a tractor and trailer with room to climb aboard. Zena was delayed somewhat as she was carrying more of the food. The ISIS fighters caught up with them near the end of the line of the people fleeing Tel Azer toward Mount Sinjar.

They captured Zena and the other women and put them into their vehicles. A Yazidi man in the distance who saw the girls being forced into the ISIS vehicles took his rifle and shot an ISIS fighter who was driving another truck. He heroically commandeered the vehicle and drove through the fighters and was able to rescue Zena's two sisters-in-law and her mother-in-law.

Once they were in his vehicle, he drove as fast as he could toward the mountain, then stopped some distance away from the bottom and told the women to run up the mountain. He left the car there and ran on foot up the mountain with them. They were able to make it out unscathed, but Zena was not so fortunate.

ISIS took Zena and the other girls they captured to Baaj, a Muslim Arabic city, and slowly accumulated more girls over the next several days. They blindfolded the girls, loaded them in the vehicles, and covered the windows so that they could not see where they were going. They were taken into Mosul, which was the local stronghold for ISIS in Iraq. Once in Mosul, ISIS separated the older women and women with small children from the younger women and girls of nine or ten years up to their early twenties, who were more valuable to them and more desired.

The young women and older girls they took to Hamam Ali, a place for washing, and left them there under guard. The women were plainly told that they needed to clean themselves well, because they would be having sex. The declaration was crude and unceremonious. The fighters further told the women that if they refused, they would be beaten to death. All of the women were frightened. A small group escaped to plan a suicide pact. They would rather die than be forced to have sex with the ISIS fighters. However, the fighters caught them and separated them before they were able to make any plans.

Instead of being taken to the market to be sold to ISIS soldiers like many of the others, Zena and some of the other young girls were taken directly to the house of Muslim residents in Mosul. Zena was left with Muslims who were not a part of the invasion of Mosul, but instead were Arab Muslim residents of Mosul who were rewarded for their loyalty to ISIS.

Zena was given as war booty, and the Mosul resident was allowed to use her as he wished. He could keep her, sell her, or marry her. He chose to bring Zena into his family to be a full-time slave. She was expected to clean the house and cook for the family. She was repeatedly and harshly physically abused when she did not perform a given task to the satisfaction of the family.

Zena was also mentally tortured. They threatened to beat her to death, kill her friends, and take her to Syria where she would be injured if she didn't comply with their demands. After twenty days, she tried to commit suicide by electrocuting herself, but the family stopped her. They were afraid that ISIS would harm them for not keeping her alive. Zena wasn't expendable. She was a valuable slave. She was an asset, and if she died, her value to ISIS would be gone. The family was scared that Zena might try to commit suicide again, so the woman of the house took her to the ISIS security forces in Mosul and dropped her off. They did not want the responsibility of her death on their heads.

Zena was put in a compound with other women. The guards were watching to make sure that she did not try to kill herself again. After two weeks in the compound with the other girls under the watchful eye of the guards, things changed dramatically. Without warning, the US forces bombed the warehouse where Zena was being kept and there was a huge explosion.

The bombing of the compound sent the guards running in different directions. There was smoke, fire and complete chaos. When Zena saw the chance, she made a run for it. She was able to find shelter in a nearby house that belonged to an Arab Sunni Muslim family. They promised to help her, but as soon as they were able to take her mobile phone away from her, they took a picture of her and sold her to another family in Mosul for $2,000 USD. The family who bought her eventually sold her back to her family for a ransom of $4,000 USD. The need for money in Mosul continues to grow, and selling the slaves back to their families has become a lucrative way to bring in an additional income.

Altogether, Zena was a slave with ISIS and ISIS supporters for almost three months. After Zena finally returned to her family, since rape victims are often considered shameful, Zena never shared the details of her rape.

Zara

This story was given during an interview with Zara's brother on March 16, 2016, by Dr. Paul.

Zara was only sixteen and was pregnant with her first child when ISIS invaded her town in Sinjar. She and her husband, Khudea, didn't have a car, so they started to walk to Mount Sinjar on the road. They were late to leave, at around 8:00 or 9:00 a.m., long after ISIS had attacked the village. The Peshmerga military forces had convinced them they would protect them from ISIS. This created a false sense of hope that led Zara and her family to foolishly stay longer than they should have. They had passed a place known as Jedali on the road to Mount Sinjar when ISIS caught up with them. They were at the back of the line of people fleeing on foot and were not able to run faster to get away.

When they saw the first ISIS truck arriving, Khudeda's uncle fired on it with his Kalashnikov rifle. His rifle jammed after only firing off a few rounds, which is a common problem with the Kalashnikov. ISIS fighters overtook them, shooting two people with the machine gun mounted on the top of their vehicle before they stopped to capture Zara, her husband, and his family. ISIS captured Khudeda's father and his elderly mother, along with Zara, Khudeda, Khudeda's four brothers, and a young cousin who had been orphaned.

The jihadi fighters took the men and boys to Tal Afar where they were separated. Zara and Khudeda's grandmother were taken to Gazarek, where they were separated into two holding areas in different locations, one for young women and the other for older women. ISIS showed Zara a video to identify her husband so she could live with him because she was pregnant. ISIS fighters are not allowed to have sex with pregnant women.

Zara was able to identify her husband in the video of men captured who were being held in Tal Afar and being forced to pray. ISIS brought him to the same area and she was reunited with her husband. They were given a house in Tal Afar.

Khudeda's father and two older brothers were never seen again. His four small brothers and young cousin were allowed to come and live with Khudeda and Zara. His grandmother was also returned to them to live in their house. Khudeda and his oldest brother were forced to clean the streets every day. All the women were forced to stay at home. Several months later, ISIS came to their house and took the two men to jail in Tal Afar. They took Zara, and the small boys were taken away for religious training. Khudeda's grandmother was taken and placed with the older women again.

Zara was taken to the city of Hit in Anbar Province after ISIS conquered the middle portion of Iraq. While there, one of the jihadi fighters hit her with his fist in the abdomen to try to make her miscarry her baby. The fighter knew he could sell Zara, and she would be worth more money if she was not pregnant. Unfortunately for him, the baby survived. Even though she was pregnant, the Arab Muslim mayor of Hit was attracted to her. He decided to buy Zara for $1,000 because she was very beautiful. He said he would marry her after her child was born. The mayor had two other girls whom he raped while he waited to be with Zara.

One of the young girls he raped later gave birth to a little girl, and the other gave birth to a boy. The mayor didn't rape Zara, but Zara was given house work to do until she could give birth to the baby.

Zara knew that each day she was in the mayor's house was a day closer to a forced marriage, and she was willing to do everything in her power to keep that from happening. Suicide was not really an option if she wanted her baby to live, so she desperately looked for ways to escape.

Fortunately, Zara became friends with a nearby neighbor who allowed her to make secret phone calls from their mobile phone. Zara was able to call her family and also used Facebook messages to give them updates. She was also able to tell her family where she was. Zara's family raised money in hopes that they could pay a ransom and buy her freedom. However, before the money was paid to ISIS, one of the two girls who was being held in the same house as Zara knew an underground human trafficker who had a way to get them to safety.

The trafficker was able to help Zara and the two girls and their two babies escape from the mayor's house and meet with Iraqi soldiers. The soldiers took them to Vian Dakhil, the only female Yazidi member of the Iraqi Parliament, to find safety. Immediately, Zara was rushed to the hospital in Dohuk where she gave birth to a little girl. The little girl was not born in slavery, but to a healthy mother in the relative safety of Kurdistan. Eventually, she was able to return to her family.

Nofe

The details of this story come from a March 6, 2016, interview between Dr. Paul Kingery and Nofe after she returned from captivity. This is one of the more difficult stories to share.

Nofe comes from a large family, as is common among the Yazidi people. She was living with her husband, children, father, mother, brother, brother's family, sister, and sister's son when ISIS invaded her small town in Sinjar. Nofe is the eldest daughter and is in her thirties.

She is the mother of a thirteen-year-old son and a twelve year old daughter. (The story only mentions one 12 year old daughter whom she was able to hide not twin daughters as was originally written here.)

Nofe had just prepared lunch for her children on the afternoon of August 15, 2014, when she heard gunfire and shouting coming from the area around the village school. She did not have to guess what the noise was. Friends and neighbors were already aware that ISIS had been invading surrounding villages. Nofe lived in one of the few Sinjar villages that did not attempt to evacuate to the Sinjar Mountain. Ahmed Jasso, the leader of the village (also known as the muqtar) told everyone that living under ISIS would not be much different than life had been under Saddam Hussein.

Everyone in the village remained in their homes and did not try to escape. Sudden gunfire and screams from the village school could mean only one thing—the invasion of ISIS had begun. Nofe did not go outside to see what was happening. Few did. Most remained in their homes and hoped for the best. A few men from the village gathered up their weapons to provide some resistance, but not enough to make any difference. Later that day, over the loudspeakers, Jasso was forced to inform the entire village that ISIS was now in charge and that all villagers would be given three days to convert to Islam or face death.

There was a knock at Nofe's door. It was ISIS. They came into the home and demanded that Nofe's husband and father hand over all of their weapons and ammunition. After ISIS left, the entire family was terrified. They did not know what to do. They knew they could not convert to Islam, a religion they viewed as evil and brutal.

On the second day, the muqtar's voice once again came over the loudspeakers. Again, speaking on behalf of ISIS, he demanded that everyone convert to Islam. Nofe and her family were growing more concerned. They had run out of food. The water and electricity had been cut off. They had nowhere to turn.

On the third day, the local ISIS leader, Abu Hamza, made Muqtar Ahmed Jasso speak once again over the loudspeaker, telling the people to bring all their belongings and come to the school, saying that ISIS was going to take them safely to the mountain. Reluctantly, hundreds of villagers slowly emerged from their houses. One by one, the families went to the local school with their valuables.

No one wanted to go, but they were given very little choice. All the village weapons had been confiscated. They did not have any way of protecting themselves, and they did not have a way to escape.

Once Nofe and her family arrived, they were forced to wait until everyone from the village was present. ISIS fighters surrounded the school and demanded all their money, valuables, house keys, car keys, and even their ID cards.

The families were then split into two groups. Women and children were taken to one side of the school courtyard, and the men and boys with facial hair were taken to the other side of the school yard. The men were loaded into trucks without much of a fight. They were experiencing a mixture of fear and false hope. Without weapons, they were helpless. The moment they handed over their weapons to ISIS, they were submitting themselves to the mercy of the jihadists and could only hope and pray that the rumors they had heard were false.

The rumors, however, proved to be true. The men were all driven to an area where long trenches were freshly dug by an excavator. They were offloaded and lined up along the shallow trench. They were turned and faced away from their captors. The men were then forced to kneel down. At the command of Abu Hamza, the ISIS fighters opened fire. Every one of the Yazidi men was executed.

The ISIS fighters went back through the bodies and shot anyone who was still alive. Like vultures, they collected ID cards, wedding rings, and any other valuables they could find on the dead bodies.

Nofe heard the men bragging about this when they returned to the village. "What have you done with them?" one woman called out. "They were killed because they refused to follow Allah," was the answer that came back. Muqtar Ahmed Jasso had complied with all of the orders of ISIS in hopes that his people would be left unharmed, but when it was clear that they were all about to be either killed, forced to convert, or enslaved, he grabbed the microphone to issue one last call of defiance through the loudspeakers, but it was too little too late. The damage had been done. ISIS had complete control. A Saudi man, who was working under the command of ISIS leader Abu Hamza, killed Muqtar Ahmed Jasso on the spot.

With the men gone, the women were helpless. One of the women being held hostage was the nineteen-year-old-daughter of Muqtar Ahmed Jasso. She was beautiful and was considered to be a prize catch. The fighters looked at her like she was a piece of meat they could not wait to devour.

One of the fighters claimed her as his own, but that did not sit well with the others who wanted her as well. Another fighter who had been hoping that she would be his prize lashed out in lust and killed the fellow jihadi. However, his newly held possession was short-lived, because she was given over to the leader as soon as he arrived. It was determined that she was much too valuable for a lowly fighter and should be given to the highest ranking officer.

ISIS demanded all of the ID cards from the Yazidis. Nofe pretended that she had already handed hers over, but she had hidden her family's ID cards in her clothes. She also put a few of the ID cards in her daughters' clothing as well with hopes that the ISIS fighters would not find them. She knew they might be their only ticket to freedom The ISIS fighters knew that some of the women were secretly holding on to their ID cards. "If you do not all hand over your ID cards or if you attempt to hide them, we will cut off your hands and your feet when we find them," they threatened.

Nofe did not completely believe the threat. She knew the women were more valuable with their hands and feet. They never found her ID cards, even though they made the threat several times.

Nofe was allowed to keep her children with her when they loaded her into another vehicle to take her to the Arab Muslim village of Solaq, where they were put into a large warehouse-like building that was initially built for the Kurdish president, Masoud Barzani.

The Saudi man who worked together with the commander and had killed the muqtar immediately showed his power by removing the picture of President Barzani, breaking the frame on the ground, and stomping his feet on the picture. Soon after they arrived, the jihadi soldiers came to take Nofe's son. "Your son will be taken to learn the Koran," one of the soldiers said as they approached. They demanded that he be given over.

Nofe knew they wanted to train her young son to be a soldier for Allah. ISIS would take him away, torture him, and brainwash him to be a suicide soldier. When they reached out for him, she clutched him close to her and let out an involuntary scream. The soldiers grabbed his arm and tried to pull him away, but Nofe fought back. Her mother instincts kicked in. One of the soldiers lifted up his rifle and brought it down with all the force that he could muster and hit Nofe in the head. The trauma from the blow knocked her back and loosened her grip.

She opened her mouth to beg them not to take her baby boy, but her words fell on deaf ears. Women all around her were wailing as their young boys were taken from them as well. Nofe's husband, father, and all the men in her life had been taken away and killed. Now her boy was taken from her too.

All she had left was her young daughter, but she too was in danger of being taken away.

The ISIS fighters came back to take the young girls away to be sold. The young virgin girls were the most valuable, and there was no age that was too young for the sick minds of the ISIS fighters. Prepubescent girls sold for higher prices than those with children. Miraculously, Nofe was able to successfully hide her daughter behind her. She was safe. For the time being. In the days that followed, Nofe was not able to eat or sleep. Her grief was too heavy.

After a few days, ISIS gave all of the women a chance to convert to Islam. Nofe was too weak, tired, and defeated to resist. She, like most of the women around her, did not put up a fight. Like the millions of women before them in the long history of Islam, they unwillingly converted in order to survive another day.

The few elderly women who did not convert were taken outside and given one more chance to believe in Allah. When they did not convert, they were placed into a shallow grave. ISIS did not want to waste their ammunition, so they called in the excavator, which took large buckets of fresh soil and dropped it on the women while they stood in the freshly dug trench.

One after another, large buckets of dirt were dropped on the women, burying them alive. Some died from the crush of the weight upon their bodies. Others struggled under the soil, unable to move, unable to breathe, until the life slowly ebbed out of their bodies as they suffocated. The young women watched this with horror, their hands over their mouths, afraid to cry out. Nofe was still too grieved about the loss of her son to watch. She couldn't stop crying, and could hardly bear the news the other women were telling her about the massacre of the older women.

Immediately after they finished killing the older women, the ISIS fighters returned. They loaded all of the remaining captives into four big trucks and took them to Talafar. Nofe was still hiding her twelve year old daughter in her clothes. They were taken off the trucks and ushered into a school building in Talafar.

Nofe Is Sold

Three weeks later, Nofe was taken to a Muslim home where she would provide free labor. She was given food and water once a day. Most of the married women with children were used for free labor, but ISIS fighters were free to come into the homes and have sex with them as they wished. Their bodies were no longer their own. They belonged to the Muslim captors. Nofe cooked and cleaned for a Muslim family for four months before she was again loaded into a truck and taken to Raqqa, Syria, where she was placed in another holding warehouse. The younger, more beautiful women were sold to soldiers every day. One by one they were taken out to be given over to their buyer.

On March 12, 2015, a man in his midforties by the name of Abu Annas Almagharabi came and took Nofe and her daughter. He didn't say anything to them; he just motioned for them to come with him. They didn't dare disobey. He was a man of medium height, thin build, and had a long dark, black beard. His curly black hair swirled around his wire-rimmed glasses. Everything about him seemed dark. Even the clothes he chose to wear were long black Afghani or Moroccan robes. He only spoke Arabic.

Nofe and her daughter were brought to a small house in a more rural area. When they entered into the house, Nofe saw a man in a wheelchair who was missing both legs. His name was Abu Waleed Almugarabi. He was about thirty years old and had lost his legs in an attack from the American military.

"You will be married to this man," Abu Annas said directly, indicating Waleed, who was in the wheelchair. Nofe had no choice in the matter. She was not being asked to marry Waleed. She was being informed of a decision that had already been made. Abu Annas was just stating a fact. Nothing more needed to be said.

"Now go and clean him up," Abu barked.

Nofe looked at him and saw that he was covered in his own urine and feces and refused to clean him up. The sight of him disgusted her. Without a second thought, Abu began yelling at her and began to beat her. Nofe quickly realized that nothing Abu said was a suggestion. It was an order. If Abu told Nofe to do something, then Nofe had to do it. No questions, no refusal. Nofe took the man to wash him up. She gagged several times and eventually vomited.

In the other room, Abu gave Nofe's daughter pills and then tied her hands and feet together. Nofe knew what was coming. She tried to stop Abu, but it was useless. He beat her until she was black and blue, then he beat her twelve-year-old daughter in front of her eyes. After he beat her, he tied her up and made her watch as he raped her daughter on the floor. Nofe's daughter quickly passed out from the drugs and the pain. Abu continued raping her even though she was unconscious.

Nofe was totally helpless. There was nothing she could do. Everything she had in life was now gone—her home, her parents, her husband, her boy, and now her daughter. Even her freedom was taken away.

After Abu was finished raping her daughter, he propped up on his knees, faced his body to the east, and began praying to Allah. He bowed toward Mecca several times as he gave thanks to Allah for his great reward. It is a horrifying practice among many Islamic militants.

After he prayed, he cut the young girl loose. Her limp hands fell to her side. She remained unconscious for over an hour. The fact that she was not lucid was a small grace for Nofe as she reached over and cradled her baby. Nofe's daughter could not walk for three days. Abu then forced marriage upon Nofe. Under the watchful eye of Abu, she was forced to have sex with Waleed, the legless man.

Abu controlled her every move. For four months, both she and her daughter were raped repeatedly by Abu and Waleed. After four months, Abu decided to sell them to other willing customers. Without warning, Nofe was sold to a man who did not want to buy her daughter as well. Nofe's daughter was sold to another man. It happened fast and without warning.

Nofe never saw her daughter again. Nofe was sold with increased frequency and was raped every day. Eventually, she made it to freedom in Kurdistan, but she never saw her children again. She now lives in a Christian village where many other Yazidis just like her have found a home. The excruciating emotional and physical pain she has suffered makes her story one of the most painful that I have shared. But the world must know what is happening in the horrific tragedy of the Islamic sex trade.

How can they ever be rescued if no one knows the horror of the truth?

TWENTY-EIGHT

Christians and Yazidi Survivors Find a Home

In the weeks that followed the initial attack on Mount Sinjar, convoys of buses and trucks began the arduous task of bringing the remaining Yazidi and Christian survivors from Syria back to Iraq. The Kurds treated them better than ISIS, but there was still very little love between the two groups.

The refugees were brought from Syria, across the border near Fishkabur, through the foothills of the Qandil Mountains, and along the fertile Tigris River Valley to a town north of Mosul called Dohuk. According to a 2013 census, Dohuk had a population of about 350,000. Today that population is higher than 1.5 million.

There was nowhere to put all of the displaced people seeking shelter, so many of the new arrivals had to find a way to provide for themselves.

Dr. Paul Kingery, director of MedEast, an NGO in Iraq, immediately swung into action to provide aid to those arriving in Dohuk. Thousands of weary and traumatized victims were overwhelming for the entire NGO community, including Dr. Paul's MedEast.

Many of the gaunt faces of the displaced women and children were full of fear. The men did not know what to do next or where to go. They were at the mercy of the Kurdish government. They were all famished, exhausted, and longing to return to their normal lives. Most of them had loved ones—brothers, sisters, children, parents, grandparents—who did not escape. The shock of that reality had not yet begun to sink in.

Dr. Paul spent time with the people who were pouring into Dohuk. He listened to their stories and made notes of their needs. He had been working in Iraq for more than six years and was familiar with serving in war-torn settings, but the details of the tragic stories that the Yazidis and Christians were sharing were unlike anything he had ever heard. For the next several days, Dr. Paul brought bread and bottled water, as well as soccer balls for the children, water coolers, and other types of aid to the people staying at a school across the street from his office in Dohuk, but the supplies needed for the thousands of people coming in were more than his resources could handle.

The Kurdish government began to provide bags of rice, beans, oil, tea, sugar, and salt, but the Kurdish government was also struggling financially. They had been abandoned by the Iraqi military forces and were left to fend for themselves. Providing aid while building an indigenous defense plan against ISIS was not easy.

Paul M. Kingery

A Yazidi woman, Dalal, showing a photo of her brother who was murdered by ISIS while fleeing to Sinjar Mountain, the day after she arrived for sanctuary at Nawroz School, Dohuk, Iraq, August 2014.

The United Nations began to set up camps to receive the refugees, but that presented several problems. The United Nations camps were heavily staffed with Muslims, many of whom did not like the Christian and Yazidi people. Both minority groups who had been attacked by ISIS did not feel safe revealing who they were to the Muslim leaders at the UN camps.

The refuges had nowhere to turn.

Then something unexpected happened for several thousands of the refugees seeking shelter. They were able to find a remote little village sanctuary outside of Dohuk, a town just north of Mosul. The village was set back in the mountains, away from all the hustle and bustle of Dohuk and the United Nations presence. It was the small rural Chaldean Christian village of Seje with an old church building offering Chaldean services. There was also a small primary school offering education in the native Chaldean language. There were only about five hundred villagers living there in the peace and quiet of the remote mountain. The village had about one hundred homes that used a single water tank for water and did not have a stable source of continuous electricity.

The village had something else that especially appealed to the refugees. There were about 240 houses that were, bare block buildings that had been partially built before the war. Because of the violence in Iraq, the homes were never completed. Not only did they lack weather-proof roofs; they also had no wiring for electricity and no plumping. They provided very little, but for the thousands of refugees who fled there, it was an oasis.

Unlike the United Nations refugee camps, the refugees would not be assigned to tents and given rationed food by Muslim administrators. They would have safety, autonomy, and freedom to move about without large barbed-wire fences and armed gates. It was not perfect, but for many of the refugees who had just narrowly escaped death, it was like heaven.

Nearly a thousand Christians from Nineveh Province fled to the small village when ISIS invaded. Assyrians, Chaldeans, Syrian

Orthodox, Syriac, and Armenian Christians poured in to occupy the unfinished block buildings. Other camps were built for the Christians on the edge of the village. Some of them were completed with sturdy structures made with prefabricated walls, while other Christians were given tents. Many were sent to live in the small primary school building.

They were soon followed by six thousand Yazidis who somehow received shelter as well.

A displaced Faqier Yazidi girl from Tel Azer in the new village, Iraq, March 9, 2016.

Families piled up in the unfinished houses, sometimes as many as forty people per house, one family to a room. The rooms had no windows or doors, only gray cylinder blocks as a division between them.

Seje and the Tigris River Valley from the mountains behind at the beginning of spring,
March 1, 2016.

*Displaced Faqier Yazidi children singing with Dr. Paul Kingery
after their resettlement in Seje Village, August 2015.*

Prior to the invasion, it was illegal for Yazidis to rent or own property in Seje, but the law did not address squatting, and so the village soon filled with Yazidis outnumbering the Christians six to one and the nature of the village changed entirely.

*A skeleton block home in which displaced families were temporarily resettled in Seje,
March 17, 2016.*

In the first days there, many of the refugees had no water, electricity, or toilet facilities. With no plumbing or proper toilets, they all had to use the open fields, ravines that filled with water in the spring, or a roofless skeleton house nearby that provided privacy to relieve themselves. With several thousand people, this quickly became a sanitation hazard.

Water was carried from the homes of Christians in small plastic jugs. There was little food to eat until some weeks later when government rations of wheat flour, sugar, salt, beans, and other dry goods, and Dr. Paul's vegetable distributions, finally arrived. A few Christian families took pity on the refugees and helped them with food and some unused water tanks.

The August sun beat down on the houses, and the blocks retained the heat during the night, so they had to sleep on the roofs in order to find cool air. There were wild dogs in the area, so they couldn't sleep downstairs for fear the children would be dragged away and eaten by the dogs in the night. They had no mats for sleeping at first, but slept on the hard, concrete roofs with clothes folded under their heads. There was no kitchen, no washing machine, no electricity, no water piping, and no place to take a shower.

Displaced Faqier Yazidi Hassan Ibrahim Khalaf and his granddaughter eighteen months after the ISIS invasion of Sinjar, Iraq, March 9, 2016.

Most of the people had very little money and no source of income. The little cash that had been carried over the mountain with them was spent on basic dry food, simple cleaning materials like soap, mops, and pans, and cooking tools, pots, and dishes. It was not much, but the village became a safe haven that many of them would eventually call home.

PART FOUR:
God's Solution to a World Crisis

TWENTY-NINE

Meeting the Needs

Before the winter set in, youths working with MedEast as volunteers and other MedEast staff built wood frames and plastic window enclosures throughout the 240 unfinished houses. The arriving refugees needed everything, and there was no time to waste. If the refugees were going to survive the winter, they would need clothes, jackets, winter coats, socks, shoes, hygiene kits, and food—lots of food.

MedEast knew that the Yazidis and Christians arriving in the village were the lucky few who had survived genocide. However, they would never get their homes back. Even if they could go back to their hometowns, it would never be the same. Their churches and temples were destroyed. All of the top clergy members who knew the roots and meaning of their language, traditions, and ceremonies were either dead or gone. But there was no time to worry about that now. If they could not get food and water, there would not be any of them left to find a path back to their ancient ways.

A displaced and fatherless Faqier Yazidi family from Tel Azer, Iraq, temporarily resettled in Seje, March 12, 2016.

Babies suffered from lack of milk because the mothers were too malnourished and dehydrated to nurse them. Powdered milk was available in the market but was not provided in the aid packages from the government. Instead of the milk they needed, babies were fed a gruel made from wheat flour and water. The babies were not impressed with this substitution. The older children and adults were suffering from a complete lack of protein for several months.

Some of the new arrivals were fortunate enough to have escaped with their vehicles, even pickup trucks, but would not part with them, even in exchange for food, because they could not afford taxi fares to get to the cities to find work, buy food, or move their family about to meet their general needs.

MedEast and a Chinese ministry called Back to Jerusalem adopted the village and worked with others to provide for the needs. (The amazing work of the Back to Jerusalem ministry will be shared in the coming chapters.)

The distribution was difficult. People surrounded the house from every side and pressed through the windows to get vegetables rather than waiting in several lines that were formed. The international volunteers were soon afraid for their own safety. Workers were also giving out new shoes at the same time, which the people desperately needed, which meant they pressed into the workers with even more urgency.

At one point in the distribution, the two muqtars (village leaders) showed up. Seje had two primary leaders, Muqtar Sabri Yako Yousef, who was in charge of one side of the village, and Muqtar Kareem Sabri Kareem, who ruled over the other side. Their leadership was challenged with the arrival of the Yazidis and Christians because their loyalties initially lay with the Christian believers. There was a natural tendency to help their own and cast aside the Yazidi people, who they considered to be unclean, uneducated mountain people who (supposedly) worshipped the devil.

However, under the guidance of Dr. Paul, MedEast was able to work out the cultural differences for the early stages of the food distribution.

A displaced Faqier Yazidi girl living in Seje after the ISIS invasion of Sinjar District.

A displaced Faqier Yazidi boy from Tel Azer, Iraq, in Seje, March 17, 2016.

Displaced Faqier Yazidi children from Tel Azer, Iraq, in Seje, Iraq, on March 17, 2016.

A displaced Faqier Yazidi boy from Tel Azer, Iraq, living in Seje, Iraq after the ISIS invasion of Sinjar District, March 8, 2016.

A fatherless displaced Faqier Yazidi boy from Tel Azer volunteering during a MedEast vegetable distribution after the invasion of Sinjar District, August 2015.

Paul M. Kingery

A displaced Faqier Yazidi girl from Tel Azer, Iraq, in Seje, Iraq, March 17, 2016.

Paul M. Kingery

Displaced Faqier Yazidi boys in Seje after the invasion of Sinjar District, March 8, 2016.

A displaced Faqier Yazidi boy, Jameel Khuro Hassan, from Tel Azer, Iraq, in Seje, Iraq, on March 17, 2016.

Displaced Faqier Yazidis Barakat Mahlo Khudeda and his daughter, Vean, in Seje, Iraq, after the ISIS invasion of Tel Azer, Iraq, March 8, 2016.
Barakat, his wife and their daughter escaped Mount Sinjar and are safe.

On top of providing food, clothing, shoes, and hygiene kits, another problem needed to be resolved quickly—sanitation. Toilet facilities for six thousand people were desperately needed. Diseases would easily spread like wildfire if urine and fecal matter piled up in the small village.

MedEast and Back to Jerusalem worked together with others to build toilets for almost every home in need. This was one of the first steps to making the refugees feel at home and help fight the spread of communicable diseases. In addition, the ministries worked together to provide an education for the several hundred children who no longer had a school to attend. Going back to school would not only provide the children with a sense of normalcy in their lives, but would be a great way to build social bonds with other children to help heal the emotional scars of having lost so much.

American professor Dr. Paul M. Kingery teaching English to displaced Yazidi girls in Seje Village, Iraq, September 3, 2015.

A displaced Faqier Yazidi widow from Tel Azer receives a traditional dress made by Yazidi girls working for MedEast in Seje, Iraq, after the ISIS invasion of the Sinjar District, August 2015.

THIRTY

A Supernatural Plague Hits ISIS?

ISIS leadership stood up to the world's largest militaries, and they were not defeated. Even though their capabilities were extremely inferior to other armies in the world, they have capitalized on the unwillingness of world powers to engage them on the ground in Iraq.

They seem unstoppable.

When they slaughtered the men of Iraq, no one tried to stop them. When they ripped the young children from their homes in Mosul and Sinjar, no one prevented them. When they took young women and little girls to be sex slaves, no one stood up for the weak to protect them. But maybe, possibly, something else is providing resistance against the flow of evil. It almost seems that there has been a supernatural plague that has been hitting ISIS. No one can say for certain whether it is a holy judgement, but you can be the judge.

In early 2016, reports began to emerge from ISIS-controlled areas about a mysterious flesh-eating disease that was attacking the militants.

The reports turned out to be true. Hundreds of ISIS fighters have been stricken with a flesh-eating disease called Leishmaniasis. Some of the reports seem to be a bit exaggerated, but what was not exaggerated is that thousands of ISIS fighters have been infected with the disease. That means many members of ISIS who brought so much fear and death to the minority people of Iraq—Christians and Yazidis alike— have encountered a torment of their own.

Experts have been comparing the disease to Ebola and warn it could rip through the Middle East as the putrid conditions of many of the ISIS-controlled areas make it fertile breeding ground for the parasitic infection to spread. The horrific disease, which often attacks the face, is becoming rife in ISIS strongholds because the terrorists are leaving bodies to rot in the streets. They are also destroying medical facilities and killing medical personnel, which has exacerbated the problem.[108]

Cutaneous leishmaniasis is spread by little sand flies, an enemy ISIS cannot control. Actually, they are unwittingly creating the very conditions that allow these flies to thrive and attack them. The skin-eating disease was a very rare condition until ISIS seized control of swathes of Syria and Iraq, killing thousands of health workers and leaving rotting dead bodies as their calling cards.

The disease is not common anywhere else in the world, and its attack on the human body is almost like something out of a science-fiction novel. It is caused by protozoan parasites usually carried by sand flies. If the infected flies bite you, then the disease immediately begins eating away at the skin and causes large open wounds that eat away at flesh.

Between 2000 and 2012, there were only six reported cases of the disease in Lebanon, but in 2013, when ISIS began their terrorist attacks, instances of the disease started to grow. In 2013 alone, there were 1,033 cases.[109] I read 22,365 cases at www.rt.com/news/325054-flesh-eating-disease check reports

Dr. William Schaffner told RT News, "It is very possible in the area where there is a lot of military activity and population movement, those are the circumstances in which an outbreak of the leishmaniasis can occur. If someone dies who gets the infection then flies will settle on the bodies. Then they multiply. You get many more flies

---

108. http://www.express.co.uk/news/uk/674828/Flesh-eating-disease-ISIS-spread-to-Europe.
109. Ibid.

that are infected. And then when the living people are in the same are, the flies bite the living people."

Loosely translated, this means that ISIS has created their own plague, and the plague is taking a toll on the ISIS fighters. The jihadis are falling ill in droves to the deadly flesh-eating disease. It is spreading at a fast rate. In fact, there have already been more than 100,000 cases reported.[110]

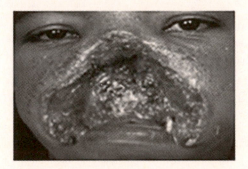

Above is a picture of the impact of the flesh-eating disease.[111]

The jihadi fighters are refusing to acknowledge the problem, and even when they are diagnosed with the disease, they refuse treatment. The disease is very easily treated with medicine, but is fatal if left untreated.[112] This is making the spread of the disease even worse.

The US State Department released this picture on Twitter to promote a disease control update:

There have been many concerns about the disease spreading into Europe as refugees continue to pour in from Syria and Iraq, but that has not proven to be the case yet. Oddly enough, it seems that for now the disease is pretty much contained to ISIS areas and those who are in the immediate region of ISIS-controlled areas.

---

110. Ibid.
111. http://cystbursting.com/most-popular-cysts/leishmaniasis/attachment/leishmaniasis-28/.
112. http://www.mirror.co.uk/news/world-news/isis-danger-being-wiped-out-5448779.

Global Engagement
@TheGEC

#ISIS dumps bodies in streets, result: spread of flesh-eating disease Leishmaniosis. goo.gl/rUCWJD

9:20 PM - 3 Dec 2015

231 50

Follow

So is this judgement or merely the repercussions of bad hygienic policies? You can be the judge.

THIRTY-ONE

Dealing with the Pain

The trauma from the massacre lurks around the corner for every survivor. When survival is no longer a factor, then the reality of the tragic events begins to settle in. The grief is sometimes too much to bear.

Some survivors are able to make it to safety, only to wonder why they wanted to survive at all. Mothers who have lost their homes, husbands, and all of their children do not want to continue living. The pain is just too much and the hurt is too deep.

When the Yazidis were on the mountain running from the jihadis who were hunting them, their instincts for survival took over. They did not want to die. They wanted to live. They did everything in their power to escape. They hiked up impossible mountain ridges without food and water. They endured the scorching sun and unbearable heat. They walked for miles through the desert with no thought of what they would do once they found safety. They did all of that on the fuel of hope that they would live to see another day, but many of them made it to the end, only to wish that they hadn't survived at all.

ISIS was able to kill more than those they massacred during their acts of genocide. They were able to do far more damage than could be calculated during their attacks. They sucked the hope of survival out of the people.

The Christians who survived wanted to either die or escape to Europe. The Yazidis wanted the same. The Christians and the Yazidis want to leave the homeland of their people who have inhabited the land for hundreds of years before the Prophet Muhammad was ever born. Their leaders were banished or killed. Their books were burned and destroyed. Their thousand-year-old temples were bulldozed to the ground or blown to smithereens. Their people were slaughtered by the thousands. There is simply nothing left for them. They are now a nomadic people without a home. Their cultural heritage has been stripped from them forever.

In Seje where so many Christians and Yazidis found refuge, they also found nightmares waiting for them.

Just a few days after arriving in Seje, one young Yazidi wife found her worse fears waiting for her. Everything she had gone through took on new meaning when she finally gave birth to her baby that she had been carrying through the entire ISIS attack. She was one of the lucky few to survive, but she did not feel so lucky. She felt cursed, cursed with life.

She and her young family moved into one of the unfinished houses. The unfinished house was nothing more than bare, gray cylinder blocks piled up on top of a cold concrete floor. It was nothing like her warm home that she was forced to leave. Back home she had a warm comfortable bed with big, heavy blankets to crawl into when the winter cold winds blew outside. It was a place that she could cuddle up with her husband and baby and forget about the world.

As she contemplated all that she had lost, she was unable to see the fortunate situation she was in. She slipped into a deep, dark place of unhappiness which was partially fueled by postpartum depression and posttraumatic stress syndrome. Feeling helpless and hopeless, the young mother searched for the only escape she could find. In a moment of deep depression, she covered herself in kerosene and set herself on fire. Her family members quickly tried to put out the fire and save her life. They rushed her to the nearest hospital, but their efforts were not enough. Seven days later she died. She had given up the will to live long before she lit herself on fire.

Other young women in the village also saw suicide as a practical escape. One middle-aged man attempted to do the same thing and set himself on fire, but his family was able to stop him in time.

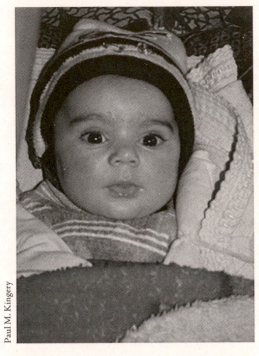

Paul M. Kingery

Infant Faqier Yazidi boy Dawood (David) born before his mother committed suicide in February 2016 following the ISIS invasion of Sinjar District.

THIRTY-TWO

The World's Genocide Solution

I spoke with seven women who had escaped ISIS after more than a year in captivity. They told me how they had been bought and sold multiple times, raped by different 'owners,' locked in rooms for months, beaten and had their children taken away," wrote Skye Wheeler, a women's rights emergency researcher at Human Rights Watch and a contributing writer for *Newsweek*.[113]

Skye has worked in several regions around the world talking to women who have been raped. She spent time on the ground interviewing women who had been raped in the most brutal manner, and after meeting with the women, she wrote, "ISIS uses shock and horror to get the world's attention. The world should respond not just with anger, but by helping women like Ramia, and her children, to get safe care, rehabilitation and justice."

After Skye met with more than fifteen women who escaped from captivity, she addressed what she believed to be the most important issue facing these women. She wrote, "Incredibly, Yazidi women who have been raped by ISIS fighters and become pregnant cannot get a safe and legal abortion anywhere in Iraq. Iraqi and Kurdish laws should be changed to allow abortions, at least in the case of rape, and safe post-abortion care."[114]

---

113. http://europe.newsweek.com/yezedis-islamic-state-christians-sex-slaves-human-rights-iraq-447842?rm=eu.
114. Ibid.

Surprisingly, Skye's solution to death, destruction, and murder against the innocent in Iraq is more death, destruction, and murder against the innocent in Iraq. She even went on to write, "Another priority is to ensure justice for the victims by holding perpetrators accountable."[115] In her opinion, holding the perpetrators accountable is also a priority, but it comes second to access to abortion. Unfortunately, because leaders and scholars around the world are at a loss about what to do, they listen to people like Skye Wheeler.

Everyone is grasping for a solution to the advancement of ISIS. Several contenders running for the United States presidency in 2015 and 2016 were specifically asked what they would personally do to destroy ISIS.

Jeb Bush, the brother of former president George W. Bush, who has unlimited access to the world's best political advisors, said that he would pivot to Syria to ensure the downfall of President Bashar al-Assad.[116] He is not alone in this idea. This has been the same strategy that President Obama and then secretary of state Hillary Clinton have been pursuing for years. In fact, it is this same strategy that led to the US inadvertently arming ISIS and supplying money for their training.[117]

However, President Assad's troops, backed by the Chinese and the Russians and aided by the Peshmerga, have been the only real force that has kept ISIS fighters at bay. While he has not been an honest Boy Scout by any stretch of the imagination, removing him is definitely not the key to destroying ISIS. In fact, if he were to lose power, it would create a similar void that occurred in Iraq, and leave an opening for ISIS to fill that would expand their power, not diminish it.

During his presidential campaign, Donald Trump outlined his strategy against ISIS, stating, "I would bomb the s**t out of them. I

---

115. Ibid.
116. http://townhall.com/tipsheet/danieldavis/2015/08/12/bush-puts-forth-isis-strategy-n2037900.
117. http://www.globalresearch.ca/u-s-supplies-isis-through-turkey/5512221.

would just bomb those suckers, and that's right, I'd blow up the pipes, I'd blow up the refineries, I'd blow up every single inch, there would be nothing left."[118]

Unfortunately, bombing is not a new strategy to destroy enemies and has rarely been effective. America did not hold back on bombing Iraq during 2003, and there are few people today who would argue that Iraq is better off now than in 2003. Nor did bombing change the course in Vietnam or North Korea.

Will an Economic Solution Help?

There are those who believe there is a political or economic solution to defeating ISIS. In February 2015, American State Department spokeswoman Marie Harf said, "We cannot win this war by killing them [ISIS], we cannot kill our way out of this war." Instead, she said, the administration should "go after the root causes that lead people to join these groups—including lack of opportunity for jobs." She went on to say, "We can help them build their economies so they can have job opportunities for these people. We can work with countries around the world to help improve their governance."[119]

Among the glaring problems with Marie Harf's solution is the fact that few countries have financially invested into Iraq's economy as much as the United States—building schools, roads and infrastructure, allowing full autonomy over their oil, and investing in their oil infrastructure. Even after their military defeat, the US invested in their government structure, handed out small business loans, and opened up the international market place to Iraqi businesses.

Marie also fails to take into account that most ISIS recruits and volunteers are coming from wealthy Western nations with a plethora

118. http://www.realclearpolitics.com/video/2015/11/13/trumps_updated_isis_plan_bomb_the_shit_out_of_them_send_exxon_in_to_rebuild.html.
119. http://www.dailymail.co.uk/news/article-2957350/State-Department-says-win-war-against-ISIS-killing-Obama-administration-avoids-mention-Christian-beheading-victims-religion-launches-new-hashtag-diplomacy-effort.html.

of job opportunities, heavily subsidized education programs, and equal-opportunity loans. An economic solution is not the answer.

Others are putting their hope in the locals who were hit the hardest and are willing to fight back.

Not all Christians were killed. Some of them escaped, and now some of them are ready to fight back. And in March 2015, the first Christian-only brigade in Iraq was formed. Christian fighters paraded and jumped through rings of fire in front of Kurdish and Assyrian officials near their training base on the border of Syria and Turkey.[120] "Around 600 Peshmerga from our Christian brothers in the Nineveh plain joined this course, which focused on physical training, military lectures and shooting exercises," said Abu Bakr Ismail, the commander of the training academy. "All the participants are volunteers…and want to liberate their land from IS and then protect it," the Kurdish special forces major general said.[121]

Iraq's Peshmerga fighters have received very limited assistance from other governments and militaries around the world, even though they have proven to be one of the few forces effective against ISIS. The new Christian brigade was an answer to prayer for the Peshmerga because they would be able to provide much-needed help in retaking Mosul and other surrounding villages. (Mosul is still in ISIS hands at the time of this writing.) Called the Tiger Guards, the brigade was first unofficially employed in 2004 to provide protection for churches after the fall of Saddam Hussein, when Muslims began to attack Christians and their places of worship.

The Christians are not alone. Yazidis are also forming military units and fighting back against ISIS. Specifically, former Yazidi sex slaves.

"They rape us. We kill them!" This is the war cry of former Yazidi singer Xate Shingali who helped form an all-female fighting

---

120. http://www.al-monitor.com/pulse/afp/2015/03/iraq-syria-conflict-us-christians.html#ixzz4D8iXW2f1.
121. Ibid.

unit called the "Sun Girls Brigade."[122] The Sun Girls Brigade gives a home to many of the women who were forced to watch their husbands, fathers, and brothers beheaded, were separated from their children, and were mercilessly raped over and over again. Many of the sex slaves had nowhere to go when they finally escaped from ISIS; their homes were all occupied by ISIS, few of them had family left, and many who did were rejected by them because of the shame brought on by rape.

The Sun Girls Brigade brings these girls into a sorority that promises revenge and retribution. Xate Shingali (pictured above), a former folk music icon, created the Sun Girls Brigade in 2015 when she was given 123 female fighters between the ages of seventeen and thirty. "We have had only basic training and we need more...but we are ready to fight ISIS anytime," Xate said.[123]

Jane is one of the young female fighters with the Sun Girl Brigade. Jane and her little sister were raped every day by a depraved jihadist before they were sold by their rapist at a slave auction. An even younger Yazidi girl named Bahar, 14, reported how she was forced to undergo medical exams to prove she was a virgin before she was sold at an auction to ISIS fighters. Young virgins brought more money.[124]

As much as the thought of revenge and retribution might excite the human side of our nature, the truth is that these brigades have made little to no progress destroying ISIS or stopping the continued genocide. As plan after plan continues to prove fruitless, the feeling of desperation grows for those fleeing from the hell hole in Iraq. Bystanders in Christian countries have seen the destruction and

---

122. http://www.dailymail.co.uk/news/article-3197565/They-rape-kill-Yazidi-singer-forms-female-fighting-unit-revenge-ISIS-forcing-sisters-sexual-slavery-beheading-brothers.html.
123. Ibid.
124. http://www.dailymail.co.uk/news/article-3197565/They-rape-kill-Yazidi-singer-forms-female-fighting-unit-revenge-ISIS-forcing-sisters-sexual-slavery-beheading-brothers.html.

helplessness and have offered another plan: get them out of Iraq and let other nations provide the refugees with safety.

But how will that work?

THIRTY-THREE

Man's Answers Won't Stop Genocide

Mosul, Iraq's second-largest city before ISIS took it over, has completely changed. According to ISIS, much of their previous way of life is *haram* (forbidden), so people anticipate being punished for practically everything. Even simple, innocent leisure activities like a family picnic are forbidden because it is considered to be a waste of time and money.[125]

"Islamic State is doing everything to keep Mosul in its grip. So far, no one has been able to take it back. It's the capital of their caliphate here," said Fuad Hussein, chief of staff to the president of the semiautonomous Kurdistan region of Iraq, which borders Mosul.

The city seems clean and orderly. Criminals are immediately punished and daily patrols drive around looking for the slightest infraction. "Theft is punished by amputating a hand, adultery by men by throwing the offender from a high building, and adultery by women by stoning to death," one Mosul resident told the BBC. "The punishments are carried out in public to intimidate people, who are often forced to watch."[126]

No one is shown mercy. Money is tight, and few jobs are available. A widowed mother of four children was caught stealing and had her hand chopped off.[127] Women are forced to cover up from head to toe

125. http://www.bbc.com/news/world-middle-east-32831854.
126. Ibid.
127. http://www.theatlantic.com/international/archive/2015/06/isis-mosul-iraq/395531/.

(including gloves), and floggings are often given in the public square for small infractions like smoking cigarettes. Witnessing public punishments and raping captured slaves seem to be the only real leisure time activities allowed for the residents of Mosul these days.

The education and medical facilities are severely undermanned because the doctors and professors who defied or questioned Islamic State laws have all been executed by public stoning or crucifixion. Prisons are filled with people awaiting their sentences from the Islamic court.[128] "Nearly no one gets out alive," one of the residents of Mosul said.[129]

People around the world are sick of watching the genocide in Iraq take place without being able to do anything about it. They feel helpless and are certain their politicians are incapable of solving the problem. Many feel that it would be more helpful to allow the victims to enter other countries rather than sending troops to Iraq.

And enter they did. Hundreds of thousands of them.

In 2014, soon after ISIS invaded Iraq, former UK prime minister David Cameron said, "The UK has a long tradition of providing sanctuary for those fleeing persecution. I am proud that the UK offers genuine refugees and their children an opportunity to build a new life."[130]

Unfortunately, what followed has been a nightmare. Many of the people who have been targeted by ISIS are not getting the proper help they need and other migrants who were not persecuted are moving into Europe on a massive scale. Instead of solving the problem, it seems the migration has only spread the problem.

The desire of Christian countries to help refugees is an honorable quest, but the open-border welcome has brought in a lot more than

---

128. http://www.wsj.com/articles/iraqi-city-of-mosul-transformed-a-year-after-islamic-state-capture-14338886260.
129. Ibid.
130. http://refugeeweek.org.uk/political-party-leaders-show-their-support-for-refugee-week/.

was intended. According to the latest UN report regarding the 2015 refugee crisis, 72 percent of the refugees received in Europe were young males of fighting age, with only 15 percent being children and 13 percent women.

Germany's chancellor, Angela Merkel, became known as the Angel of Mercy because of her efforts to bring refugees to Germany.[131] But after opening its borders, Germany's crime rate sky rocketed with assaults, robberies, and what Germans classify as "predatory offenses against personal freedom," including threatening behavior, with over 200,000 cases in 2014,[132] and the number of crimes committed by refugees in Germany is expected to double to more than 400,000 in 2015.[133] Update statistics They had attacks or rapes during holidays last year??

Sweden, which is well known for its generous open-door policy toward refugees and its peaceful stance in the international community, took in a large number of refugees. The Swedish people bent over backward to bless the people coming into their nation. Some priests, like Eve Brunne, even proposed removing crosses from the churches and replacing them with arrows pointing toward Mecca to make the Muslim refugees feel more welcome.

Now Sweden is considered to be the rape capital of Europe with 77 percent of rape cases caused by 2 percent of the Muslim population.[134]

There are at least fifty-five "no-go" zones in Sweden where Swedish police are no longer allowed to patrol because the Muslim control of the area is so strong that the police will be attacked and

131. http://www.theatlantic.com/international/archive/2015/09/germany-merkel-refugee-asylum/405058/.
132. http://www.express.co.uk/news/world/644827/refugees-committed-crimes-Germany-migrant-crisis-last-year.
133. http://www.gatestoneinstitute.org/7470/germany-migrants-crime.
134. https://muslimstatistics.wordpress.com/2015/03/19/sweden-77-6-percent-of-all-rapes-in-the-country-committed-by-muslim-males-making-up-2-percent-of-population/.

their patrol vehicles destroyed.[135] They have essentially lost control of portions of their own nation where Muslim immigrants have taken over. Swedish police who responded to a refugee center because a young boy was being raped were chased out by refugee men protecting the attacker. The police had to run for their lives.[136]

The refugee crisis from Iraq is considered to be the primary reason behind the historical exit from EU founding member Britain from the European Union.[137] Britain has long been considered the cornerstone of the European Union. But the suicidal decisions of the EU to equally distribute refugees who did not share the values of the countries of the EU and had zero desire to integrate left Britain feeling that their voice had little impact on the decision-making process in Brussels.

The challenges in Iraq were not helped or solved when the EU took in large numbers of refugees, and one of the main reasons is because the real victims of ISIS were still being neglected.

Yes, the child or Christian mother coming from Iraq might have their life changed forever, but taking in young Muslim men from the most dangerous and destructive locations on earth is actually allowing the perpetrators to follow their victims instead of removing the victims from the source of the pain. This policy also allows the perpetrators to expand their pool of victims.

For many European law makers, it has become clear that allowing massive migration of refugees from Iraq and Syria has not solved anything. In fact, it has only made the problem more complicated. But if that is not the answer, then what is?

It seems that the world has run out of solutions and is not sure where to turn. This is where the church can step in and provide aid from one of the most surprising sources: the Bible.

---

135. http://www.svd.se/55-no-go-zoner-i-sverige.
136. http://www.express.co.uk/news/world/644315/Sweden-migrant-crisis-refugee-asylum-seekers-Alexandra-Mezher-breaking-point.
137. https://www.rt.com/news/349055-refugee-crisis-brexit-austria/.

THIRTY-FOUR

Biblical Solutions Have Power

Iraq is the home to many groups of people who are largely unreached by the Gospel. Even though it is the cradle of civilization and was once the location of the first Christian kingdom, Islam has essentially waged jihad on every Christian in the region.

Iraq is in the heart of the final frontier of the Gospel message that exists between the Great Wall of China and the Western Wall of Jerusalem. This land "between the walls" has the highest level of poverty, the lowest level of medical care, the lowest quality of life, and the highest victimization of genocide.

Iraq has long been home to some of the greatest ancient societies—such as the Sumerian, Akkadian, Assyrian, and Babylonian Empires—but they have been strangled by the choking power of Islam. ISIS has done their best to erase the history of anything that does not reflect Islam by engaging in religious cleansing on a massive scale, because they know the importance of ignorance. They are very aware of the dangers that remain if the message of Christ is allowed to be spread unhindered.

In order to keep a society in darkness, the enemy has to use all of its power, energy, and hate to enslave citizens, whereas the liberty of the Gospel can destroy the confining walls of evil with only a whisper. The Gospel message is entirely disruptive and menacing to societies that perpetuate genocide. It destroys the goals of the destructive, which means that it might just be the single best solution to preventing or stopping genocide.

What if future genocides can be prevented by what we find in Matthew 28:19–20 and Acts 1:8, which is the active command to spread the Good News to all the world?

We already know that ISIS has their own form of the Great Commission like that found in Matthew 28:18–19, but their version comes at the end of a sword. The cold, hard truth is that evil, left to fester, both persecutes and grows. Like a cancer, it does not stay isolated and localized; it spreads and infects. Evil conquers and controls. It imposes and kills. It rapes and destroys and is eventually genocidal.

Lies and death are best combated with truth, love, and life. It is only through the love of Jesus Christ that societies can be transformed and evil can be stopped, but if that is true, then wiping out ISIS is not the answer, because that would be employing the evil tactics of Islam instead of the commandment of love that Christ gave in the Bible.

Christians have had the answer the entire time, and the people of Iraq were without it because believers did not enact the Great Commission as commanded by Jesus Christ. The genocide in Iraq is, in fact, an "ecclesiastical crime," because the followers of Jesus have selfishly left the lost of the world to perish without the Truth.

ISIS is evil and without Christ. They are doing exactly what they are expected to do. The knee-jerk reaction is to blame ISIS for their behavior, but can a dog be blamed for being a dog? Is it possible for man to be "good" without Christ? How can a group that vehemently denies Christ be anything other than Christ-less? Is there a moral law inherent in a Christ-less society?

A society without Christ is much more hideous than we would like to admit. The evil in our souls knows no boundaries and would surely scare us if it were every fully revealed.

Didn't Jesus say very plainly that no man is "good" except the Father (Matthew 10:17)? The law is written on our hearts (Acts 2:14–15), so surely breaking the law is also known in our hearts, making us aware that we are not good. The further we are from the Law-Giver, the further we are from the law itself, and the further we are from the law, the further we are from being good. For example, lust can bring guilt to the heart, but how can we know how to identify lust as a sin without the law that forbids us to covet (Romans 7:7)?

The Good News is not brought to man because man is naturally good. If man were naturally good, he would not need the Good News. The Good News is brought to us because we are naturally bad and have a tendency to do evil things. As Paul pointed out, we know what to do to be good, but we do not do it. We know what we should not do, but we do it anyway:

> For we know that the law is spiritual; but I am carnal, sold under sin. For what I am doing, I do not understand. For what I will to do, that I do not practice; but what I hate, that I do. If, then, I do what I will not to do, I agree with the law that it is good. But now, it is no longer I who do it, but sin that dwells in me. For I know that in me (that is, in my flesh) nothing good dwells; for to will is present with me, but how to perform what is good I do not find. For the good that I will to do, I do not do; but the evil I will not to do, that I practice. (Romans 7:14–19)

Translation? Man is naturally evil and is not able to do good because sin dwells in the heart of man.

We are all aware of the law that is written on our hearts, but our hearts are full of sin, rendering us unable to be good.

ISIS is a dark reflection of what can lie in the heart of every man without exposure to the truth, which is both the law and the Good News. The Truth of God's Word is not debatable. It brings life to the lifeless and law to the lawless.

Muslims, both moderate and extreme, are without the truth and have no choice but to follow the sin in their hearts. This is not a popular belief in a pluralistic world, but the Good News of Jesus is either true or it is not; it cannot be both. The Good News is not just true for me; it is true for everyone. It is the truth that defines both good and evil. We are often taught that evil is the extreme form of something that is bad—e.g., genocide—however, all it takes for evil to exist is for man to defy God's law.

God is pure truth, goodness, and holiness, so to defy Him and His law is evil. In the holiness of God, nothing is partly evil or partially good; it's either completely good or completely evil.

Some teach that God created hell to use as a disciplinary measure after death; however, hell can be witnessed in any situation where God is opposed. The areas where ISIS rules are living hell and are the result of actively opposing God and His law. If the people of Iraq want to escape hell, they must first deny evil. Denying evil starts with turning away from evil and toward God. Only the truth can set us free from evil (John 8:32). It is impossible for us to say that we want to enjoy the benefits of the truth but not accept *the* truth, Jesus Christ.

The laws of man cannot help anyone escape the impact of evil, because the laws of man are reflections of the decrepit state of the sinful hearts of man. When laws are merely written to enforce the desires of man, then governments are capable of legislating unspeakable evil.

Sharia Law is now the law of Mosul, Iraq, but it is evil and immoral, even though it is legal and completely enforceable, because it violates God's law. Laws that bring freedom, justice, and equality can only be correctly instituted when they are based on biblical laws. George Washington once said, "It is the duty of all nations to acknowledge the providence of Almighty God, to obey His will, to be grateful for His benefits, and humbly to implore His protection and favor."[138]

---

138. Douglas Groothuis, "Addressing the Problem of Evil," *Christian Research Institute*, ECFA, 2009, accessed May 25, 2016.

But how can people believe in Him and implement His laws if they have never heard? "How shall they hear without a preacher? And how shall they preach unless they are sent?" (Romans 10:14–15).

People in Iraq have not been exposed to the Good News of Jesus Christ. They are suffering in Iraq because Christians have neglected the Great Commission. Hell is ever-present because the Light of the world has not been shown. If Christians want to destroy the dark clutches of evil in Iraq, it must be done with Light, not darkness. If ISIS is to ever be conquered, it must be done through the sacrifice of Christian messengers delivering the truth of God's Word, not via secular combat forces.

But how do we do that, and where do we start? One organization of committed missionaries, Back to Jerusalem, has made an uncompromising commitment to spread the message of Jesus Christ right in the middle of world terror.

THIRTY-FIVE

Iraq and the Chinese Vision of Back to Jerusalem

Toward the end of 2015, a Chinese missionary leader, Pastor Joshua, from China's underground house church, arrived in Iraq for the first time. He had already sent four missionaries from China to Iraq after seeing the genocide that took place in 2014. As he stepped out of the airport, he noticed a military base across the street. Soldiers were patrolling the fence line. By his side was another young, bright-eyed Christian missionary from China who was ready and eager to serve.

Joshua comes from one of the larger underground house church networks in China that currently has several million members. His entire life is committed to training up and sending out Chinese missionaries who have a vision to serve in the unreached areas between China and Jerusalem.

The missionaries Joshua sends out from his church in China are not sent legally. The Chinese government does not approve of Joshua's church, of which he is one of the leading pastors. They certainly do not approve of international missionaries being sent from China to share the Gospel in other parts of the world.

"I almost didn't make my flight out of Beijing," Joshua said after he stepped off the bus into the arrival hall of the Iraqi airport. "Last week our church in Henan Province was raided by the police. We had about a hundred evangelists from all over China who came together and somehow the police found out about it. I was warned about the raid before the police arrived, so I made it out before they caught me—otherwise I would have never made it on my flight to Iraq."

Unlike most missionaries around the world, Chinese missionaries are most often sent to countries where the government does not approve of their activities while coming from a country (China) where the government's disapproval is just as absolute.

Joshua is helping Chinese Christians leave their home nation of China, not in search of religious freedom from other nations or to obtain asylum protection, but instead to share the Good News of Jesus Christ with countries that are experiencing the same depravity they have experienced for over a half century.

"Our goal is not to help Christians find safety in Christian nations," Joshua often says. "Our goal is to bring the message of Jesus Christ to those areas of the world that have still not heard."

China's Astounding Revival

Joshua is a part of a much larger movement in China that is fulfilling the Great Commission. China is experiencing one of the largest revivals the world has ever seen. The number of new believers in China is astronomical and is estimated to be as many as one million per month. The new body of Christian believers in China is expected to soon surpass the number of official members in the Communist Party, if it hasn't done so already!

In some megacities in China, like Wenzhou on the east coast, currently one out of every four people are now Christian. This phenomenon has led to a burning fire for missions and outreach.

The movement is not a new one. It was birthed in the Chinese church almost a hundred years ago. Since its mission cannot be legally carried out by the churches that are registered with the government, the main engine behind the movement is the illegal underground house church. The origin of the underground house church movement is rural in nature, but their future is bound to change due to the rapid urbanization of China, which is occurring so quickly and broadly that even Wikipedia has a page devoted to it.

Currently, according to our own estimates, China is nearly 10 percent Christian. This number can be confusing, because it would be obvious to anyone in China that one out of every ten people on the street in China is not Christian, unless it is a place like Shandong, Anhui, Henan, or Wenzhou. However, the estimate becomes tenable when Henan—the most populated province in the nation with a high percentage of local Christians—is factored into the mix. In addition, there is a growing number of Christians in the minority areas around Guangxi, Yunnan, and Sichuan, where entire people groups consider themselves to be Christian, which also increases the national percentile.

Places like Sichuan and Henan have been the most populated provinces in China for years, but this has altered in recent years. Urbanization has led to the separation of Chongqing from Sichuan Province, and today Guangdong has passed up Henan as the most populated province in China. People from rural areas throughout China are racing to production powerhouse provinces like Guangdong. Large numbers of rural Christians have also started moving to the urban areas and are filling up factories, roadside shops, and office buildings throughout the cities, taking the Gospel with them.

During the twentieth century, Christianity took hold in the rural areas of China and spread like wildfire. It has continued on into the twenty-first century. The rapid rate of growth has been hard to calculate and continues in those areas even while many believers move to the urban areas. The Lord is definitely using the mass migration to the cities for His purposes. It is almost as if the Chinese evangelists were not moving fast enough to get the Gospel out of their provinces so the Lord sped up the process by sending the missionaries to a single location—the city. This momentum of migration is now fulfilling the dreams of the early Chinese Christian leaders who envisioned China joining the Great Commission movement westward toward the Middle East.

Why Would China Send Out Missionaries?

At first glance, the Chinese would seem to have a large enough challenge to just evangelize their own nation. Why in the world would they be so audacious as to think they are ready to help the efforts in Iraq?

Most of the Chinese Christians who have a vision to take the Gospel message to places like Iraq come from poor, uneducated families with agrarian backgrounds. By many standards, they have not been educated properly in theology or missiology that would equip them to carry out such a huge and dangerous task in Iraq. Most of them have nothing more than a primary school level education.

They do not speak the Iraqi language, they do not share the Middle Eastern culture, and many of them have very little exposure to Islam. In almost every way the Chinese Christian missionaries seem to be ill-equipped for mission work in Iraq.

However, there are a few things that make them uniquely qualified. First, they too come from a background of persecution. On the surface, the persecution from ISIS looks completely different from the persecution the Chinese have been suffering from the atheists for generations, but a closer look shows many similarities. Both use similar employments of fear tactics, control mechanisms, and public pressure.

The Chinese Christians earned their education, not in the safe halls of institutions insulated by free countries, but in the fiery furnace of persecution. They know all too well what it is like to rely on the leading and guiding of the Holy Spirit to persevere, even to survive.

They know what it is like not to have access to Bibles, training materials, and Christian books. They are familiar with one of the most notorious Internet control mechanisms in the world with the Great Firewall of China that blocks them from access and exposure to Christian blogs, teachings, and music. In many ways, they are very uniquely trained to help those who have been persecuted in Iraq and have an empathy that goes beyond just "feelings."

This movement by Chinese Christians is known as the *Back to Jerusalem* vision, which, in practical terms, is a vision of the Chinese church to send at least 100,000 missionaries from China to the 10/40 Window. In other words, it is the Great Commission. This is a sign of a healthy and vibrant church.

To categorize the Back to Jerusalem (BTJ) vision as only a goal would be wrong. It is, in fact, a reality. At the time of this writing, there are Back to Jerusalem missionaries from China in North Korea, Vietnam, Laos, Cambodia, Burma, Pakistan, Kazakhstan, Iran, Jordan, South Sudan, Egypt, Dubai, and Iraq.

BTJ is a rallying call to wake up China to become a mission-focused country. There is excitement in the air when Christians in China share about the Back to Jerusalem vision. Many Chinese see this time in history as their turn to be responsible for carrying out the Great Commission as so many others have in the past.

Many books and reports on happenings in China are about the revivals that took place in the 1980s and ⊠90s, which have led some missionary experts to conclude that the revivals in China are dying down and coming to a close. However, these reports usually fail to take notice of a new wind sweeping throughout this most populated Asian nation.

How is most of the world missing it? Foreign Christian delegations and potential missionaries are seeing the bright lights of Shanghai, the tourist attractions in Beijing, and exploring the huge shopping areas in Shenzhen without getting a true picture of what

God is doing in China. Though the churches are growing at amazing rates in these places, too, there are new revivals taking place in less-frequented parts of China to the west that are on the borders of closed countries. In the last five years, the Chinese have been experiencing revivals where believers can clearly hear the voice of God calling them to go west.

Chinese Missionaries Go West

In one Chinese underground house church network, known as the "Five Brothers," one of the leaders, Pastor Ezekiel (not his real name), shared about an amazing time of revelation that took place at one of their meetings in 2010:

> In 2010 we have seen a huge revival take hold in all of China! I was there in the 1980s when China began its famous days of massive revivals, but I tell you that this revival is even stronger. This spiritual revival is happening everywhere, and we have received a clear vision from God.
>
> Before, it was our goal to train missionaries in languages and cross-cultural skills, but many of the missionaries who had been trained couldn't go because they felt too weak and incapable. Missionaries have been training all over China for years, but most of them have never had a clear vision of where to go in the Muslim, Buddhist, and Communist world.
>
> Now we are having prayer meetings where God is talking to us clearly and telling us where to go. God is specifically calling people to the western borders [of China] and to the minority groups. In the past, Chinese Back to Jerusalem missionaries would go to other countries and cultures to preach the Gospel, but the vision and the calling were never really clear. The leaders often appointed people to go to different areas because of availability, not based on the calling of the Lord.

Now, believers all over China are seeing visions like the ones that the apostle Paul had. These visions are of specific people in specific countries speaking specific languages. Some of the believers who are having these visions are even being specifically told that they will be martyred.

One night I was in western China and the Spirit of the Lord filled the room. Everyone fell to their faces and started crying and calling out to the Lord. During these meetings I couldn't sleep for two days and two nights. I couldn't stop praying. The Holy Spirit was so strong. Young people began to call out, "Yes, Lord, I am willing to die in that country for you. Yes, Lord, I am ready to have my name put into the Lamb's Book of Life."

One night, during one of these meetings, a young man came to me and asked me to pray with him. I told him, "Everyone is praying. Why do you want special prayer? Just join everyone else." The young man was persistent. He told me that God told him to go to Palestine and preach the gospel, but he was afraid. He said that God was telling him clearly that Palestine will be the mission field that he will be sent to, but he was afraid of the violence toward Christians there. I told him not to fear because if God had called him, God would be with him and would strengthen him. I placed my hands on him and began to pray.

After praying he replied, "God has told me clearly that I am to go to Palestine. It is there that I will be martyred, but I will not fear. I will preach the gospel of Jesus Christ because it is the Truth for all mankind. It is the power that saves!"

As this young man stood there, his young wife came and stood beside him. She quoted from the book of Ruth 1:16-17, "Where you go, I will go, and where you stay, I will stay. Your people will be my people and your God my God. Where you die, I will die, and there I will be buried. May the Lord deal with me, be it ever so severely, if even death separates you and me." That night forty-four young people came forward and said that they too were willing to sacrifice their lives, if need be, in Muslim countries.

Revival has also been taking place in the hard-to-reach areas of western China like Xinjiang. Since 2008, not many foreigners have been living in Xinjiang. Many of those who were living there prior to the Beijing Olympics were forced to leave. At that time, many of them were given only forty-eight hours to sell their car and apartment, find places for their clothes and furniture, and arrange everything to get to their next destination.

Believers from the underground house church in eastern China began to send large numbers of young bold missionaries to Xinjiang in the west. It is one of the most difficult places to share the Gospel because there is not only aggression against Christians, but an overall hatred for Han Chinese as well.

Today, in Muslim-dominated cities throughout western China, there are small churches popping up everywhere. Bible schools for the Uyghur minority people, who are primarily Muslim, are now in full operation in China to handle all the new believers.

These revivals are getting Christians excited about the new role of China and the Back to Jerusalem vision. The impact that God is having on China and the spiritual fruit of the Chinese serving around the world is already very visible.

Now missionaries from the underground church in China are working and serving in Iraq. It should be clear, though, that their goal is not to build a church in Iraq that looks like the church in China. Their vision is not to build a Chinese Christian empire in Iraq, but to instead support the local Christians in Iraq and serve the efforts that are already there.

The Chinese missionaries in Iraq are partnering with nations from around the world to serve the people of Iraq and make the name of Jesus known to as many people as possible.

THIRTY-SIX

Combating Evil:
A Practical Plan

Christians around the world can no longer wait to get involved in Iraqi mission efforts. ISIS is not retreating.

Back to Jerusalem missionaries from China are partnering with MedEast and PCCR (Plain Compassion Crisis Response) to change the course of the history of Iraq forever. Their efforts might actually have more of a positive impact on Iraq than the entire history of foreign military conquests in the nation.

Chinese Back to Jerusalem missionaries are training and being sent out from many different camps around Asia to take the Gospel message to people in Iraq who have suffered the most from ISIS. Many of these people groups in Iraq who have been hit hardest by ISIS are considered to be unreached—having never heard the Gospel message.

The Chinese have a three-phase plan to meet the challenges presented by ISIS.

The three phases are:

1. To provide emergency aid to the Iraqis who have suffered from genocide.

2. To provide missionaries and Gospel materials to the areas hit hardest by ISIS.

3. To target ISIS with the Good News of Jesus Christ.

Those who have suffered the most are those who have seen and experienced the genocidal attacks of ISIS firsthand. Outside of the Gospel, their needs are mostly humanitarian. Many are in desperate need of emergency items.

Back to Jerusalem missionaries have a long history of providing aid to areas after natural disasters like earthquakes, tsunamis, and floods, but this is the first man-made humanitarian disaster that Back to Jerusalem has ever officially undertaken.

Emergency aid is still desperately needed. Most families who have fled from ISIS did not take anything with them except for the clothes on their backs. Back to Jerusalem, MedEast, and PCCR work together to provide necessities like food, clothing, water, shelter, and sanitation.

Outside of the immediate disaster relief, there are three ways that the missionaries are meeting the needs of phase one:

1. Provide basic food.

2. Provide basic education.

3. Provide basic safety.

Providing food means more than just simply buying a bunch of rice and vegetables and handing them out. Instead, missionaries are focused on providing long-term solutions by implementing local agricultural projects so that refugees can grow their own food. One of the ways they plan to accomplish this is to use a system known as "aquaponics." Aquaponics is a form of farming that Back to Jerusalem missionaries have long adopted and shared with the most rural and urban areas around the world.

Aquaponics was brought to China for BTJ by Travis Hughey, who is an expert in organic farming. It is a sustainable food source that uses fish waste to feed and fertilize vegetables. Aquaponics does not require soil, so it can be used in the most unforgiving land on earth. Instead of soil, vegetables are planted in rock beds. The water flows through the rock beds to provide nutrients to the plants, and the rock beds provide a natural filtration system that cleans the water flowing back to the river.

Right now, genocide victims in Iraq have to rely on places like Turkey or Iran to provide imported food while they face continued conflict with ISIS. Aquaponics systems are helping alleviate this need. The hope is that this method of farming will provide food for the long term and remove the dependency on outside aid.

One of ISIS's goals is to kill and rape the young Yazidi and Christian children of Iraq. Those who escaped lost everything, including the chance of obtaining an education. BTJ, together with MedEast and PCCR missionaries, built a school in Seje to provide an education for the hundreds of children who were targeted by genocide in that area. In addition, the school does not just meet the educational needs of the children, but also offers day classes for adults who wish to increase their employability by learning English. Men and women who escaped the clutches of death are now rebuilding their lives and have an opportunity to take advantage of these certified language courses provided by Dr. Paul Kingery.

Another incredibly profound problem that needs to be addressed is the sex slavery trade. Accurate counts of murders and kidnappings by ISIS are hard to come by. The Kurdish prime minister's office issued their figures on March 10, 2016. That office indicated that 4,029 Yazidi women and girls had been abducted, but only 1,429 have come home, leaving 2,600 who are still in captivity or who died in captivity.

The Yazidi girls are either given or sold to fighters first, are warehoused, or are left with caretaker Sunni Muslim families in Mosul, then sold to other men for cash. The buyers are not always ISIS fighters. Most people make the assumption that this is the case. But the local Muslims in the areas that have been overrun by ISIS are more than happy to participate in the killing, enslavement, and abuse of Christians and Yazidis. Today, many of the homes, cars, and personal items that used to be owned by Christians and Yazidis are now owned by former Muslim neighbors, not ISIS. This ownership is not limited to property and other goods. This ownership also relates to women, girls, and young children.

As seen in the Sinjar massacre, the abducted girls are often sold and resold repeatedly while in captivity, their "ownership" being passed from one man to another. In each transfer, there is the humiliating and sickening experience of being looked over by several men or many men, usually in Mosul, Iraq, or Raqqa, Syria, with gawkers appraising the female, touching her, and running their hands over her body in a way that violates the victim further. Often the smaller children of a woman are sold with her, and occasionally subjected to the whims of sick pedophiles.

Muslim men often pray before or after raping a female slave, and sometimes explain how they are saving her soul by making her Muslim through sex rather than her willing conversion. The new owners will tell the young girls that it is their right to "marry" (rape) them as spoils of their involvement in the war. The men will make the women or girls false promises about houses, money, and care for their children, then sell them off when they grow tired of them.

Because the rapists routinely force the use of contraceptives on their victims, few are impregnated. In cases of pregnancy, abortions are sometimes forced, or the woman will be violently hit in the abdomen in an attempt to cause spontaneous abortion. Very few give birth to the children of terrorists.

In rare cases, concerned moderate Muslims will buy girls and set them free, helping them return to their families. Occasionally, moderate Muslims, often of modest means, will take pity on the girls when they show up at their houses seeking help during an escape. These families send the victims on to safety and to their families at mortal risk to themselves and their families and without compensation.

It is more common, however, for Arab Muslim families to sell the girls and women for profit. Sometimes they will act sympathetic to the victim and pretend they are saving them. There have also been reports of Muslim-owned houses that were used by the smugglers as a sort of false "freedom train" through which the victims would pass on their way to safety. However, any idea of this being an actual "freedom train" is shattered when the lucrative financial payments are made to the smugglers for their services.

The sex slaves who are fortunate enough to escape and find their way back to their families are often surprised when they discover that their families do not want them back. The sexual abuse that many of the young women endured cause them to be marked with a virtual "Scarlet Letter" by the Yazidi traditions once they return to their families.

In the conservative ancient cultures of Iraq, some families feel the social shame of having a daughter or sister who has been repeatedly used and abused by Muslims. This makes them unclean in the eyes of the culture and renders most of them an unsuitable marriage partner.

In some of the refugee camps, the Christians and the Yazidis meet renewed persecution from the Muslim majorities. Young Christian and Yazidi women who are known to have been raped can quickly find themselves targets of predators in the camp. Since many of them are so young, without an education, rejected by their families, having nowhere to turn, they can eventually end up as victims again in the sex trafficking circles.

Some of these women who were rejected found their way to the same village where BTJ and MedEast are serving together. Many of them needed a safe place that they could call home. As a part of Phase One, a safe house was needed to serve these girls who were coming out of slavery.

THIRTY-SEVEN

Safe House

In October 2014, the Research and Fatwa Department of the Islamic State (ISIS) issued a pamphlet about owning female slaves. It contains more information on the subject than we shared earlier. The pamphlet was dated Muharram 1436 and was printed by ISIS's publishing house.[139]

The pamphlet clarified the position of Islamic law as it pertains to having sexual intercourse with female slaves. The pamphlet was translated by MEMRI Jihad and Terrorism Threat Monitor (JTTM) in the form of answers to common questions.[140]

According to the answers about female slaves,

> Al-Sabi is a woman from among ahl al-harb [the people of war] who has been captured by Muslims.

> What makes al-sabi permissible [i.e., what makes it permissible to take such a woman captive] is [her] unbelief. Unbelieving [women] who were captured and brought into the abode of Islam are permissible to us, after the imam distributes them [among us].

> There is no dispute among the scholars that it is permissible to capture unbelieving women [who are characterized by] original unbelief [kufr asli], such as thekitabiyat [women from among the People of the Book, i.e. Jews, Christians, Yazidi]....

---

139. http://www.memrijttm.org/islamic-state-isis-releases-pamphlet-on-female-slaves.html#_edn1.
140. Ibid.

It is permissible to have sexual intercourse with the female captive. Allah the almighty said: '[Successful are the believers] who guard their chastity, except from their wives or (the captives and slaves) that their right hands possess, for then they are free from blame [Koran 23:5-6]'...

If she is a virgin, he [her master] can have intercourse with her immediately after taking possession of her. However, is she isn't, her uterus must be purified [first]....

It is permissible to buy, sell, or give as a gift female captives and slaves, for they are merely property, which can be disposed of [as long as that doesn't cause [the Muslim ummah] any harm or damage.[141]

This ISIS pamphlet provided the guidelines when ten-year-old Ama (not her real name) and her sixteen-year-old aunt were taken captive by ISIS.[142]

After being taken from their homes, the two girls were held captive in the Tel Afar district of western Mosul. Ama, who turned eleven in captivity (official reports say she was twelve when she escaped), faked an illness that made it difficult to sleep so she appealed to her captives for sleeping medication.[143]

When they gave her the medication, Ama hid it and saved it up over a period of time. When the time was right, she crushed up the medication and slipped it into the tea of her captors so they would fall into a deep sleep. This presented Ama and her aunt with the first opportunity to escape since they were captured in August 2014.

They waited till midnight to leave the house, because if they were caught outside at night in Mosul, the security forces might have them both executed. Once everything was quiet, Ama and her aunt made a run for it. They ran north toward the desert mountains with no light

---

141. Ibid.
142. Story told by Iraqi MP Vian Dakhil during recorded BTJ interview in April 2016.
143. https://www.rt.com/news/340574-isis-sleeping-pills-yazidi/.

except for the moonlight on the ground. After nine hours of hiking, miraculously they were able to make it to the Kurdish front lines.

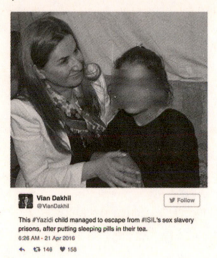

Vian Dakhil
@VianDakhil

🔵 Follow

This #Yazidi child managed to escape from #ISIL's sex slavery prisons, after putting sleeping pills in their tea.
6:26 AM - 21 Apr 2016

↩ ⇄ 146 ♥ 158

Once the two girls made it to the Kurdish area, they were taken to a UN camp for refugees where they were able to meet with Iraqi parliament member Vian Dakhil. "If anyone is able to help," Vian told BTJ during a podcast interview, "if anyone can help us, please, because we need everyone to help—with anything. You cannot imagine what the situation is with the refugees or the situation is with [Ama] when she is coming from ISIS. She is damaged. She is damaged on the inside [vagina] after what happened to them when they are under ISIS control…it is very important that we rebuild [and help] the girls after what has happened to them."

To help young girls coming out of slavery, BTJ and MedEast collaborated on a plan for the establishment of a safe house.

First, the safe house aims to allow the women who have escaped a hostile environment to find a safe haven to recover. The safe house also provides counseling to help deal with the emotional and physical trauma from their time in captivity. The safe house offers practical skills and training, which act as a kind of therapy. The lower floor is used for sewing and craft-making activities to train the young girls and women to produce income for themselves.

The safe house is located high in the mountains, tucked away in the foot hills of Seje where MedEast has their headquarters. The serene location is conducive to healing for the participants. Behind the house is an entrance to a gorge, with mountain trails on either side, and an undisturbed two-kilometer-long mountain path for refuge and contemplation, which is ideal for quiet meditation and reflection.

House mothers, who are older, retired expat women, are always in the home to help the girls and women, and Western-trained female psychologists with credentials in counseling trauma victims are present from time to time to assist them with recovery.

Before the building of the safe house was even started, the sewing program was underway, providing training to displaced Yazidi girls on how to make dresses for widows and orphan girls. This helped the girls earn money that supported them as they attended high school.

Dresses and crafts, like handbags, were also sent to the US for marketing through the PCCR volunteers going back home. Ramonda Samawi, of Lebanese descent, but with training in tailoring in Riyad and Paris, led the MedEast sewing program in the beginning, then returned later at intervals to provide ongoing support.

The safe house and the sewing training was the beginning of healing and a new life for the devastated young women.

THIRTY-EIGHT

Business as Mission

The young girls who come to live at the safe house will not only find security, acceptance, and love. They will also find access to very practical training that can help them establish businesses that will open doors and provide opportunities for them in the future.

Back to Jerusalem is working with missionaries from China who are skilled in starting international businesses. These missionaries are using their expertise to train former sex slaves not to just find a job but to start their own companies. One of the best ways to ensure that these young women will not fall victim to social predators again is by expanding their options to create a secure financial future.

Back to Jerusalem has been using business as a way to bring the Gospel into closed countries for many years. It is not a new concept and is in no way unique to the Back to Jerusalem ministry. In fact, it is a very biblical concept that can be found in the New Testament. Unlike the Western Christian mission model, which requires continual funding from churches, the Chinese are going with very little funds and support and relying instead on an ancient biblical model that requires one to be engaged in the market place. The Chinese are teaching the young women to work like they do and survive the way that Paul did, by becoming "tentmakers" (Acts 18:3).

The Chinese BTJ missionaries understand that long-term missions in a place like Iraq cannot be done without sustainability. While most Christian organizations might focus on financing various humanitarian projects that require ongoing support, Chinese missionaries are forced to find ways to be financially sustainable. The Chinese have adopted a new approach, which is called Business as Mission, or BAM, and BAM has emerged as a significant new model for mission work.

China has been a titan in today's globalized economy, and this has created strategic opportunities for Chinese Christian businesses in some of the most unlikely corners of the world, including Iraq.

Business as Mission is a relatively new term but is based on biblical concepts. Other expressions used for BAM include "transformational business," "tentmaking," and "kingdom business." These are very generic terms, but the way they are used among the Chinese in the BTJ context changes the way missionaries can engage with former slaves in Iraq.

The Chinese missionaries' vision of working with the slaves is to provide more than just employable skills. Employable skills are not enough in Iraq, because these young women have been marked in their community with the stigma of being brutally raped. Virginity and purity are held in the highest regards for females in the Yazidi society. After their abduction and abuse, through no fault of their own, many of the young women are rejected by both their families and their communities.

If they are not able to find suitable husbands who are willing to accept them with their dark history, then they will be forced to provide for themselves. That means they will need jobs. Northern Iraq is not exactly a booming economy these days, so the chance of finding an employer who is willing to hire them is pretty low.

Women in this type of situation often become victims of prostitution or get trapped in the underground sex trade and human trafficking industry. To keep that from happening, the Chinese recognize that it is not enough just to teach these former slave women to be employable, but they must learn to identify needs in the market and use that knowledge to learn how to provide a product that will meet that need.

If we look at the Bible, we see amazing examples of God taking ordinary individuals and making them businessmen, kings, leaders, judges, crop owners, and soldiers who not only survive, but are able to use the gifts God has given them to have an impact on their community.

Iraq does not have the most ideal economy for new businesses, so these young women must learn to adapt and adjust to unfair business trade rules and patriarch-controlled environments. Chinese female missionaries are well equipped with the tools needed to help these women, as they are accustomed to these environments and know what it takes to set up businesses in Tibet, North Korea, Cambodia, South Sudan, Iran, and Syria, as well as in Taliban-controlled areas of Afghanistan and Pakistan.

Their business as mission model is unique and provides a natural connection with young women who have been abused by ISIS. Chinese women working at the safe house will spend days, months, and even years discipling the local women on how to accomplish this.

The Chinese have the ideas and tools to start mission-minded businesses in areas that have been hit hardest by ISIS. When most businesses are pulling out and shutting their doors, the Chinese are moving in. They know how to squeeze every penny out of a profit, even in a war zone. The Chinese also know how to function in areas of hostility toward Christianity. Chinese businesses have been used as a cover for church activities for years since the areas where the Chinese are experiencing revivals forbid any kind of proselytizing.

Of course, securing the investments needed is always a challenge, but God has provided the Chinese BTJ missionaries with some very unique opportunities around the world.

When Mao Zedong first took over China in 1949, a huge flood of Chinese immigrants began to flood the neighboring Asian nations. Today, those individuals who fled more than sixty years ago have thriving businesses. They also have a second and third generation of well-educated children and grandchildren who are doing very well financially.

Amazingly, many of these *huaqiao* or foreign Chinese have become Christians and have missionary hearts to join their countrymen in taking the Gospel to the final frontier—all the way Back to Jerusalem. Wealthy Chinese business investors from Hong Kong, Taiwan, Indonesia, Singapore, Malaysia, Indonesia, Philippines, and other nations are joining the poor rural Chinese missionaries on the field in Iraq and are willing to invest. What makes these investors unique is not that they are wealthy Chinese business owners in foreign nations outside of China. What makes them unique is that they are business investors who are looking not for the tangible return on investment but for the salvation of souls.

This is a whole new breed of businessmen who are kingdom minded. It is a growing phenomenon that used to be very prevalent in the West with businesses putting biblical ethics and Christ first. Businesses in China are picking up where many traditional Western Christian businesses have left off, but with a twist.

The BTJ missionaries who are going to Iraq are not your normal missionaries; they are uneducated farmers and street vendors who are accustomed to having church services, Bible schools, and church activities in the secret rooms of factories, office cubicles, or shops. They are not necessarily involved in full-time ministries that are sustained by donor donations, but instead are more apt to find business opportunities in the communities where they are serving.

China has become the factory of the world, producing goods that are needed by consumers all over the globe. Many of those factories are owned by overseas Chinese who allow their facilities to be used as churches, Bible schools, and missionary training centers.

Pastor Joshua of Back to Jerusalem has provided the biblical training for all of his Iraqi missionaries in a clothing factory that produces clothing for Nike, Adidas, and Levi Jean Company. Of course, Nike, Adidas, and Levi Jean Company management at their headquarters do not realize that their facilities are being used for this purpose, but the owners of the factories who secure the contracts for production do—and they fully support the mission efforts of BTJ.

The same economy and strategy that has allowed Chinese Christians to operate in closed countries around the world, including China, is being employed in Iraq. Iraqis still have a need for televisions, mobile phones, earphones, routers, cameras, cars, shoes, watches, socks, furniture, alarm systems, and so on. Where do you think they buy their goods? Like most everyone else, they buy them from China.

The goal of the BTJ missionaries is to provide both the knowledge and the resources to the women who have had everything ripped from them and help them be financially independent. The hope is that these women can use what Satan intended to destroy and turn it into an asset to reach others.

Other organizations have a different approach with their aid. Their goal is to provide food and shelter for the rest of the women's lives, but what happens when the money runs out? What happens when the security forces leave? Others think sending these young women to other countries where they will find safety and opportunities is the answer. But what about the young ladies who do not get to leave? What about them?

What if, in the deepest and darkest areas of the world, one woman who has been through it all finds a path out of poverty and escapes the perils of her past? What if one woman, who was brutally abused by ISIS and imprisoned as a sex slave, finds the true meaning of life through Jesus Christ and uses her experience to reach other women?

The BTJ missionaries from China are willing to use all the tools at their disposal, including business, not to create dependency, but to create opportunities of independence that can carry the Gospel message for generations to come.

THIRTY-NINE

Missionaries and Gospel Materials

As we have already noted, many of the people fleeing from ISIS belong to unreached people groups who have never heard the Good News of Jesus Christ. This is not just the Yazidi people. The Shia and Sunni Muslims who have fled from ISIS are also unreached people groups.

In fact, some of the Christians who are fleeing from ISIS in Mosul are cultural Christians, but have never consciously made a decision to follow Jesus Christ. They grew up in the cultural communities that were planted by the disciples of Jesus. They still speak the same language that Jesus spoke, but in spite of their rich heritage, many of them have never made a decision to follow Jesus Christ or share their faith with others.

As the refugees spill into the village where BTJ, MedEast, and PCCR are serving, they are carrying a lot of emotional and spiritual baggage with them. Many of them are dealing with nightmares and deep, raw trauma from the near-death experience they survived. The aftereffects of rape, murder, and poverty can be deadly if people have no emotional and/or spiritual support. The refugees are in desperate need of Christian materials as well as people to present those materials. Those who are suffering from loss and depression need both missionaries and Bible materials in the local language to convey a healing message for them.

Historically, many of the unreached people from the Iraqi areas that have been hit hardest by ISIS purposefully restricted their contact with outsiders and remained largely homogenous for generations; this has kept them from being exposed to the Gospel. Now that they are on the run from ISIS, they find themselves disoriented, dispersed, and more vulnerable to outside influences than ever before. For the first time in a long time, these unreached people groups have access to the Gospel.

Dr. Paul, with MedEast, PCCR, and Back to Jerusalem missionaries from China spend week after week participating in church services in the village homes that are open to everyone who wants to attend.

The missionaries from China also build relationships by engaging refugees and learning the language so that they can understand how best to share the Gospel with them. They often invite the refugees to their homes and show them the various farming methods they are using in their gardens to grow food. They use the aquaponics units to introduce the refugees to the different methods that can be used to cultivate fish on a very small budget. Several of the refugees come to their homes for evening meals, which opens the locals up to the Gospel message, but, unfortunately, also makes the young Chinese missionaries vulnerable to robbery.

Because local refugees are able to go into the home where the Chinese are living, they are able to learn information that could help locals burglarize their home. One Chinese family who lived in the middle of the community serving the refugees there had all of the money the family had to live on for several months stolen from them one month after moving there.

It was yet another reminder that serving in war-torn areas of the world is not always easy. But it is worth it.

Sharing Jesus Through the Gospel Cloud

Getting the Gospel into the hands of the refugees is a challenge. But since most of them still have their mobile phones, the Chinese missionaries decided to use a unique way to provide Gospel materials.

Back to Jerusalem invented a new device that has been extremely effective during the testing stage in Iran. The new device is known as the Gospel Cloud. During the testing stages, the Gospel Cloud was used to make files available in very crowded areas to everyone who had a wireless device, like a mobile phone, tablet, or laptop.

It is a very powerful device and the way it works is extremely simple. The Gospel Cloud unit is a small mobile device, the size of a mobile phone, which missionaries can easily carry in their pocket. It sends out a Wi-Fi signal that extends roughly one hundred meters; but instead of connecting users to the Internet, it acts as its very own server, and it only allows the user to access a Web page that has been designed specifically for spreading the Gospel. The Wi-Fi connection can be easily detected by any mobile devices. Any person close enough to the Gospel Cloud can sign on anytime and have access to Gospel materials to download on to their device.

The Wi-Fi signal is labeled "free Wi-Fi." Those who sign on believe they are on the Internet, but they are not. When they open the browser and type in "www.google.com" or "www.youtube.com," they will be directed to Back to Jerusalem's own Web site.

Again, the user does not really know that he or she is not connected to the Internet, because the device simulates the experience of surfing on the Web. The website has a home page that offers free movies, music, and e-books for instant download, or they can be streamed directly.

To fully understand this concept, think of what you encounter when you first sign on to the Internet at a hotel or an airport. First you click on the Wi-Fi icon to connect to the Internet. From there you often see a pop-up page known as a "portal page" where you must agree to some terms and conditions or watch some advertisements before you can sign on and explore the Internet. Oftentimes you will even be asked to enter your credit card information and pay a fee to use the Internet.

The Gospel Cloud works the same way, except that the user never has to agree to any terms or conditions or pay a fee. They also never really leave that portal page. He or she navigates only deeper and deeper into it by clicking on icons or buttons leading to free e-books, music, or videos.

People are free to browse through the Web pages of content and download a free Bible in their language, or free Christian music, or even Christian movies that teach about Jesus. They are free to sign off anytime. The good thing about being in the middle of the desert in a refugee village is that there are not a lot of Wi-Fi options competing with the Gospel Cloud. Boredom is in our favor.

In the future, Back to Jerusalem missionaries plan to offer language training, updated local news information, and other types of information and tools related to the Gospel and the message of the Good News.

The Gospel Cloud is battery operated, so missionaries can set it up anywhere in the village and retrieve it at a later time. They also have solar units that will allow them to strategically place the Gospel Cloud in areas without electricity for long periods of time. Because the Gospel Cloud is not connected to the Internet, it cannot be stopped or controlled by outside government entities. Our content cannot be blocked by the government or by ISIS.

In addition to this, Back to Jerusalem has added a bonus feature that is particularly exciting for Chinese BTJ missionaries. There is a box on the home page that allows missionaries to anonymously chat with anyone in the village who is signed on to the unit.

When people in the village sign on, they will find a little box in which they can ask questions or become engaged with a missionary whose identity and location remain anonymous. That means that a female believer from China can chat with a male member in a completely safe environment, without revealing her identity and without the male discovering that he is being evangelized by a woman.

Because we have invented this little tool, it will be very difficult for anyone to find it or to stop it.

This project might seem completely insane to those who do not understand the power of the Gospel. The Bible says, "God has chosen the foolish things of the world to put to shame the wise, and God has chosen the weak things of the world to put to shame the things which are mighty" (1 Corinthians 1:27).

Back to Jerusalem, MedEast, and PCCR are currently using every means available to share the Gospel message with those who have been hit hardest by the terrorism of ISIS.

FORTY

The Good News of Jesus Christ

Spreading the Good News of Jesus Christ is the boldest and most extreme measure to take in a country hostile to Christianity, but it is absolutely essential to stopping genocide in Iraq. In order to fight the genocide, it is important to move past the symptoms and get to the heart of the problem.

According to the United Nations High Commissioner for Refugees (UNHCR), well over 1 million refugees reached the shores of Europe in 2015.[144] That is likely only a fraction of the actual number. More have entered in 2016.

"Over one million people have landed on Europe's shores, fleeing war and persecution, seeking a better life for their families," said Vincent Cochetel, UNHCR director of the bureau for Europe. "Tragically, over 3,700 other children, women and men did not survive the perilous journey by sea and their hope for a fresh start died with them.

"If there were more legal avenues for refugees to reach Europe, perhaps some of those who died at sea could have found peace and safety instead. For the refugees who risked everything and have now safely reached Europe, we hope they will be received in the context of the European values of dignity, solidarity, and human rights, so that they may find their new beginning," Cochetel added.

---

144. http://www.unhcr.org/news/latest/2015/12/5683d0b56/million-sea-arrivals-reach-europe-2015.html.

Vincent Cochetel's answer to the perilous problem in Iraq is that Europe should have a streamlined way to allow refugees from war-torn areas to enter its countries.

But the question should be asked: Why do refugees flee to Europe? When they flee from the war in Iraq, what are they looking for? Are they looking for peace? Kuwait and Saudi Arabia are on the border of Iraq and are peaceful Muslim countries. Iraqis, Saudis, and Kuwaitis are all Arab nations, so the language, practices, and religious beliefs are all relatively the same.

Are the refugees looking for economic opportunities? If so, then why not go to Qatar, Dubai, or Bahrain? These countries are literally oozing with wealth and job opportunities. Above all else, the refugees from Iraq have to flee through Turkey to get to Europe, so why not stop in Turkey? Turkey has many opportunities that Iraq does not have and has a culture that is far more conducive for a Muslim from Iraq than Europe.

If the UNHCR cannot ask this first basic question about the problem, then there is no reason for them to make suggestions in their report about how to fix it! The problem is that leaders and policy makers are pussyfooting around the real problem and trying to treat the symptoms, but treating the symptoms without identifying the root problem is a very dangerous proposition.

If someone comes to the hospital with a communicable disease, it does not help anyone to send that person to a place full of people where that disease does not exist, because now a new group of people will be needlessly exposed to that disease. The disease has not been defeated or stopped. Instead, it has been multiplied. That would be medical malpractice.

Likewise, treating the influx of refugees from genocidal areas without tackling the root of the problem is social malpractice that multiplies the problem.

Why are the refugees fleeing to Europe and not stopping in Dubai or Qatar? Why are the refugees willing to die on their way to

Greece instead of stopping in Turkey? Few people will actually tell you why because it does not sound like a very nice thing to say. The truth might hurt people's feelings, but truth does not care about your feelings.

The thing that no one is willing to say is that Islam is socially inferior to Christianity. That is not the same as saying that Muslims are inferior to Christians, because that would be a false statement. But Islam creates hostile environments that lead to racism, violence, and emotional, spiritual, academic, and economic poverty.

Repeating that last paragraph can cause a lot of turmoil today (and possibly death), but if the world is not willing to have integrity and honesty in identifying the problem, then it is impossible to identify the answer. If the world is looking to Europe or America for answers in combating genocide, then the question must be raised about what these areas have that the Middle East does not have.

Islam has a very long history of genocide that was both practiced and endorsed by their founder—the Prophet Muhammad. To fight the act of genocide by embracing the religion of genocide does not make any sense.

Instead, in order to fight genocide and destroy it, a fundamental spiritual transformation has to occur. This comes not from the impotent secular forums of polluted international communities nor from the opposing forces of genocidal Islam, but instead can only come from the saving work of Jesus Christ, the messianic sacrifice by the one who gave His life for all mankind. The One who said, "You have heard that it was said, 'You shall love your neighbor and hate your enemy.' But I say to you, love your enemies, bless those who persecute you,… that you may be sons of your Father in heaven" (Matthew 5:43–45).

Honestly, at first glance that seems like the absolutely worst idea on the planet—fighting the violence of ISIS with the love of Jesus. Initially it comes across as absolute lunacy. How can abstract love combat tangible evil manifested as genocide? It seems absurd. The entire strategy instantly invokes images of hippies from the 1960s stuffing flowers into the rifle barrels of riot-control police.

However, the violence and injustice in ancient Europe did not disappear as a result of the force of armies. Instead, each country fell to their knees because of the blood shed by martyrs out of their love for those whom they served. Jesus brought nations to Him, not because He was a military conqueror like Muhammad, but because He gave His life as a living sacrifice for all mankind, whom He loves dearly.

The Bible teaches that ISIS is not beyond Christ's salvation. In fact, outside of the blood of Jesus, none of us is better than the worst jihadist of ISIS. Jesus taught that when someone thinks evil thoughts in his or her mind, that person has already sinned (Matthew 5:21–22, 28). According to the measuring stick of righteousness that Jesus introduced, we are all murderers, blasphemers, adulterers, liars, and thieves. Some of our sinful thoughts we would not want to whisper in an empty room by ourselves with the lights off.

We all can be as evil as the jihadists, but as Christians, what makes us different is the love of Christ, and if that formula worked for us, there is no reason why it will not work for them.

Once it has been established that the love of Christ in the Gospel message is what they need, then the next question is will it work? Has it worked in the past? Do we have any biblical examples of it working in the past?

Can ISIS Be Reached with the Gospel?

According to Pastor Joshua of China's underground church, there are biblical examples.

Pastor Joshua and I sat in a Chinese restaurant in Phnom Penh, Cambodia, contemplating the idea of helping refugees in Iraq. At that time, most of the aid was being sent to the refugees who were spilling across the border into Turkey.

Pastor Joshua is one of the most important strategists for the Chinese BTJ vision. He has funding from both Chinese and South Korean businessmen who are working and running businesses in China. He has an almost endless supply of young, spiritually hungry, sold-out missionaries from the various underground churches in China, and he has had the unique experience of suffering for his faith. Joshua has been beaten, thrown in prison, and kept from his family for long periods of time because of his belief in Jesus Christ. But Joshua would not stop because he could not stop.

Few things can prepare a pastor for the challenges of working in genocide areas like living through the Cultural Revolution in China where cultural genocide was the norm for more than two decades. The number of people who have been killed in genocide in Iraq pales in comparison to the millions who died in the Cultural Revolution of China in the 1960s and 70s under dictator Mao Zedong.

Pastor Joshua knows without a shadow of a doubt what brought China out of that darkness; it was the same thing that brought him out of it personally—the love of Jesus Christ. Nothing can keep him from hiding the one true answer. For him, this phase is a natural part of the Great Commission.

Many falsely think that the term *underground church* implies a secret society of Chinese Christians who hide their faith so that others will not know they are Christians and who practice Christianity only in the privacy of a secret closet or room. Nothing could be further from the truth. Chinese Christians like Pastor Joshua burn with an unexplainable fire to share their relationship with Jesus with others, no matter what the consequences. The term *underground* refers to the legality of the fellowship. The churches have to often meet in unregistered locations because the government refuses to officially recognize them.

When contemplating how best to help the victims of genocide, Joshua looked for a way to bring the Gospel message to ISIS. He had been so deeply involved in the work in Cambodia that he had not had time to watch the news about what was going on in the rest of the world, but when the subject of ISIS was brought up, he immediately noted, "We need to share Jesus with them."

Joshua may have more people in his church than the entire population of Norway, but, honestly, he can be so beautifully ignorant of the normal response of more mainstream, conditioned Christians sometimes. He did not think about his statement before he added, "Are the members of ISIS any different from the apostle Paul? Didn't Jesus die for them as well?"

His stance challenges Christians to think of things in a new paradigm. His experience with persecution in China allows him to come to conclusions that cultural Christians in the West do not naturally arrive at.

Who is ISIS? When we think of them, do we think of them as militants in the way that the newspapers or magazines describe them or the way that the young slave girls see them?

If our villages had been ransacked by ISIS, our fathers had been slaughtered, our sons kidnapped, and our young girls raped, would we not all have a deep, seething hatred in our hearts that yearns for the harshest revenge known to man?

But Joshua's proposal does not originate from hurt and anger. His proposal comes from somewhere else that is not natural to humans. His words echo Ephesians 6:12–13:

> For we do not wrestle against flesh and blood, but against principalities, against powers, against the rulers of the darkness of this age, against spiritual hosts of wickedness in the heavenly places. Therefore take up the whole armor of God, that you may be able to withstand in the evil day, and having done all, to stand.

As much as we detest what ISIS stands for, we must resist the desire to hate the individual men, because Jesus died for them, too. Is it too much to believe that the ISIS fighters have been deceived and they too are victims in the same way as the ones they victimize? Doesn't Jesus love them, too? Didn't He create them in His image? And if He loves them, are we not commanded to love them as well?

Gulp.

That is a hard concept to swallow—no doubt about it. After all of the incomprehensible pain they have brought, after all of the destruction and death, how can anyone be asked to love them? It seems too great a task. The burden is too grand for us to even propose to those who are suffering in Iraq today.

When we think of all the killing, maiming, raping, and torturing that ISIS has inflicted on so many people, it might feel impossible to ever feel anything but hatred for them, but all Christians have been commanded to love their enemies. There has seldom been a greater example of an enemy than ISIS, or a greater challenge for the command to love.

Pastor Joshua's words point to a much greater source of Love than this world is capable of, and if genocide in Iraq is to ever be stopped, then the cycle of hate must end at the root.

The idea is hard to swallow, and the ability to carry it out seems virtually impossible. Everyone in the world is running away from ISIS. Anyone who does not deny Christ is enslaved or killed. Who would be crazy enough to willingly go back to ISIS-controlled territory and attempt to do the unthinkable: proselytize?

FORTY-ONE

Evangelizing in ISIS Territory

"Your threats do not frighten us and you will never win over us," declared Abu Mohamed al-Adnani, the official spokesman for ISIS during an audio message posted on Saturday, May 21, 2016.

"You think defeat is the loss of a city or a land? Were we defeated when several cities of Iraq were taken away from us and we went to the desert? Will we lose if you control Mosul, Raqqa and other cities that were previously controlled by us: Definitely 'no,' because defeat is only the loss of the wish and will to fight. **"There is only one way for the US to gain victory and that is by taking the Quran out of the hearts of Muslims,"** Adnani claimed.[145]

This is one area where Back to Jerusalem missionaries whole-heartedly agree with the spokesman of ISIS. The only way for ISIS to be defeated "is by taking the Quran out of the hearts of Muslims."

But how will they know that the only truth is found in the Bible, not the Quran, unless they hear, and how will they hear unless someone is sent (Romans 10:14)?

How can missionaries from China get the Gospel message to the people of ISIS? Well, this is not an impossible task. It is never an impossible task. This is when small tools like the Gospel Cloud unit will come into play. If missionaries are able to get units into ISIS areas, then the Wi-Fi capabilities can be turned on. When ISIS

---

145. http://rudaw.net/english/middleeast/22052016.

members sign on to the free Wi-Fi provided by the Gospel Cloud unit, they will have the opportunity to see and hear the story of Jesus and receive the answers that they seek—often for the first time. Then the Holy Spirit will continue to work in their hearts, confirming many things that have been challenging them. The answers will not be a new revelation as much as they will be a confirmation of the things the Holy Spirit has already been speaking to them.

In addition, Back to Jerusalem missionaries from China have more than just one egg in their basket, although some of their plans cannot be shared in this book.

In June 2016, Back to Jerusalem began providing electronic Bibles that were invented for use in North Korea for PCCR. The newly invented Bibles were modified so they could also be used in Arabic speaking areas. The Bibles are called SUPER Bible (Small Unit Powered E-Reader) because of their long-term capacity. They can be used for up to seven years without charging or changing the battery!

Back to Jerusalem has been using the SUPER Bible for several years in North Korea with amazing success. North Korean Christians are able to read the Bible for several years without having to worry about buying new batteries or finding a place to get it charged.

The idea of solar chargers always come up when electronic Bibles are mentioned, but the current state of solar energy does not provide the adequate amount of energy that is needed to power an electronic reader for any significant amount of time unless it is a larger unit, which is not conducive for small, clandestine units like the SUPER Bible.

Back to Jerusalem, partnered with PCCR, has the ability to deliver these units to those that desire them with an LR-RAD delivery system.   The LR-RAD unit cannot be described in this book because of security reasons, but the capabilities, which work in conjunction with local authorities on the ground, allow the SUPER Bibles to penetrate the heart of ISIS-controlled areas.

This SUPER Bible project goes to the heart of Abu Mohamed al-Adnani's fears. According to his own words, he does not fear the US military or their ability to take cities, because Islamic militants believe that this war is a part of the ultimate Islamic Armageddon. What they fear is that the truth of God's Word will penetrate the hearts of their people. To protect themselves and the people against the Gospel, they must use violence and terror.

On top of the SUPER Bible and the Gospel Cloud Unit, Back to Jerusalem missionaries are working on another breakthrough invention that is sure to make the ISIS commanders upset. The inspiration for this unit came right from the set of a Hollywood blockbuster spy-thriller.

It is known as the "Pill Bible."

In the movie *Bourne Identity*, Matt Damon plays a secret agent known as Jason Bourne. In the beginning of the movie, his body is pulled from the night waters by a random fishing vessel. The captain of the ship becomes a makeshift surgeon and removes the bullets from Jason Bourne's back. While doing this, he notices an abnormal lump in the skin and uses a scalpel to cut around it. He finds a small pill-sized unit that he examines closely. He rinses it off with water and finds that it is a small projector that uses a small powerful red beam of light to project a bank account number to a Swiss bank account.

This is the inception of the Pill Bible idea. Basically, the Pill Bible is about the size of a small pill or half the size of your thumb nail. It is powered by a motion device that, when shaken, creates energy. The energy that is created from movement powers a light. The light is not very noticeable at first, but when pointed at a wall or flat surface, that light creates a sizable projection. Amazingly, the projection is a Bible scripture. As the projection of the scripture is held on the wall, the Bible Pill can then start to slowly scroll through scriptures so that the person holding the pill can read through the Bible.

The Bible Pill is so small that an LR-RAD unit is able to take many of them at a time to distribute throughout the most closed-off areas of ISIS territory. If ISIS jihadi members storm into a home or room where the Bible Pill is being used, then the user can simply swallow the Bible Pill.

You know how some people take the "pill" so they will not get pregnant? Well, we use the Pill to help people get pregnant – to be impregnated with the Gospel of Jesus Christ and give birth to revival!

Back to Jerusalem believes that the enemy desperately wants to keep people from ever being exposed to the words of Jesus Christ because there is both life and hope in His words. The bondage of hopelessness is destroyed and the shackles of slavery are broken by the Gospel. The Good News of Jesus Christ will not only set ISIS victims free, but it will give the jihadists themselves the chance to experience real love and liberty.

What if an ISIS member who is fighting for Islam sees and hears the message of Jesus Christ from the Gospel Cloud and makes a decision to follow after Christ with the same passion that he follows after Islam? What if he gets a SUPER Bible or Pill Bible into his hands and becomes a follower of the only true God?

Spreading the gospel message to ISIS is a critical part of stopping the hate that fuels genocide. Fighting ISIS with a fire-on-fire type of battle will not provide a long-term solution to the problem. The end of genocide and the road to long-term peace are possible only through Jesus Christ. Every other route is a waste of time. Only the love of Christ can fully conquer the hate of ISIS and wipe away the scars and the pain of their victims.

FORTY-TWO

Join the Effort to Stop Genocide in Iraq

If we want to see an end to genocide in our lifetime, then we are going to have to be humble in our approach to the answer. We must be humble Christians, which means we must be both intellectually and spiritually humble. As such, we must approach the Bible with the acknowledgement that maybe we do not know everything there is to know about the words we read in Scripture.

When we look at the world around us and then look to the Bible for answers, we have to honestly ask ourselves, "What can we learn from Scripture? What can it teach us?" For that we must be willing to throw away preconceived ideas and look at the Word of God with fresh eyes and beg for the Holy Spirit to lead us, and we must be willing to accept what He is telling us.

That might seem easy in theory, but it is becoming increasingly difficult in today's Western Christian circles, because many of the things we understand about the Bible have been taught to us for generations. What if what we understand has been wrongly taught? What if a misinterpretation of the Bible's call to evangelize the world has been passed on to us?

This is why it is so very important for us to ask the Holy Spirit to speak to us directly from Scripture and to override the pride in our hearts that presumes understanding. To approach the Scriptures humbly requires no less than this.

A concept that we need to examine in light of what Scripture really says is the idea of "safe spaces." *Safe spaces* is a new term on college campuses in the United States today. These are places where university students can go to find safety from ideas that hurt their feelings. It is a place that is free from micro aggressions, where feelings are elevated above seeking knowledge. It would seem that, of all places in the world, college campuses should be the one place to explore new ideas and challenge our own understanding of the world. However, the reality is that these "safe spaces" take away that privilege.

In many ways, churches have started to follow universities and have become "safe spaces" where feelings are put before revelation. By creating the church as a "safe space," we are basically saying that we would like revelation as long as revelation does not hurt our feelings. Many Western Christians have bought into the idea that we should insulate Christians from anything that might make us feel uncomfortable. Lord forbid, we are ever uncomfortable!

Unfortunately, anyone requiring a "safe space" in the kingdom of God to protect their feelings from words and ideas that might be offensive to them cannot possibly participate in the Great Commission and will not be able to share in the suffering of Jesus. There are no safe spaces in the Bible. The truth of God's Word does not exempt itself from being true because your feelings might be hurt.

Do not misunderstand, the Bible is full of love, grace, and peace, but it does not care one bit about your precious feelings. If your feelings are hurt by something in the Bible, then it is your feelings that must change to conform to the Bible and not the Bible that must change to conform to your feelings. You do not get a pass. There are no safe spaces from the Truth.

It is not certain where the idea of "safe spaces" originated, but it certainly seems that they do not exist in the Bible. The very idea of picking up your cross daily and following Jesus runs contrary to the idea of "safe space." Only in His will and truth do we find solace from the tempest. To do that, we must be spiritually humble enough to acknowledge that the Bible has all the answers and we do not.

God is not required to confirm our assumptions. Building assumptions rooted in human thought and not derived from what we read in the Bible is a dangerous practice that handicaps our ability to participate in the Great Commission.

There are two common misconceptions about Christ that people assume when they explore the Bible for the first time, and they keep us from being a real threat to the kingdom of evil:

1.Many people in the world have made the assumption that the Bible and its teachings are supposed to be nice to everyone and accept every idea as equal. Therefore Christians who follow the Bible must also be nice to everyone and accept every idea as equal, essentially giving credence to sinful behavior. (This is mainly because they look at the product and not the process). Some people call this tolerance.

2. Following Jesus equals successful living and successful living equals more money, a better job, great kids, a good family, and a fun time every single day of your life.

Both of these assumptions are false, at least according to a basic understanding of what the Bible says concerning the life of Jesus and His followers.

Let's tackle the first one, which is that the Word of God is supposed to be nice. This is a biblical worldview that endorses sinful behavior.

This worldview of the Bible and Christianity comes from evaluating the end product instead of the process. Of course, the Bible is full of love, grace, and peace, but if the Bible is evaluated properly, there is also an overwhelming amount of rebuke for those who attempt to justify their sin and ignorance.

Notice the reaction of Jesus toward the Samaritan woman at the well or the woman caught in adultery. Those who humbled themselves before Christ and allowed themselves to be crushed and wrecked before His holiness found love, peace, and forgiveness. Those who assumed they were righteous and did not humble themselves or allow themselves to be crushed, like the Pharisees, and attempted to justify or sanctify their sin and disbelief, were rebuked in the strongest ways. The manner in which they were rebuked was not "nice" at all.

If God is going to use us to fight the darkness that perpetuates genocide, we must first be willing to be humbled and crushed before Him. There is no other way. Our sin has no safe space.

If we have a desire to be coddled, then it may be because we do not harbor the truth and instead follow a gospel of selfishness and darkness. Darkness and sin need coddling, not truth. Sin needs light to be driven out. Light cannot be driven out by darkness, so there is no need to fear new ideas and approaches. If in doubt, allow the Light to shine freely in your life. Sunshine is the best disinfectant.

If we desire to join the effort to stop genocide, we must be ready to be baptized. Baptism is the public confession of an outward change. It is the public acknowledgement that we are leaving the world and following after Christ. Before we are baptized, we are very much a part of the world. We are born into the world and accepted by the world.

But when we are baptized, we come up out of the water changed and transformed. We are no longer a part of the world, but are born again in Christ. We are a new creation, and just as Christ was rejected by the world, so will we be rejected by the world. The "safe spaces" for our sins and worldly ways are left behind. For the follower of Jesus Christ, there is no "safe space." Jesus promises rejection, persecution, and condemnation by the world for those who follow Him. This is the opposite of a safe space.

The Bible challenges you to unlearn the things you have learned in the world. We are challenged not to see the Bible through the eyes of the world but to see the world through the eyes of the Bible. The world has preconceived ideas about what Christians should be. They have created boxes that Christians need to fit into, and they expect the followers of Christ to fit into those boxes.

For instance, the world says that certain sins are not necessarily sins at all and for Christians to say that they are sins according to the Bible is—well—not very loving. The world says that stance is not very accepting. The world says that if Christians were truly loving and understanding, they would show love to the sinner by accepting his or her sin.

Instead of Christians clinging to the truth of the Bible and accepting the rejection of the world because of its perverted definition of sin, Christians have accepted the world's definition of love and adopted the world's definition of sin. And since the world's definition of sin is perverted, it needs protection from the truth of the Bible. That protection is what we call a "safe space" in the church. It is the lie that needs protection—not the Truth.

As a Christian reading the Bible, we are challenged to investigate new ideas and explore new aspects of Christ, even if we find the results to be offensive to our human nature, and even if the world around us finds those truths to be offensive. And the world will indeed find the conclusion of the Bible to be extremely offensive and intolerant.

The last words to leave the lips of Jesus were that of a suicide mission. He sent His disciples into the deepest, darkest, most hostile regions on earth and told them to share the Gospel message. In practice, this is dangerous, especially in areas like northern Iraq. Now, we can follow the storyline to logically deduce what comes next. If they crucified Jesus, what are they probably going to do to us? Paul used imagery to paint us a large, clear, unmistakable picture: "I am crucified with Christ; it is no longer I who live, but Christ lives in me" (Galatians 2:20).

This reality counters our second assumption in Western Christianity that following Christ will make us financially successful and experience absolute bliss.

Joining the effort to stop genocide is difficult because it requires us to put to death our secular Christianity. It requires us to follow Jesus as He is *really* portrayed in the Bible instead of how we think He ought to be portrayed. It forces us to abandon the life we have prepared for ourselves on earth and removes the cute and convenient box we have tried to put Christ in. It requires that we boldly and humbly give our life in complete service to Jesus, and accept whatever path He takes us on.

If you want to help stop genocide, you can contact your local mission's effort to see what other ministries are doing to take the Gospel message into ISIS-stricken areas. Look for more than just poverty-alleviation programs or refugee aid efforts. While these are great and necessary, they merely treat the symptom and not the root cause. Seek and join others who have a passion to take the Good News to the heart of the enemy's territory.

If we want to stop genocide, we must first be willing to lose our life for the sake of Gospel.

Apart from the love of Jesus Christ and His followers who are willing to do whatever is necessary to share the truth of the Gospel, there is no other way to bring an end to the crisis in Iraq, or the hatred and violence in any other part of the world.

"In My Arms"

by Dr. Paul M. Kingery
January 26, 2016, Seje Village, Iraq

You ran from certain death and straight into my heart
You held me in your arms and couldn't bear to part
I wiped away your tears, but couldn't stop my own
You felt the greatest pain a heart has ever known

I cried with thundering voice unto the farthest star,
What man has caused this child to run away so far?
What evil heart has shed this child's precious blood?
And caused a thousand more to perish in the flood?

Then deep within my soul I found your brokenness
A vessel for my love and soothing tenderness
I washed your bleeding feet and poured into your hands
A balm for every wound a father understands

I raised you up to walk so slowly at the first
And poured some water out to quench your burning thirst
I helped you rise to stand and wouldn't let you fall
We took the first small steps together walking tall

I offered you some bread to feed your hungry soul
And broke it for you there to soothe and make you whole
You looked into my eyes and saw my depth of love
Then raised your weary head to see the light above

In time your wounds were healed and sorrow slipped away
The pain a memory of a distant former day
Your life was filled with love and joys you'd never known
And in my arms you knew you'd never be alone

I never left your side in years that passed us by
My ears were never far from every plaintive cry
My hand was always near to show you I was there
I never laid upon you more than you could bear

The ones who sought your life the fire will sweep away
But now your soul is saved unto a better day
And I have gained a child whose heart is dear to me
And we will share our love throughout eternity.

304